DORDOGNE

BEAUJOLAIS

TARN

VAUCLUSE

SOUTHWEST PROVENCE

CÔTE D'AZUR

MTWTFSSMTWTFSSMTWTFSSMTWTFSSMTWTFSSMTWT

(take)

advantage of us

This is your own personal Smithcard, which entitles you to a year's free membership. The moment you register it, you can access the members' area of our website, and start finding out about exclusive last-minute offers from our hotels. The card also provides members-only privileges when you book hotels, such as a free bottle of champagne on arrival, upgrades, discounts on room rates and more. To start receiving special hotel offers, activate your card now by registering online at www.mrandmrssmith.com (it only takes a minute).

Look out for the Smith at the end of each hotel review.

A Mr & Mrs Smith membership card
should be affixed here

If it has been removed, you can still buy the book
and we will send you a replacement card. Please
send proof of purchase, with a return address, to
Spy Publishing Ltd,
277–279 Chiswick High Street,
London W4 4PU
United Kingdom

Register now
Activate your **BlackSmith** membership today, and receive our newsletter the *Guest Book*. It is packed with news, travel tips, even more offers, and fantastic competitions. We promise not to bombard you with communications, or pass on your details to third parties; this is between you and us.

And there's more…
If that isn't enough, you can even get access to VIP airport lounges, flight and car-hire offers, and your own personal travel concierge, simply by upgrading your membership to either **SilverSmith** or **GoldSmith**. Visit www.mrandmrssmith.com/members for more details.

Small print: all offers are according to availability and subject to change.

bon voya

Welcome to our new guide to beach boutique and countryside chic, which is undoubtedly the most varied hotel collection we have yet produced. To whet your wanderlust, we signpost you to chic châteaux, beachside fincas, even a hillside hideaway accessible only by cable car.

We must confess this has been the most enjoyable Smith project so far. But combing the northern shores of Reykjavík and trawling the sunny South of France wasn't always a day at the beach… Still, blue skies, the scent of pine, the odd rosé-fuelled lunch (research teams have to eat, you know), and balmy evenings by the sea all helped us through our duties – as did the overwhelming warmth of our Continental cousins.

Among the reviewers we asked to make like spies, so that we could give you the lowdown, were bon vivant Howard Marks, hat (and hotel) designer Philip Treacy and interior stylist extraordinaire Ilse Crawford. As well as accounts of their adventures, we include inspiring insider guides to all our destinations (you can print off portable versions from www.mrandmrssmith.com).

The idea of our books is to make your planning carefree and your escapes utterly enjoyable. That's why we now have a hi-tech website where you can discover exclusive hotel offers, check availability and use our simple booking service. You can also access an expanded version of the Coast and Country collection, as well as find fantastic stays all over the world. We hope you enjoy every trip. Until the next time…

Best wishes and bon voyage,

Mr & Mrs Smith

contents

REYKJAVIK
ICELAND

FRANCE

BEAUJOLAIS   SOUTH TYROL

DORDOGNE   PIEDMONT

TARN   VAUCLUSE
SOUTHWEST PROVENCE
COTE D'AZUR

PORTUGAL   TUSCANY

SPAIN   ITALY

CASCAIS

SOUTHERN EXTREMADURA   SARDINIA

SORRENTO   PUGLIA

SEVILLE PROVINCE   MALLORCA
RONDA   IBIZA   GREECE
COSTA DE LA LUZ

AEOLIAN ISLANDS

SANTORINI

5

(at a glance)

LESS THAN €100
Escondrijo Costa de la Luz p260
Le Manoir de Raynaudes Tarn p92

€100–€149
Château les Merles Dordogne p24
La Coluccia Sardinia p180
Farol Design Hotel Cascais p236
La Fuente de la Higuera Ronda p302
Hospedería Convento de la Parra S Extremadura p250
Hotel Signum Aeolian Islands p144
Toile Blanche Côte d'Azur p52

€150–€199
Villa Bordoni Tuscany p212
Château de Massillan Vaucluse p34
L'Hôtel Particulier Southwest Provence p76
Jardins Secrets Southwest Provence p70
La Maison du Frêne Côte d'Azur p58
Hotel Raya Aeolian Islands p138
Les Terrasses Ibiza p276
La Villa Piedmont p154
Villa Fontelunga Tuscany p218

€200–€299
101 Hotel Reykjavík p124
Astra Apartments and Suites Santorini p104
Atzaró Ibiza p270
Can Simoneta Mallorca p286
Hacienda de San Rafael Seville Province p312
Hostellerie de Crillon le Brave Vaucluse p40
Masseria Torre Coccaro Puglia p170
La Minervetta Sorrento p192
Oustau de Baumanière Southwest Provence p82
La Sommità Puglia p164
Son Brull Hotel and Spa Mallorca p292
Villa Sassolini Tuscany p224

€300+
Château de Bagnols Beaujolais p14
Perivolas Traditional Houses Santorini p110
Vigilius Mountain Resort South Tyrol p202

1–9 ROOMS
Escondrijo Costa de la Luz p260
L'Hôtel Particulier Southwest Provence p76
Jardins Secrets Southwest Provence p70
La Maison du Frêne Côte d'Azur p58
Le Manoir de Raynaudes Tarn p92
Les Terrasses Ibiza p276
Toile Blanche Côte d'Azur p52
Villa Fontelunga Tuscany p218

10–19 ROOMS
Atzaró Ibiza p270
Villa Bordoni Tuscany p212
Can Simoneta Mallorca p286
Château de Massillan Vaucluse p34
Château les Merles Dordogne p24
La Fuente de la Higuera Ronda p302
Hacienda de San Rafael Seville Province p312
La Minervetta Sorrento p192
Perivolas Traditional Houses Santorini p110
La Sommità Puglia p164
La Villa Piedmont p154
Villa Sassolini Tuscany p224

20–34 ROOMS
Astra Apartments and Suites Santorini p104
Château de Bagnols Beaujolais p14
Farol Design Hotel Cascais p236
Hostellerie de Crillon le Brave Vaucluse p40
Hospedería Convento de la Parra S Extremadura p250
Oustau de Baumanière Southwest Provence p82
Hotel Signum Aeolian Islands p144
Son Brull Hotel and Spa Mallorca p292

FRANCE

TWTFSSMTWTF **SS** MTWTFSSMTWTFSSMTWTFSSMTWTFSS
FRANCE

Beaujolais

COUNTRYSIDE	A VINE ROMANCE
COUNTRY LIFE	HAUTE CUISINE HEAVEN

MTWTFSSMTWTFSSMTWTFSSMTWTFSSMTWTFSSMTWT

FRANCE

BEAUJOLAIS
Distinguished wines, world-renowned cuisine and ornate châteaux of honey-coloured stone – Beaujolais is everything the Francophile dreams of. Located in the heart of France, this is a rural idyll of old villages, vineyard, lush farmland, forest and gentle hills, where the graceful Saône and Rhône rivers merge. A bright firmament of Michelin-starred restaurants offer gourmet tables overflowing with fine Burgundy and some of the best cuisine in France. Horse riding, ballooning and cycling will let you savour the rich landscape of Beaujolais, and even burn off a few calories after a night on the gastronomy.

GETTING THERE
Planes Lyon St-Exupery airport sees regular flights throughout the year from numerous destinations.
Trains High-speed TGV trains connect Lyon to the rest of France. London to Lyon takes four to six hours by Eurostar, via Lille or Paris.
Automobiles A car is recommended if you want to visit the vineyards, châteaux and historic towns scattered throughout the region.

DO GO / DON'T GO
Visit in May to see cherry blossom in bloom, or in autumn when turning leaves give the region a spectacular colour. The third Wednesday of November sees the town of Beaujeu come together to get a first taste of the year's Beaujolais Nouveau. The winter months can be rainy.

BEAUTIFULLY BEAUJOLAIS
Follow the wine route through the region by visiting the villages of Brouilly, Saint-Amour, Fleurie, Morgon and Moulin-à-Vent. Your hotel can organise a visit to the nearby cellars of Francisque Rivière.

LOCAL KNOWLEDGE
Taxis In towns, pick one up from a taxi rank or hail one on the street. If you're travelling in more remote areas, try to book a car in advance or prepare for a long walk.
Tipping culture Restaurant and café bills usually include a service charge (*service compris*) but it's customary to leave a small tip. For taxi drivers, add ten per cent to the metered charge.
Siesta and fiesta Many restaurants close after 14h and reopen in the afternoon around 16h. Shops also break for lunch, except in big-city centres; most close on Sundays.
Packing tips A pair of running shoes – the food is so good that you'll have to up your fitness regime to cope.
Recommended reads *La Symphonie Pastorale* by André Gide; *Madame Bovary* by Flaubert; *French Women Don't Get Fat* by Mireille Guiliano.
Cuisine Haute! Haute! Haute! More (Michelin) stars than the Milky Way. Highly prized local ingredients include tender Charolais beef and excellent wines, such as Chablis and Beaujolais. The area has also given us favourites like boeuf bourguignon and coq au vin. Cheese lovers should try Epoisses, a creamy cow's cheese said to have been Napoleon's favourite.
Currency Euro.
Dialling codes Country code for France: 33. Lyon: 04.

DIARY
July Lyon's Roman amphiteatre hosts Les Nuits de Fouvière, a festival dedicated to the performing arts. **Third Wednesday of November** The new Beaujolais wine is unveiled in the town of Beaujeu en Ligne. **December** The Festival of Light is held just before New Year in Lyon, when windows are lit with candles and there is a lantern procession through the city. Concerts and operas are held at the same time (www.lyon-france.com).

WORTH GETTING OUT OF BED FOR

Viewpoint In the heart of the Pouilly-Fuissé vineyards, the Rock of Solutré overlooks the entire Bresse region. President Mitterrand used to climb this limestone escarpment once a year.

Arts and culture Pay a visit to one or more of Burgundy's splendid châteaux. The moated Château de Cormatin, between Tournus and Cluny, contains wonderfully opulent rooms (www.chateaudecormatin.com). The formal gardens of the 17th-century Château de La Chaize are breathtaking (www.chateaudelachaize.com).

Activities The hotel can organise numerous activities, from hot-air ballooning, horse riding, wine-tasting and guided tours of Lyon and the historic castles and villages of Beaujolais.

Daytripper Lyon is a great place to visit for a day. Bring some flat shoes for the cobbled streets of Old Lyon, then follow the labyrinthine underground passages, used by the city's 18th-century silk-makers to carry their delicate fabrics under cover from Silk Hill down to the river barges.

Perfect picnic The summit of the extinct volcano of Mont Brouilly has super views over the Beaujolais region. There are wonderful picnic spots down by the river at Montmerle-sur-Saône.

Something for nothing There's excellent cycling through peaceful villages between Cluny monastery and Juliénas. There are some hills but also some wonderful views.

Shopping There's a daily food market on Place aux Herbes in Mâcon (except Mondays) and on Saturday morning on Quai Lamartine. There's also a great covered market in Villefranche on Sundays. Open-air stalls on Croix-Rousse hill and Quai St-Antoine in Lyon are great for local specialities like St-Marcellin cheese and boudin noir (black pudding). Historic master pâtissier Pignol on Rue Emile Zola sells delicate confections. The city rivals Paris for designer shopping, particularly on Rue Emile Zola, Rue du Président Edouard Herriot and Place Kléber. Lyon is also famous for its silk scarfs.

CAFES

Mix with the locals at Bagnol's tiny café, opposite the hotel gates. In Lyon, Place Bellecour is ideal for sampling relaxed café culture.

BARS AND RESTAURANTS

Maison Troisgros in Place Jean Troisgros in Roanne (04 77 71 66 97) is run by one of France's thrice-Michelin-starred chefs. The magical food, monastically calm kitchen and immaculate cellars make this an unmissable destination. The Troisgros bistro next door does simpler food with a touch of glamour. The art deco **La Rotonde** on Avenue du Casino in La Tour-de-Salvagny (04 78 87 00 97; closed Sunday and Monday) has fine formal dining. **Léon de Lyon** on Rue Pleney (04 72 10 11 12) is a century-old temple to haute cuisine. Its bistro is ideal for lunch. Minimalist, Asian-inspired **Nicolas le Bec** on Rue Grolée (04 78 42 15 00) is new-wave French cooking and offers all the latest foams and froths. **Grand Café des Négociants** on Place Francisque Régaud (04 78 42 50 05) has fine food in plush gilt-and-mirror surroundings.

NIGHTLIFE

Lyon has an excellent **Opera House** on Place de la Comédie (08 26 30 53 25). The building is a striking 18th-century edifice with a modern glass-roof extension by Jean Nouvel. Hip **Victoria Hall** on Rue du Repos is an urbane cocktail bar that wouldn't be out of place in Manhattan. The clubby, informal atmosphere at **Le Boudoir** on Place Jules Ferry is great for late-night drinks.

Château de Bagnols

DESTINATION BEAUJOLAIS
STYLE FIVE-STAR CASTLE
SETTING FAIRY-TALE GARDENS

M T W T F S S M T W T F S S M T W T F S S M T W T F S S M T W T F S S M T W T

FRANCE

'A staggering building
complete with moat,
drawbridge and towers
in the honey-coloured
pierre dorée stone'

For more than a decade, I had dreamt of the Château de Bagnols. When I was editor of *Elle Decoration*, I saw incredible pictures that lodged in my imagination, images from childhood: *Beauty and the Beast*, *Bluebeard's Castle*, *The Princess and the Pea*… The extravagant interiors looked about as far from the idea of a boutique hotel, and from the modern design that filled the pages of my magazine, as was possible. Intensely beautiful, the pictures that struck me most were of its beds, which simply beggared belief – insane four-posters piled high with mattresses and hung with heavy red-brocade drapes or antique silks. This was the stuff of the films – of Peter Greenaway and Luchino Visconti. However, it was a dream, and I never went.

Now, finally, invited to review the hotel with my husband, it was time to visit Bagnols. Would I be horribly disappointed? Were those pictures a stylised sham? As we arrived in the village of Bagnols, 12 miles from Lyons, and spied the extraordinary castle walls, the answer was, clearly, no. This is a really staggering building in a tiny village, its historic might absolutely apparent. Complete with moat, drawbridge and towers in the honey-coloured stone called *pierre dorée*, the schoolbook stronghold is punctured by neat, cruciform arrow holes. (You might call it a hole-istic experience, perhaps, to be the recipient of an arrow from one of those.)

The interior of the château does not disappoint. It is the brainchild of a truly cultured woman, Lady Helen Hamlyn, who also owns the house by architects Mendelsohn and Chermayeff in Old Church Street, London – one of England's first modernist houses. The rooms in both the original 13th-century castle and the 'new' (ie: 15th-century) block are beautiful. Our bed was as sublime as I had hoped, decorated with fragile antique textiles and made up with tactile Swiss bedlinen (which you can buy, too). Next to the bed, the water tumblers were made of silver, giving us a visceral introduction to what it must have been to be

a French aristocrat. The bathroom was grand, too, with an antique marble bath and local products including a really, really strong lavender bath foam – the type that works against typhoid and tigers. We also had a huge sitting room, filled with bleeding-heart-coloured sofas, and another tiny room covered with early frescoes. It blows your mind.

The kitchens are central to the building and, thanks to a clever sleight of design, you walk through them on your way to anywhere, past the teeming, steaming theatre of food preparation. The grounds are lovely, with dense borders of lavender and a formal garden where we took drinks before dinner. The swimming pool is round, with grass growing right up to its edge. Alas, all this whimsy and wonder has to fit into a 21st-century reality, and the food and service at Bagnols are of a very French kind, rather than tallying, to my mind, with the beyond-beautiful environment. The human contact is formal and, operationally, the hotel deals in star ratings and status rather than princesses and peas.

The Château de Bagnols is certainly the most beautiful hotel I have ever stayed in. To have a heavenly time, order room service (after all, how often do you have your own four-poster?). The rooms are so exquisite it is mad not to stay in for the evening and do your own variation on 'You be Louis and I'll be Marie Antoinette.' Just don't lose your head. We also dined in the very grand Salle des Gardes, where we had cherry *clafoutis* for pudding; in contrast, we lunched under the trees, on goat's cheese and red wine.

During the day, go out and explore, do your own thing; the château has bicycles you can go off on, for picnics and jaunts. We made use of their nicely produced book of trips that you can enjoy by bike or car, which took us to just the sort of places we love. We spent a morning at an over-the-top food market at Villefranche, where we did the rounds of the vast quantities of local produce, buying huge bags and bundles to take home, including an array of fresh goat's cheese and a sausage called Jésus (the old ladies laughed when I asked them why, ↓

leaving me none the wiser), as well ogling as all those great, artistically ordered piles of fruit and vegetables.

Hanging out in yeasty cellars and debating the relative values of 2004 and 2002 is very much our idea of fun, so we also enjoyed a visit to a much-awarded local winemaker, Alain Chatoux, who makes Beaujolais and some very decent white. If you think there is no significant difference between men and women, you might think again after a session of wine-tasting. Down in Mr Chatroux's chilly *cave*, we noted that Mr Smith preferred the powerful kick of a 2003 or a 2005 vintage, while Mrs Smith put her money on the lighter, chillable 2002 or 2004. An interesting experiment, and not one without its non-scientific compensations.

For a change of aesthetic, we drove an hour to see the modernist convent La Tourette by Le Corbusier. One of his last works, it is a building that expresses the interior life of man, and embodies his search for intensity and soul. Built around the progress of the sun, the building allows light to enter the building in many different ways.

Slits of light accompany you down corridors; you enter a chapel through a transformational wall of light; and altars are dramatically lit with wizard fingers of light. It is incredibly moving. We weren't sure how to follow that, except by plunging back into the brocade-draped, fresco-covered, sumptuous worldliness of our quarters at Château de Bagnols – from the sublime to the luxurious, you might say.

Reviewed by Ilse Crawford

NEED TO KNOW

Rooms 21, including eight junior suites, four suites and one apartment.

Rates €475–€875 for the rooms; €2,395 for the apartment; from €16,500 a night for exclusive occupancy of the entire château. Breakfast, from €30.

Check-out Midday.

Room service 24-hour service, with a reduced menu after 22h.

Facilities Library with Internet access. Guided walking, horse riding, golf, tennis, cookery classes and wine-tasting. Bicycles to hire at €40 a day. Luxury chauffeured cars available for transfers and touring.

Poolside Heated outdoor pool in summer.

Children Welcome. There are English-speaking babysitters, a children's menu and extra beds (at €95 a night) available in some rooms.

Also Small dogs are permitted in the hotel. Smoking is allowed on request.

IN THE KNOW

Our favourite rooms Room 8 has an arched ceiling, painted walls and a gilded four-poster bed. Room 1 has a tower bathroom and a crimson-hung four-poster.

Hotel bar There's a small bar on the first floor, open until the last guest leaves.

Hotel restaurant Michelin-starred La Salle des Gardes serves modern cuisine, as well as traditional dishes and spit-roasted meats and game, in the former guards' room and on the south-facing terrace. Lunch is served 12h–13h30; dinner, 19h30–21h30.

Top table Dine by the fire in winter; outside under the century-old lime trees in summer.

Dress code No jeans: châtelaine chic for her; jacket for him.

LOCAL EATING AND DRINKING

Just to the north of Lyon, the Michelin-starred **L'Auberge de l'Ile** on Place Notre Dame, L'Ile Barbe (04 78 83 99 49), is a *très romantique* 17th-century house surrounded by wooded gardens. It has a cigar room but is decidedly unstuffy. **Guy Lassausaie** on Rue de Belle Cise in Chasselay (04 78 47 62 59) is another excellent Michelin-starred option with a contemporary atmosphere. **Le Vieux Moulin** on Chemin du Vieux Moulin in the village of Alix (04 78 43 91 66) is a stone-built Rhône-side mill, converted into a relaxed country inn where you can fill up on rustic French fare, from mustardy sausages to frog's legs.

 Wine-tasting at a local vineyard (very occasionally this will be unavailable due to harvest times, etc).

GET A ROOM!

Use our online booking service at www.mrandmrssmith.com to check availability and make reservations. Register your Smithcard to find out about current member offers for this hotel.

Château de Bagnols
Bagnols, Beaujolais
+33 (0)4 74 71 40 00
info@bagnols.com; www.bagnols.com

Dordogne

COUNTRYSIDE	BUCOLIC BACKWATERS
COUNTRY LIFE	WINE, WOODS AND WINDING RIVERS

MTWTFSSMTWTFSSMTWTFSSMTWTFSSMTWTFSSMTWT

FRANCE

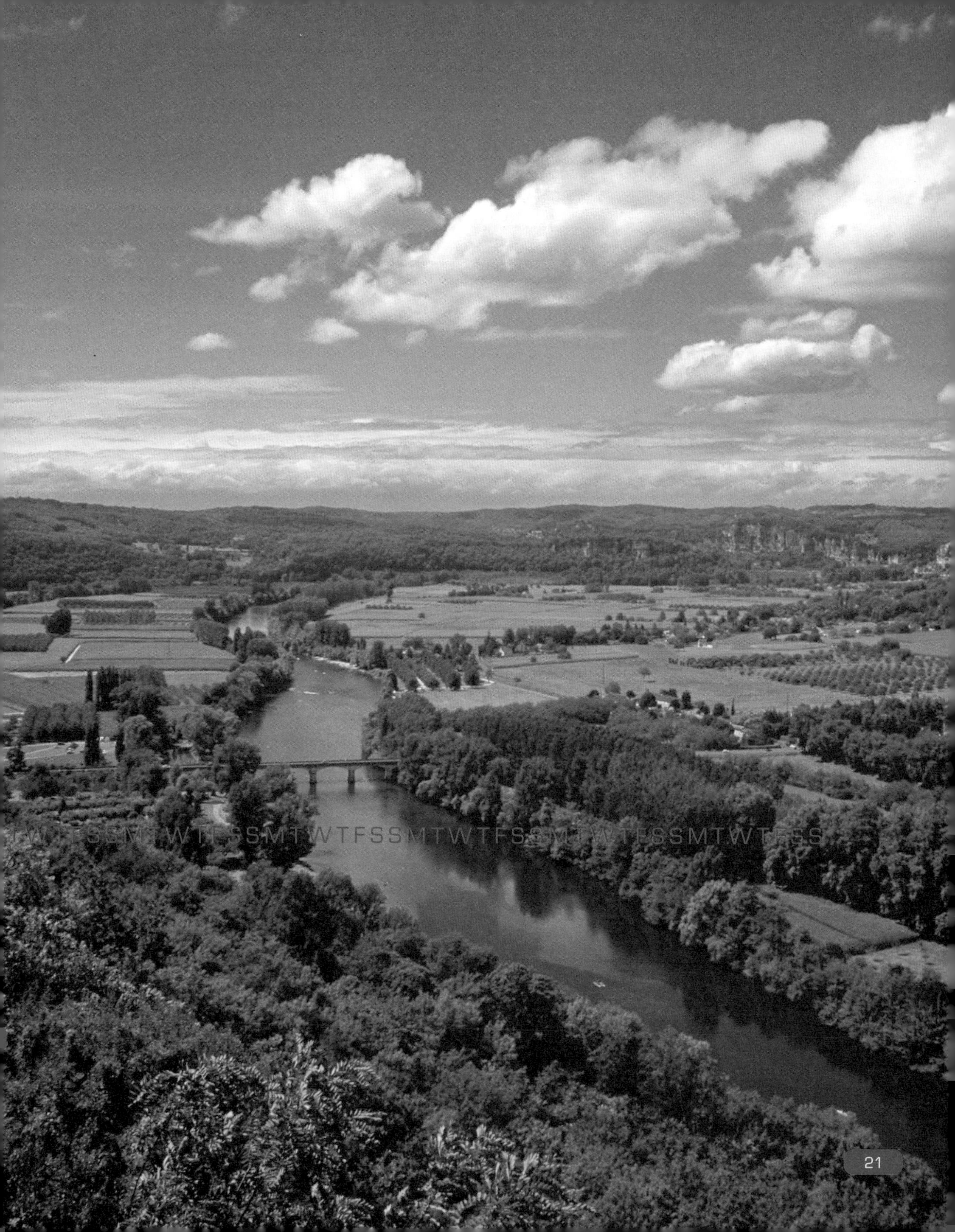

DORDOGNE

In the warm valleys of southwestern France, where the Dordogne, Isle and Lot rivers wriggle their way to the Atlantic, the lush landscape, sunny days and mild temperatures combine to produce perfect conditions for grapes and truffles. Happily these are also ideal surroundings in which to linger and enjoy the world's finest wines and the region's gastronomic specialities. The names of the honey-coloured mediaeval towns, villages and châteaux of the Périgord are instantly recognisable to gourmets, from the vineyards of Bergerac and St-Émilion to the truffle stalls of Périgueux. Here, time is measured in vintages and happiness comes by the glass.

GETTING THERE

Planes The low-cost airlines fly to Bergerac airport, 5km southeast of the town centre. There are also regular flights to Bordeaux throughout the year.
Trains The high-speed TGV from Paris to Bordeaux takes three and a half hours. It's eight hours from London via Eurostar. Bordeaux to Bergerac takes one hour.
Automobiles A car is indispensable for exploring the vineyards and countryside.

DO GO / DON'T GO

Spring is sunny but changeable, with May and June absolute perfection. Summer is busy but ideal for canoeing on the Dordogne. September and October see fine weather and the all-important grape harvest. Winters are usually wet and mild.

DEFINITIVELY DORDOGNE

The Périgord 'black diamond' truffles are famed for their earthy taste and aphrodisiac qualities, and can cost up to €600 a kilo. They grow well in the Dordogne and the main markets during the harvest season of December to early March are Périgueux, Sarlat and Brantôme. Out of season, look for truffles preserved in cognac.

LOCAL KNOWLEDGE

Taxis There's no chance of hailing a cab out in the sticks. In Bergerac, call 05 53 23 32 32 to pre-book your ride. Or burn off those foie gras calories and hire bicycles from Apolo on 05 53 61 08 16.
Tipping culture Service charges are always added to restaurant bills, but a few extra euros are appropriate for waiters and taxi drivers.
Siesta and fiesta Shops tend to shut 12h30–14h30. Restaurants are often closed on Sundays and Mondays outside the summer months.
Packing tips A pinny for wannabe chefs, scales for the gourmands.
Recommended reads *Cyrano de Bergerac* by Edmond Rostand; *The Generous Earth* by Philip Oyler.
Cuisine The Périgord conjures up gastronomic dreams of wine, walnut oil, mushrooms and truffles, not to mention the ducks and geese reared to produce foie gras. A Périgord speciality is roast goose fried in its own fat with Landaise potatoes. If you can possibly eat any more, try some goat's cheese or walnut tart with strawberries.
Currency Euro.
Dialling codes Country code for France: 33. Bergerac: 05.

DIARY

Early May The châteaux of St-Émilion open their wine cellars for a day, usually on a Sunday; some offer free samples. **Late June** Every two years Bordeaux holds its three-day Fête du Vin, with wine tasting, concerts and auctions. **14 July** Bergerac's magnificent four-day food and wine festival sees tables in the streets and free concerts in the evening (www.pays-de-bergerac.com). **Mid-August** Brive-la-Gaillarde has a ten-day festival of classical music concerts. **Third Sunday of September** The start of the wine harvest is announced from the Tour du Roi in St-Émilion, accompanied by parades; see www.saint-emilion-tourisme.com for details.

WORTH GETTING OUT OF BED FOR

Viewpoint The village of La Roque-Gageac, near the charming mediaeval town of Sarlat, clings to the cliffs overlooking the Dordogne valley. The most striking view is from the ruins of the troglodyte fort at the top of a vertiginous ladder.

Arts and culture The Dordogne is dotted with castles and châteaux. Two of the best are the Renaissance Château de Puyguilhem near the town of St-Jean-de-Côle and the very grand Château de Hautefort, with its wonderful gardens, northwest of Brive-la-Gaillarde.

Activities There is good canoeing on the Dordogne, between Argentat and Beynac. Copeyre in Souillac hires canoes and mountain bikes (www.copeyre.com). The Bergerac area is ideal for wine-tasting; contact www.vins-bergerac.fr for details. L'Essentiel, on Rue Guadet in St-Émilion, promotes 'boutique' producers and is stylish yet unstuffy (www.essentiel-vin.com). There's a challenging nine-hole golf course at Château les Merles (www.lesmerles.com).

Daytripper Book two weeks in advance to visit the wine cellar of Château Margaux, north of Bordeaux. The neoclassical château produces some of the Médoc region's finest wine. The cellars are closed in August and during the harvest (www.chateau-margaux.com).

Something for nothing The suitably haughty statue of Cyrano de Bergerac takes pride of place in Bergerac's Place Pélissière. The statue's famously protruding nose is often stolen.

Perfect picnic There are some wonderful picnic spots on the banks of the Dordogne. Our favourite stretch is around the two mighty fortresses of Beynac and Castelnaud near Sarlat.

Shopping In Bergerac, Bille de Bois in Place du Docteur André Cayla is filled with old-fashioned wooden toys. There's so much fabulous local wine to choose from; try the velvety Monbazillac, a sweet white wine often drunk to mark special occasions. There are markets in Bergerac on Wednesdays and Saturdays, Lalinde on Thursdays, Libourne on Fridays and Sarlat on Saturday. Bergerac's fleamarket sells antiques and bric-à-brac on the first Sunday of the month.

CAFES

The best cafés in town are normally clustered around central squares, such as Place Pélissière in Bergerac, Place de la Liberté in Sarlat and Place du Marché in St-Émilion.

BARS AND RESTAURANTS

Restaurant **L'Imparfait** on Rue des Fontaines in Bergerac (05 53 57 47 92) has a pretty terrace and a daily menu specialising in fish dishes. Formal **Le Vieux Logis** in Trémolat, 20 minutes upriver from Bergerac (05 53 22 80 06), serves Michelin-starred cuisine in a former tobacco barn or outside under the linden trees. **Le Chapon Fin** on Rue Montesquieu (05 56 79 10 10) is one of Bordeaux's most romantic Michelin-starred restaurants, and also offers cookery courses. **Hostellerie de Plaisance** on Place du Clocher (05 57 55 07 55) is a Michelin-starred hotel restaurant in St-Emilion with superb food and a spectacular wine list. **Le Quatre Saisons**, on Côte de Toulouse in Sarlat (05 53 29 48 59), does tasty food including an excellent vegetarian menu, which is a welcome piece of information for any non-carnivores touring France.

NIGHTLIFE

Evening entertainment in Dordogne is decidedly mellow and unpretentious. **La Poissonnerie**, on Rue du Colonel de Chadois in Bergerac, is a great place to spend a warm summer evening to the occasional accompaniment of live Cuban music or jazz.

Château les Merles

DESTINATION	DORDOGNE
STYLE	NEOCLASSICAL NUNNERY
SETTING	BERGERAC'S ROUTE DES VINS

MTWTFSSMTWTFSSMTWTFSSMTWTFSSMTWTFSSMTWT

FRANCE

'Black satin slippers lay next to our
bed in special boxes, and a silver
bowl of berries from the château's
organic garden was waiting for us'

'We're definitely coming back,' I said to Mr Smith as we parked the hire car and walked, just after midnight, into the white, pebbled, candlelit courtyard of Château les Merles. A long table of late diners were finishing off their puddings underneath the stars. 'Hang on – we haven't even checked in yet,' he pointed out, as we sat down in a pair of white-upholstered Philippe Starck chairs and were immediately brought welcoming glasses of champagne and a plate of canapés. (These included specialities of the Périgord region: we pounced on foie gras, tomato tartlets and some deliciously crisp radishes and endive.) Within seconds, the cares of the day, the plane delays and the car-hire queue were distant memories.

The air, which was scented with the lavender and thyme that border the courtyard, further aided our relaxation. The 17th-century château was breathtaking in the crescent moonlight. After checking in, without actually having to get up from our table, we were shown to our suite. It was decorated in a style I am christening 'convent de luxe': dark wood, antiques, lots of white upholstery, crisp snowy linens and huge windows everywhere. 'Who's hidden the nuns?' I asked. But any concealed nuns were sybarites, too: black satin slippers lay next to our bed in special boxes, and a silver bowl of berries from the château's organic garden was waiting for us. There were two parallel white sofas in the little sitting room, and a dark-velvet chaise longue for stretching out and reading and chatting on, side by side. In the gleaming black and white bathroom we found a similar blend of monochrome luxury and simplicity.

Even if our beds were of that silly Siamese-twin configuration (locked together but made up separately), it wasn't the end of the world, as they were extremely

comfortable and welcoming, and we couldn't have had a more delightful awakening in the morning. Manic birdsong roused us and I pulled back the shutters to reveal the hotel's swimming pool sitting picturesquely in the lush gardens. Fear of missing breakfast (as well as general lethargy) prevented us from taking a quick dip there and then and, instead, we returned to the courtyard restaurant to sample the château's morning delights.

A table inside was spread with organic garden fruits, home-made bread, viennoiserie, a variety of cheeses and hams and other local delectables. I've never eaten a dish of freshly picked blackcurrants for breakfast before but I can recommend it. We sat for ages eking out the meal with supplementary cappuccinos and extra croissants, basking in our new setting. As we sat, we observed a few other guests in tailored shorts lugging huge golf caddies across the courtyard on their

way to the morning's round, and felt intense relief that we had no such taxing agenda ahead of us.

As breakfast drew to a close, our thoughts turned naturally to lunch, so we got into the car and drove to the local town of Bergerac, about ten minutes away. We wandered round the narrow streets of the old town, buying hats, looking at antiques and hunting slightly obsessively for some pink and gold dessert plates while dodging statues of Cyrano, the town's most famous romantic hero and, along with goose liver, the region's most celebrated export.

Lunch, at the hotel's recommendation, was at the excellent (and modestly named) L'Imparfait in a quiet back street, where we feasted in a shady courtyard on sea bream and lamb shanks. They were both exceptional. After some light shopping (more local wine, foie gras, some candlesticks), we made our ↓

way back to the hotel and stretched out on the sunloungers, coming to every now and then to summon some drinks via the phone, which was conveniently situated right by the pool.

I couldn't imagine any possible improvement on the scene, but Mr Smith, post-swim, was nursing a very understandable complaint. He wistfully mentioned to staff that he was going to miss an important football game. A huge projector screen was instantly rigged up in an empty upstairs ballroom, and cold beers (and kir royales for me) were delivered to us throughout the match. So much more civilised than our local, we observed, looking up at the chandeliers.

Evening came, and all the corridors became crowded with small girls in tutus. The local ballet academy, it transpired, was putting on its end-of-term gala at the hotel. We watched from a nearby bench, drinks in hands, as the tinies performed before us, overseen by their stern Mamzelle in black leggings. Then we dined in the courtyard restaurant where a special buffet had been prepared. The local wine and produce were just delicious, and I felt so happy I genuinely contemplated joining the dancers for their Swan Lake finale. Mr Smith, however, kept a firm hold of my elbow, distracting me with spoonfuls of chocolate mousse and raspberry sorbet, until the dangerous moment had passed.

Reviewed by Susie Boyt

NEED TO KNOW

Rooms 15, including two suites and one apartment.
Rates €110–€250, not including breakfast.
Check-out 11h, but late check-out is sometimes available.
Room service Breakfast is available between 08h30 and 10h. An imaginative 'world food' menu is available between 10h30 and 19h.
Facilities TV and DVD.
Poolside Outdoor pool, sunbathing patio with sleek black parasols open 09h–20h.
Children Warmly welcomed. Pre-booked day-care facilities are available. An extra bed is €15.
Also The château has a tennis court and a narrow and challenging nine-hole golf course (you can borrow clubs). Horse riding can be organised with the local stables.

IN THE KNOW

Our favourite rooms Suite 7 is spacious and has a fine view over the Dordogne valley. Suite 8 has high ceilings, classical styling and views over the swimming pool and golf course.
Hotel bar The Bistrot is an informal lounge bar with a menu of tasty and unfussy dishes. You can try wines from the château's own vineyards, as well as a large selection of renowned local wines.
Hotel restaurant La Bruyère Blanche at Château les Merles serves excellent New Périgordine cuisine, with a strong emphasis on fresh and seasonal local ingredients. The château sources all its wines locally in the Bergerac region.
Top table Out in the courtyard on a summer's evening.
Dress code Country chic: informal with a splash of style.

LOCAL EATING AND DRINKING

L'Imparfait on Rue des Fontaines in Bergerac (05 53 57 47 92) serves a short, seasonal menu, which changes every day according to what's good and fresh at the market that morning. **L'Enfance de Lard** on Place Pélissière in Bergerac (05 53 57 52 88; closed on Tuesdays) serves well-prepared meat dishes. Its open fire creates a cosy atmosphere in the cooler months. The vine-shaded tables at **Le Treille** on Quai Salvette in Bergerac overlook the Dordogne and are a pleasant spot for a drink. In St-Émilion, **Le Clos du Roy** on Rue de la Petite-Fontaine (05 57 74 41 55; closed on Tuesdays and Wednesdays) has inventive fish and seafood dishes, and a bulky wine list.

 Smith cardholders receive a free glass of champagne, a selection of regional amuses-bouches and a bottle of wine from the vineyards of Château les Merles.

GET A ROOM!

Use our online booking service at www.mrandmrssmith.com to check availability and make reservations. Register your Smithcard to find out about current member offers for this hotel.

Château les Merles
Tuilières, Mouleydier
+ 33 (0)5 53 63 13 42
info@lesmerles.com; www.lesmerles.com

VAUCLUSE

Vaucluse

COUNTRYSIDE	FRUITBOWL OF PROVENCE
COUNTRY LIFE	PETANQUE AND PASTIS

MTWTFSSMTWTFSSMTWTFSSMTWTFSSMTWT
FRANCE

TWTFSSMTWTFSSMTWTFSSMTWTFSSMTWTFSS

31

VAUCLUSE

Cultivated for centuries beneath the peak of the mighty Mont Ventoux, the Vaucluse is the earthy, abundant counterpart to the show-off glitz of the Riviera and the Côte d'Azur. Melons from Cavaillon, truffles from Carpentras, lavender from Sault, classic Rhône wines – tempting produce is showcased daily in the local markets. The soft valleys and craggy peaks are diverse and beautiful, Provençal sunlight alchemising vineyards and villages into instant art; walkers and cyclists can tackle the Alpine foothills or laze in lavender fields. You could spend a lifetime sampling the culture – summer festivals, specialist honeys, Avignon's mansions and museums – or you could simply tug the brim of your straw hat down a bit and lie back until it's time for that apéritif.

GETTING THERE

Planes Nîmes and Marseille airports are best.

Trains The train is a comfortable and convenient option. Eurostar from London takes seven hours, with a change in Paris. From July to September there's a weekly direct train on Saturdays taking six hours.

Automobiles Great for exploring the wine regions and the foothills of the Alps, but be careful in villages with steep, narrow streets.

DO GO / DON'T GO

Spring and autumn see the region in its sunniest mood. Only the postcard-prettiest villages get crowded, even in summer. Winter is chilly when the Mistral wind blows.

VERY VAUCLUSE

Know your food and craft markets: there's one in Avignon every day except Monday. Bédoin (Monday) is lively but touristy; Vaison (Tuesday) and Sault (Wednesday) are great for a wander; Carpentras (Friday) is best for delicious local food.

LOCAL KNOWLEDGE

Taxis It's best to book in advance. Your hotel should be able to arrange a pick-up from the train station in Avignon or the airport in Marseille.

Tipping culture A service charge is automatically added to restaurant bills, but it's usual to round up the bill or leave a few euros.

Siesta and fiesta Lunch is observed strictly between 12h–14h; you can expect to dine 19h–21h30.

Packing tips A programme for one of the summer's theatre, dance or opera festivals in Avignon or Orange.

Recommended reads *The Man who Planted Trees* by Jean Giono; *Market Day in Provence* by Michèle de La Pradelle.

Cuisine Gastro-Provençal reigns – refined dishes of lamb, game and fish with olive, lavender and herb flavours. Local wines are a must: ask for something from the village's own *vigneron* (wine-maker). Do make like a *petanque*-playing village elder and order a Ricard (a popular brand of pastis), starting with one part pastis to three parts water.

Currency Euro.

Dialling codes Country code for France: 33. Provence: 04.

DIARY

July The Festival d'Avignon brings all manner of street performers to the city, as well as formal concerts (www.festival-avignon.com). Avignon's off-beat fringe arts festival runs at the same time, filling the streets with jugglers and mime artists (www.avignon-off.org). **Last two weeks of July** Carpentras stages Les Estivales de Carpentras, an entertaining celebration of music, theatre and dance. **15 August** Sault, in the heart of the region's lavender fields, hosts the fragrant Fête de la Lavande.

WORTH GETTING OUT OF BED FOR

Viewpoint There are belvederes on the twisty route up Mont Ventoux. High above Beaumes de Venise (ask in the village), Domaine de Durban has top dessert wines and a super view.

Arts and culture The well-preserved Roman amphitheatre at Orange makes a thrilling backdrop to the summer opera festival in July (www.choregies.asso.fr).

Activities Wine-tasting routes criss-cross the region; see www.rhone-wines.co.uk for details. Provence Vélos (04 90 60 28 07) will deliver bikes and tandems wherever you request, for half or full days of backroad cycling. There's quad biking on the slopes of Mont Ventoux; contact Ventoux Quad at Crillon-le-Brave (06 19 06 05 92). Station du Mont Serein has skiing in the winter and go-karting in the summer (04 90 63 42 02; www.stationdumontserein.com). For horse riding, try Centre Equestre le Ménèque (04 90 65 66 39) near Bédoin.

Daytripper Avignon's monumental Palais des Papes was built in the 14th century, when the city was home to the popes. Modern pilgrims seeking more earthly delights can enjoy chic shopping and gourmet dining around Place de l'Horloge.

Perfect picnic Head to the market and fill your bicycle's panniers with baguettes, goat's cheese, onion tarts and some rosé. Our favourite spot is between Mormoiron and Malemort.

Something for nothing You can sample your way around the region's bigger markets, especially the one at Bédoin. Look out for wild lavender growing around Sault in July and August.

Shopping Apart from the giant blocks of savon de Marseille, the best buys are olive-wood kitchenwares and lavender bath products (we like the Popée family's tiny shop on the road from Sault up to the Ventoux). In Sault, nougaterie André Boyer sells sweet treats in an historic interior. Isle-sur-la-Sorgue hosts a celebrated antiques market every Sunday morning.

CAFES

Patisserie **Jouvaud** on Rue de l'Evêché in Carpentras is hard to resist. Avignon's English-run **Simple Simon** on Rue de la Petite-Fusterie, is good for teatime. **Cafeina** on Rue du Corps de Garde in Gigondas is a pretty salon de thé with home-made cakes (closed Fridays). At Sault, a good market-day coffee stop is **La Promenade**, with its sweeping view over the lavender fields below.

BARS AND RESTAURANTS

In Avignon, **La Mirande** on Place L'Amirande (04 90 85 93 93) is a Michelin-starred hotel and cookery school with a garden terrace. The stylish **La Compagnie des Comptoirs** at 83 Rue Joseph Vernet (04 90 58 39 29) is run by the renowned Pourcel brothers. A less swank but equally good option for lunch is **Le Bercail** on L'Ile de Barthelasse (04 90 82 20 22).
Le Grand Pré in Roaix, near Vaison-la-Romaine (04 90 46 18 12) is a swish, Michelin-endorsed operation with an elegant, romantic terrace. **Chalet Reynard**, above the tree-line, near the summit of the Mont Ventoux (04 90 61 84 55) is an Alpine brasserie and popular with mountain thrill-seekers. A favourite with ex-pats, **Le Mas de la Bonoty** between St Didier and Pernes (04 90 61 61 09) serves excellent traditional cuisine.

NIGHTLIFE

Summer nights on the town in the Vaucluse are all about village bars alfresco, where the company will include Belgian cyclists, local eco-punks and classic Gauloise-chuffers.

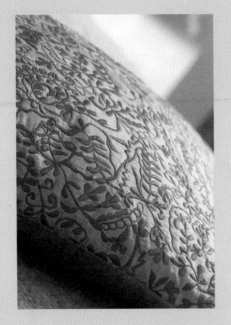

'An 18th-century chaise longue next to a contemporary sofa, antique mirrors, a Murano glass chandelier and very cool wallpaper'

Château de Massillan

DESTINATION	VAUCLUSE
STYLE	HIP HISTORICAL
SETTING	SECLUDED MEADOWS

MTWTFSSMTWTFSSMTWTFSSMTWTFSSMTWTFSSMTWT
FRANCE

TWTFSSMTWTFSSMTWTFSSMTWTFSSMTWTFSSMTWTFSS

Château de Massillan, Vaucluse, France

I was intrigued and inspired by the idea of staying in a château built for Diane de Poitiers, Henry II's lifelong consort, a lady renowned for her beauty, intellect and sense of aesthetics. It's fair to expect a small luxury hotel to be charming, but nothing could have prepared us for the dramatic sight of the Château de Massillan's starkly beautiful proportions, revealed at the end of a suitable driveway leading into leafy grounds. The Richard Long-style lavender bed in front of the main entrance added to the majestic impression, as well as reminding us well and truly that we were in Provence.

The sounds and scents that waft through the night as we walk into our castle are so characteristic of the region – cicadas, lavender, warm wind (no Mistral this evening), we'd know we're in the South of France with our eyes shut. We are greeted by smiling staff who turn out to be exceptionally professional, polite, charming and helpful. Along with a luxurious quantity of public space – with stone floors, antique mirrors,

chic chandeliers and a mixture of antiques, mid-century modern and perfectly contemporary pieces – the hotel has only 12 rooms, which makes Massillan homely rather than stately, and ensures that service is superlative.

Through to our suite, past old urns and the 21st-century fountain, which give a clue as to the style of our quarters. It is indulgently spacious, with an 18th-century chaise longue sitting next to a contemporary sofa, more antique mirrors, a Murano glass chandelier, and very cool wallpaper that turns out to be by those Glaswegian masters of fine-art wallcoverings, Timorous Beasties. The bathroom's simple design accentuates the beauty of the Provençal landscape and Massillan's lake – framed nicely as you lie in the bath.

It is no exaggeration to say that I have never come across a hotel offering such a dining experience as this. In these evocative surroundings, even the

simplest plate of cheese or Serrano ham is unforgettable. Presentation is creative and masterful, and the flavours light, delicate and fresh. Away from the big-city world of our usual life, where eating is all about refuelling and fast food, it is refreshing to eat at a relaxed pace, and to feel that the chef really cares passionately about every single dish he places in front of you. We were thrilled that supper consisted of six different courses, and perfectly satisfied with the no-choice menu, which, in fact, made it even more enjoyable.

Waking up in the morning to the sounds of the water fountain, and the light and heat of Provence, is exciting and relaxing all at once. Breakfast is a healthy and simple combination of fresh fruit, cereals, cheeses, delicious breads, and apricot jam with lavender, plus some of the best coffee I have ever tasted in France. We take a walk around the herb garden: the air still has a fresh edge until midmorning, when the sun starts to mean business. We are almost

definitely walking in the formidable steps of Diane de Poitiers. Only a handful of families have owned the château since her day; the current owners bought Massillan in 2001. You can tell that Birgit Israel and Peter Wylly work in design: it takes professionals, and ones in love with their project, to combine respect for historic features with modern cool.

Poolside at hotels is not usually my favourite thing to do, but the size of the Château de Massillan and the limited number of guests make the garden feel like our very own, and the pool becomes the focus of our stay. The beauty of the setting, the water, heat, shade when we want it, native plants and trees and hypnotic sounds of the cicadas… time seems to slow until we have reached a state of perfect laziness. I keep meaning to wander over to the salon on the far side of the courtyard to leaf through one or two of the owners' design-led book collection – much more considered than a mere handful of coffee-table books – but, incredibly, ↓

I never get round to it. We do, however, manage to sample the wonderful cocktail list. And, one lunchtime, we make a foray to the extremely local Grillade d'Helios, which might be Massillan's own restaurant it is so nearby. We share pizza baked in the wood-fired oven: so good, so simple – perfectly in keeping with our foresty setting.

We barely leave the compound all weekend and *je ne regrette rien*. By night, the courtyard is lit with sunken lights and candles, and decked with oleander and lavender. Massillan, the only crenellated castle I know of that has bedchambers in lavender blues, pale chocolates and dark honey, gets the balance between mediaeval and retro-chic just right, and the atmosphere is intimate, informal and genuinely warm. Whatever your reason for going to this place, just go.

Reviewed by Philip Treacy

NEED TO KNOW
Rooms 12.
Rates €170–€625.
Check-out Midday, but flexible depending on availability.
Room service Guests can be served breakfast in their rooms on request.
Facilities All rooms are decorated with antiques. Suites have large terraces that open onto to the courtyard.
Poolside The beautiful courtyard swimming pool is surrounded by stylish wooden sunloungers.
Children The hotel is not suitable for children.
Hotel closed From mid-October until Easter.

IN THE KNOW
Our favourite rooms The intimate suite is spacious and stands on its own in the gardens. Room 16 is the personal favourite of the hotel's interior-designer owner. Room 15 has a big sexy chandelier and overlooks the fountain and terrace below.
Hotel bar Guests may enjoy drinks throughout the hotel and grounds.
Hotel restaurant Like the hotel itself, the daily four- or five-course set menu blends classic French cuisine with contemporary flair. There is also a wonderfully comprehensive wine list. A reservation is essential. Open for dinner 19h30–21h30.
Top table Alfresco in the oleander-lined courtyard.
Dress code Birkin/Gainsbourg chic.

LOCAL EATING AND DRINKING
Formal, Michelin-starred **Le Pré du Moulin** in Sérignan-du-Comtat (04 90 70 14 55) has a rich menu of forest mushrooms, asparagus, Mediterranean seafood, and truffles, combined with aromatic Côtes du Rhône wines. In Uchaux, **Côte Sud** on Route d'Orange (04 90 40 66 08) is great for a lunch or dinner of fine gastronomy. **Grillade d'Hélios** on La Martine (04 90 40 61 81) is a casual and relaxed restaurant with hearty rustic fare and barbequed meat dishes.

 Smith members receive a selection of wines, hand-picked by the hotel sommelier, and an upgrade, subject to availability.

GET A ROOM!
Use our online booking service at www.mrandmrssmith.com to check availability and make reservations. Register your Smithcard to find out about current member offers for this hotel.

Château de Massillan
Chemin Hauteville, Uchaux
+33 (0)4 90 40 64 51
reservations@chateau-de-massillan.com; www.chateau-de-massillan.com

Hostellerie de Crillon le Brave

DESTINATION   VAUCLUSE
STYLE   PRIVATE EYRIE
SETTING   HILLTOP TURRETS

MTWTFSSMTWTFSSMTWTFSSMTWTFSSMTWTFSSMTWT
FRANCE

'As you sit on the Terrasse
Ventoux, the rest of the little
village lies beneath you, the
mountain and the vine-covered
plain leading the eyes up and away'

TWTFSSMTWTFSSMTWTFSSMTWTFSSMTWTFSS

Mr Smith is poking his head out of the car window, not unlike a handsome hunting dog wearing sunglasses and a hat. 'I'm not getting it,' he says.

'Are you really sniffing as hard as you can?' 'Yes! Slow down – it's being blown away by the wind.' I don't want to slow down all that much, since it is nearly two o'clock, and the rigid window that is French lunchtime is about to slam curtly shut in our faces. We are taking the scenic route back towards our hotel, after a morning in Sault, one of the lavenderiest towns in France, and Mr Smith is keen to inhale. The *chemin des lavandes* takes us among the rows of bushes that cover much of the valley, past smallholdings where you can buy essential oils and lavender bags. Our attempts to snort the fragrance direct from the air end in snorts of laughter, and I put my foot down, lest we go hungry.

We find friendly faces and a still-open kitchen at Chalet Reynard, an alpine-style café and restaurant near the

top of the Mont Ventoux, on whose southern flanks we are staying for the weekend. Our boutique castle hideaway, L'Hostellerie de Crillon le Brave, is pretty elevated itself, perched high on the hillside, though nowhere matches the mountain for loftiness. It reigns over this part of the Vaucluse like a lost Alp, fertile and vine-covered lower down, dramatically denuded of vegetation at the top.

After a salad among Lycra-clad cyclists (the Ventoux is a magnet for determined Belgians), we head back to Crillon for the afternoon. The village is ever-sleepy; since it's not on the road to anywhere, passing trade is minimal. We pass through the country-house reception into one of the hotel's leafy terraces, where I decide to settle down with my book while Mr Smith heads athletically to the pool. I have decided this is my second-favourite spot, hedged by a bank of herbs (wafting their scent obligingly); I am saving the Terrasse Ventoux, my number one, for the apéritif, which was such a lovely way to kick off our stay last night. If the

hotel were a ship, it would be the foredeck; the rest of the little village lies beneath you, with the mountain and the vine-covered plain leading the eye up and away. At sunset it is truly romantic – I defy any lovers, young or not-so, to sit here and not feel like holding hands.

Our room is in La Maison Reboul (the rambling property occupies half a dozen mellow-stone houses, connected by 'secret' paths). It is very private, rustic yet elegant, and one of the biggest doubles we've had the pleasure of staying in. The fabrics are pretty; the dove-grey paint accents are chic. There are botanical prints on the wall, a sofa and armchairs in a modern mixture of checks and florals. We've got Provençal tiles on the floor, and a free-standing rolltop bath on the other side of the vast bed, which is itself a most welcoming destination, with its high padded headboard and piles of pillows. The shower room is the best surprise of all: it occupies the 12th-century tower, with a window like a tunnel, at the end of which you spy a burst of light, a haze of green vines and the distant hillside.

My neck twinges faintly and I wonder… reception can't guarantee the instant conjuring-up of a masseur, as it is Sunday, but promise to give it a go. An hour and a half later, I find myself being expertly reassembled by Roger Page, the hotel's on-call massage therapist and a former professional cyclist. He sounds a wee bit cynical when I ask him about this evening's football match between Italy and France – 'big business', rather than the beautiful game, he concludes. I bid Roger *au revoir* gratefully and prepare myself for my romantic sports date. The wonderful wet room can't compete with a long, relaxing bath and a glass of champagne.

There's certainly nothing cynical about my beau's approach to the match. I have lost count of the number of times he has made me ring the hotel to make sure we would be able to watch Zidane take on the Azzuri without missing dinner; breakfast and lunch times are impressively elastic here, but the kitchen stops taking orders at half nine on the dot – we wouldn't even be into extra time by then. ↓

In the event, it is a surreal experience: pan-fried foie gras and turbot instead of lager and cigarettes; restrained murmur rather than expletive-strewn yelps and roars. When Zidane stacks it and all is lost, the staff, perhaps not permitted to weep openly, politely deflect our commiserations with 'C'est pas grave' – a rather sporting response, we think. It was worth spending the time indoors, just: summer dining usually takes place on the beautiful circular terrace, smart with olive trees and erect evergreens.

There is always someone on hand at Crillon to bring us a glass of Côtes-du-Rhône by the pool or in our room. The warmest welcome comes from Patrick Gaillard, the amiable and able general manager, who greets and waves off every guest, and gives the genuine impression that nothing is too much trouble. He clearly loves L'Hostellerie, but was happy to point us down the hill to the Vieux Four restaurant, Crillon's other dining option, when we decided we wanted a stroll with our supper on our first night here.

Our lovely room overlooks the breakfast terrace, but on our second morning here, we could still do with a map to find it. That has probably been our favourite thing about L'Hostellerie: there's always a little bit more to find, another door or gateway to a new level of sunny seclusion. Little birds visit us as we sip coffee looking out over the greeny-grey expanse. There's a lot more for us to discover here, and in the Vaucluse in general – we haven't even got round to any formal wine-tasting (as opposed to informal wine-consuming) on this trip, nor have we spent a morning meandering round a market. But we have 'done lavender'. And we've found ourselves feeling more relaxed than we thought we knew how to: this is our kind of mountain.

Reviewed by Mr & Mrs Smith

NEED TO KNOW
Rooms 32.
Rates €200–€600, excluding breakfast.
Check-out Midday.
Room service Anything from the restaurant menu can be brought to your room, until 21h30. Light snacks are available at other times.
Facilities Wireless Internet in reception, laptops available, bicycles, wine-tasting, cheese-tasting and massage on request.
Poolside Outdoor pool with panoramic country views.
Children Are very welcome.
Also Pets are allowed, with a €10 charge. Smoking is permitted in the outdoor areas.

IN THE KNOW
Our favourite rooms Room 33, aka La Tour, is a vast suite on two levels with a pair of open-plan rolltop baths with a superb view, separated by a 'champagne table'. Room 32 also has an open-plan living area, bedroom and bathroom, plus a vast shower room built right into the wall of the old citadel.
Hotel bar You can take your apéritif in any of the hotel's many nooks and crannies, indoors or out: the Terrace du Ventoux is pretty unbeatable in summer.
Hotel restaurant Set in the rustic cellar, with an open fireplace and a gorgeous terrace, serving refined but not precious Provençal cuisine, such as pan-fried foie gras, and turbot or lamb.
Top table At the front of the terrace in summer; by the fire in winter.
Dress code Linen, sunglasses, not too outré.

LOCAL EATING AND DRINKING
Le Vieux Four (04 90 12 81 39) is Crillon's other option for dinner, and a fine, unfussy one it is, too, with a lovely terrace. **La Gousse d'Ail** in Bédoin (04 90 92 16 87) is more rustic, with robust, herby cuisine. A little further afield, **La Nesque** in Villes-sur-Auzon (04 90 61 82 10) is a super local with a fine courtyard and good regional food. On market day in Carpentras, the best staging posts are **Bar-Brasserie Rich** at the end of Rue de la République, and the bars on Place Charles de Gaulle, near the cathedral. **Bistrot de l'Industrie** on Quai de la Charité in L'Isle-sur-la-Sorgue (04 90 38 00 40) makes a pleasing riverside pitstop for a cold beer and a pizza on market day.

 Smith members are treated to one complimentary champagne breakfast for two.

GET A ROOM!
Use our online booking service at www.mrandmrssmith.com to check availability and make reservations. Register your Smithcard to find out about current member offers for this hotel.

Hostellerie de Crillon le Brave
Place de l'Eglise, Crillon le Brave, Vaucluse
+33 (0)4 90 65 61 61
crillonbrave@relaischateaux.com; www.crillonlebrave.com

COTE D'AZUR

Côte d'Azur

COASTLINE   GLITTERING RIVIERA
COAST LIFE   SEA AND BE SEEN

MTWTFSSMTWTFSSMTWTFSSMTWTFSSMTWTFSSMTWT
FRANCE

TWTFSSMTWTFSSMTWTFSSMTWTFSSMTWTFSSMTWTFSS

COTE D'AZUR

On the coast that defined seaside glamour, you can never be too rich or too brown. Despite countless imitators, there is only one Riviera and one Côte d'Azur, and the original retains a distinctive cachet that keeps the starlets and socialites flocking here year-round. The high-rollers may glitter in the chic beach bars and fine French restaurants, but it's the coast itself, floating between the green mountains and the warm indigo sea, that outshines everything. The landscape of parasol pines and terracotta-hued villas is bathed in Provençal light and colour, where Picasso and Matisse paid hotel bills in masterpieces just for the chance to stay another day.

GETTING THERE

Planes Nice airport is the coast's main gateway. Nice Helicoptères (+33 (0)4 93 21 34 32) has regular flights from Nice to Cannes (€115) and St Tropez (€295).

Trains Trains run regularly to and from Nice-Ville station. The TGV from Paris takes six hours.

Automobiles Bowling along with the wind in your hair may be a Riviera fantasy but, in reality, the coast road is very congested. Even so, a car is invaluable for visiting the villages inland.

DO GO / DON'T GO

Mediterranean rules apply: spring and autumn are perfect, with July and August crowded and hot. May sees the Cannes Film Festival and Monaco Grand Prix take place.

COMPLETELY CÔTE D'AZUR

Try your luck at the roulette tables of the Casino de Monte Carlo, Café de Paris, or Le Sporting (membership is not required, but don't forget ID). Try to break their bank, not yours.

LOCAL KNOWLEDGE

Taxis You can hail taxis on the street if they display a yellow light, although it's better to use a taxi rank. Prices are expensive.

Tipping culture By law, a service charge is automatically added to all restaurant bills, but it's nice to leave a euro or two.

Siesta and fiesta Shops are normally open 9h–12h and 14h–18h. Banks close at 16h30. Restaurants are often closed on Mondays and Tuesdays.

Packing tips Your most glamorous wardrobe – nothing else will do. Very big, very dark sunglasses (to be worn at all times).

Recommended reads *To Catch a Thief* by David Dodge; *The Last Life* by Claire Messud; *Tender is the Night* by F Scott Fitzgerald.

Cuisine Provençal cuisine for ladies who lunch: elegant pasta dishes, tapenade, salads, fruits de mer. Provence rosé is delicious, but sometimes it just has to be champagne all the way.

Currency Euro.

Dialling codes Country code for France: 33. Provence: 04.

DIARY

February Monte Carlo's glamorous Primo Cup sailing competition fills the marina (www.yacht-club-monaco.mc). **April** The Tennis Masters attracts the top players (www.masters-series.com/montecarlo). **May** The world's best-known cinema event, the Cannes Film Festival, kicks off two weeks of Hollywood swagger and unrestrained movie madness (www.festival-cannes.fr). It's followed by the Formula 1 Monaco Grand Prix (www.monte-carlo.mc/formule1) and the Classic Car Grand Prix (www.acm.mc). **Last week of July** Nice International Jazz Festival takes place, principally in the ruins of the Roman amphitheatre (www.nicejazzfest.com). **16–19 August** The Pantiero Festival in Nice stages electro gigs at the Palais des Festivals (www.festivalpantiero.com).

WORTH GETTING OUT OF BED FOR

Viewpoint The restaurant terrace of swish Château Eza (04 93 41 12 24) in Eze, has magnificent views of Cap Ferrat, 400 metres below. Book in advance for a table at sunset.

Arts and culture La Colombe d'Or in St-Paul-de-Vence was once frequented by artists such as Picasso, Rouault and Léger, who paid their bills in artworks, leaving the hotel with a fabulous collection. The nearby Maeght Foundation Museum has works by Kandinsky and Chagall. Matisse designed the interior of the Chapel of the Rosary in Vence.

Activities Charter a yacht to explore the coast; contact www.aquacruise.com for details. The Verdon Gorge is ideal for rafting and canyoning; contact www.aboard-rafting.com. In the winter it's possible to ski at Isola 2000, two hours from Nice; or try ice-karting or ice-driving if you dare. Contact www.sportsloisirs.net for more details.

Daytripper The peaceful coves of the Isles de Lérins are perfect for picnics and skinny-dipping. Take the 15-minute ferry from Cannes or Juan-les-Pins.

Best beach The sandy crescent of Plage Mala, at Cap d'Ail, attracts Monégasque socialites. Plage de Paloma is a shady cove at the tip of luxurious Cap Ferrat. Private Castel Plage in Nice is where the discerning go to bronze. Plage de la Garoupe on Cap d'Antibes was immortalised by F Scott Fitzgerald in *Tender is the Night*. Z-Plage in Cannes is suitably fabulous.

Something for nothing You'll have to get your hire car round Monaco's twisting two-mile Grand Prix street circuit in around a minute and 14 seconds if you want to beat the lap record.

Shopping Galeries Lafayette near Place Masséna in Nice brings Parisian chic to the Côte d'Azur. For design boutiques, Monte Carlo's Boulevard des Moulins and Metropole Mall are hard to top. Every Saturday there's a fleamarket in the Old Port in Cannes. Cours Saleya market in Nice is antiques heaven on Mondays and foodie paradise the rest of the week. Go early.

CAFES

Watch the automobile exotica purring past at **Café de Paris**, on Place du Casino in Monaco, or ignore celebs over coffee at **Cafe Roma** on Square Mérimée, by Cannes' yacht-filled port.

BARS AND RESTAURANTS

Zebra Square at the Grimaldi Forum, Avenue Princesse Grace (+377 99 99 25 50), is great for pre-dinner drinks or late-night glam. Country-house **La Bastide de Saint-Antoine** on Avenue Henri-Dunant in Grasse (04 93 70 94 94) serves excellent French cuisine on a terrace under the trees. **Tetou** in Vallauris-Golfe Juan (04 93 63 23 26) is the best beach restaurant for bouillabaisse. Closed November to March. **Restaurant Le Moulin de Mougins** on Quartier Notre Dame de Vie, Mougins (04 93 75 78 24) has two Michelin stars. Book a table in the sculpture garden. In Cannes, **Le Mesclun** on Rue St-Antoine (04 93 99 45 19) is great for fresh fish, grilled to perfection. Dress up for a fantastic lunch or dinner on the terrace at **Restaurant La Palme d'Or** at the Martinez Hotel on La Croisette (04 92 98 74 14).

NIGHTLIFE

Jimmy'z, on Avenue Princesse Grace in Monaco, is the height of fashion, luxury and expense. The Arabian Nights garden at **Le Baoli**, in Port Pierre Canto in Cannes, is a stylish place to party under the stars. **Les Caves du Roy** at the luxurious Byblos hotel on Avenue Paul Signac in St Tropez is one of the coast's most glamorous nightspots, where looking the part is all-important.

Toile Blanche

DESTINATION	COTE D'AZUR
STYLE	CHIC CHAMBRE D'HOTE
SETTING	ARTY ENCLAVE

MTWTFSSMTWTF**SS**MTWTFSSMTWTFSSMTWTFSSMTWT
FRANCE

'The rustic house and lavender-filled garden contrast with a modern interior; polished concrete is mixed with bold colours and striking art'

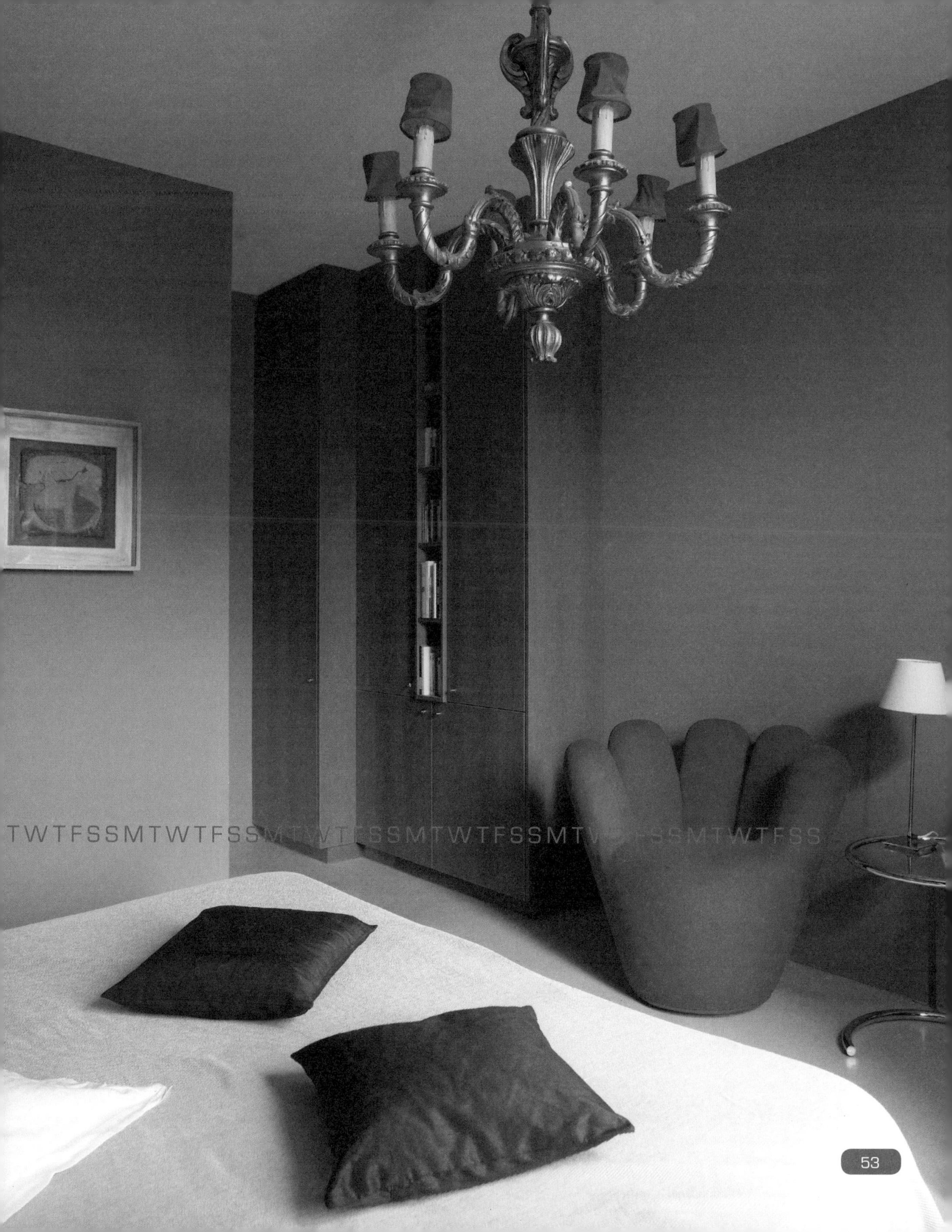

Toile Blanche, Côte d'Azur, France

As we drove towards our destination through the rolling hills of southeast Provence, down tiny tractor-filled country lanes, it was clear that this was to be a weekend for leaving city life far, far behind. Despite being a mere 15 minutes from Nice airport, we managed to get completely lost in the rural landscape; the countryside was so picturesque we were only too happy to take the scenic route. Eventually we found what we were looking for – a beautifully restored 300-year-old house, finished in Provence's signature honey-coloured render. We were greeted by the charming Madame Nadine who, like the setting itself, had a calm and gentle air.

The lack of dedicated reception area promotes a relaxed, informal feel. This informality could be said to extend to our room, where Mrs Smith discovered a neat stack of someone else's smalls in the wardrobe. When we asked if we were in the right room, Madame appeared surprised, and came up to remove the mystery lingerie. Though charmed by the huge bed and gloriously big bath, we wondered whether the lack of TV or minibar was an oversight by the hotel. We found a whimsical note explaining that the absence is quite deliberate in order to create proper downtime. It wasn't until we sipped an early evening beer on the terrace that the penny dropped...

This isn't a full-service hotel stuffed with hairdryers and staff poised to pick up your towels. Toile Blanche is a chambre d'hôte – one of those quintessentially French things that doesn't quite translate into English. It's a place to stay as a privileged guest in a family home, where hotel facilities and amenities

are swapped for the chance to gain an insight into the Riviera way of life. The owners are generally busy getting on with their lives during the day, rather than tending to your each and every need, so consequently they appreciate an easy-going attitude from their guests. At the same time, they value any opportunity to get to know you and truly want you to feel at home.

Yet this is no ordinary home. The rustic house and lavender-filled garden contrast delightfully with a very modern interior. Polished concrete walls are mixed with bold colours, intriguing sculpture and striking artwork. Pristine linen tablecloths and white parasols flap gently in the breeze: this is cutting-edge style in an idyllic rural setting.

When we quizzed one of Nadine's amiable sons about the vibrant art adorning the walls, it transpired that Leroy+Leroy are not only resident artists, but also his brothers, and Toile Blanche's talented chefs. Their parents' love of art has clearly rubbed off – even extending to their own contemporary gallery. Here is a family business par excellence: a private home in the South of France given over to culture, food and laidback living. Perfect for a Smith escape.

Just as the hotel isn't really a hotel, the restaurant isn't really a restaurant, but a table d'hôte, albeit a very sophisticated one. Each night in summer a set menu is offered for a very reasonable €40. Fresh local ingredients arrive each day in distinctly un-Sainsbury's-like wooden trays, and are cooked to perfection with a sense of adventure and fun. We'd advised our hosts that we're vegetarian, and to our delight found that this didn't mean missing out – who knew veggie haute cuisine could exist in France? Our love of apricot-hued Provençal rosé was also catered for by a well-chosen wine list.

By the end of the night we agreed that it was one of the best meals we'd ever had on French soil. That is some compliment, and it explains why this restaurant was full of locals and should be booked in advance. (Dinner is only served for three summer months ↓

and should not be missed). As our fellow dinners indulged in an incredible array of cheeses, we sloped off to bed, pausing briefly to ask at what time breakfast was served. The answer was a refreshing 'as late as you like'.

We put this to the test by moseying downstairs from a prolonged lie-in at 11h15 to find one table on the terrace still set for breakfast. We apologised for being the last guests to rise but Madame shrugged, smiling: 'Someone has to be.' Breakfast was a splendid mix of fresh fruit, cheeses and patisserie with coffee and just-squeezed orange juice. We were then left to our own devices, which meant sunbathing for Mrs Smith and a splash in the elegant pool for Mr. The tranquillity that dominates the local valley was broken only occasionally by Pico, the 25-year-old feathered member of the family. Mr Smith discovered a new talent for squawking and whistling, to Mrs Smith's embarrassment. Pico, unembarrassed, responded accordingly.

We decided (a little reluctantly) to go out for dinner the next night, and having already spent the day wandering the ridiculously quaint St-Paul-de-Vence, we headed to Haut-de-Cagnes, an untouristy mediaeval bourg where we climbed the steep alleys followed by a legion of ponderous Basset hounds. In Place du Château we came across a bucolic French scene of a boules match, so we bagged a table at Le Jimmy's and spent the evening debating, over perfect pizza and rosé, whether we could afford a local pied-à-terre.

Toile Blanche has all the essential ingredients for a boutique weekend away. The hills, cobblestone villages, pretty terrace and wolf-whistling parrot made it all the more unforgettable. But what makes Toile Blanche special is the languid pace of French family life and the phenomenal food. This is a hotel (sorry – chambre d'hôte) that could persuade even the most ardent urbanite to adopt a healthy dose of sun-kissed slothfulness.

Reviewed by Mr & Mrs Smith

NEED TO KNOW
Rooms Six.
Rates €140–€225, including breakfast.
Check-out Midday. There is a luggage store for late-departing guests.
Room service There is no formal room service at Toile Blanche.
Facilities The hotel has no TVs. There is wireless Internet in the lounge.
Poolside The outdoor pool is set on the terrace, with beautiful views.
Children The hotel does not usually cater for children. An extra bed is €25.
Hotel closed Open year-round, but the restaurant is closed from mid-September to mid-June.
Also The terrace and gardens are sprinkled with sculptures. Pico the parrot lives in the garden and has a penchant for wolf whistling.

IN THE KNOW
Our favourite rooms Bonheur is cosy and decorated in warm shades of aubergine and red. Détente is a spacious room with a great private terrace.
Hotel bar There is no bar, but pre-dinner drinks are served on the terrace.
Hotel restaurant The restaurant is open from mid-June until mid-September and has a strong reputation for delicious and creative cuisine. There is one menu, and one price: €50. Vegetarians are well catered for.
Top table On the terrace, with views over the garden.
Dress code Relaxed Riviera style.

LOCAL EATING AND DRINKING
The famous **Colombe d'Or** in Saint-Paul-de-Vence (04 93 32 80 02) has fine food and a stupendous art collection. The pretty village of Haut-de-Cagnes is perfect for an evening stroll and has several excellent restaurants. **Le Grimaldi**, on Place du Château (04 93 20 60 24), serves fine Provençal cuisine served on a panoramic terrace. Just across the square **Le Jimmy's** is perfect for pizza (04 92 13 05 93). Michelin-starred **Josy-Jo** on Place du Planastel (04 93 20 68 76) has a seasonal menu based on local produce. **Le Black Cat** jazz club next to the mediaeval castle is perfect for a late-night drink.

 Smith members receive a Leroy+Leroy print.

GET A ROOM!
Use our online booking service at www.mrandmrssmith.com to check availability and make reservations. Register your Smithcard to find out about current member offers for this hotel.

Toile Blanche
826 Chemin de la Pounchounière, Saint-Paul-de-Vence
+33 (0)4 93 32 74 21
info@toileblanche.com; www.toileblanche.com

La Maison du Frêne

DESTINATION COTE D'AZUR
STYLE ARTY TOWNHOUSE
SETTING STREETS OF VENCE

MTWTFSSMTWTFSSMTWTFSSMTWTFSSMTWTFSSMTWT
FRANCE

'All the rooms are spacious
enough to feel like your own
apartment, adorned with art,
antiques, sculpture and books'

We touched down in Nice at the start of Mr Smith's 40th-birthday weekend, observing that the South of France attracts a rather more sophisticated crowd – if you class skinny white jeans, Cavalli sunglasses and Gina sandals as sophisticated – than our fellow travellers on recent Balearic trips. There's status and money in them there Provençal hills, evidently, which at least bodes well for my secret search for a perfect, original birthday present.

And so to collect the Fiat Panda. Lesson number one: when picking up a Fiat Panda, you really shouldn't stand in the Platinum queue. Luckily, Providence smiled: the customer before us was so patronising that I gave the member of staff a sympathetic look. Hertz forgave us for standing in the posh queue, and rewarded our sympathy with a upgrade to a BMW X3 – a veritable mini Chelsea tractor, not ideal for the narrow streets of the hilltop towns, but undoubtedly a coup. Lesson number two: being nice wins the day.

Shortly after spotting the beautiful cité historique of St-Paul-de-Vence on our left, we arrived in the less touristy but equally charming hilltop town of Vence. At La Maison du Frêne, we were greeted by Thierry, the owner. Both the man and his house are stylish, witty and unorthodox. You get the impression that you are stepping into a more interesting world, where anything goes, as long as it can be loosely termed as art. Freedom of expression, creative inspiration and exceptional taste make this a boutique guesthouse you won't forget in a hurry.

There are just four rooms in La Maison du Frêne. An indulgent thought would be to bring a group of your closest friends, take all four of the rooms and have an intimate house party hosted by Thierry. All the rooms are spacious enough to feel like your own apartment, with art, antiques, sculpture and books adorning them. The books on Coco Chanel and the history of couture that lined the shelves meant I subtly binned my well-thumbed celeb magazine. We

stayed in the Parisian room. Its bed is fit for a king. Thierry puts some of his best pieces in the rooms; he is such a perfectionist that, apparently, he personally takes care of every single detail, right down to the bedding. La Maison du Frêne is an undeniably impressive labour of love. Our bathroom was beautiful: surprisingly large, with double basins and big shower with curved glass wall. There was a large hanging space for clothes and an empty fridge. What an inspired idea: choose your own contents in the local shop and avoid suffering the heavy prices of the usual in-room minibar.

The thing is, La Maison du Frêne is not a hotel; it is definitely more like a private house where you can combine complete privacy with your host's conviviality. Guests are free to do whatever they want, and are given a code to access the front door when Thierry isn't at home. If the reception area and kitchen are open, he is at home; if they are locked, you go straight up to your suite. The first day it was just the

two of us at breakfast. We sat at the kitchen table with Thierry preparing and entertaining around us. Once a director for French beauty brand Carita, and also a former hairdresser to the stars, Thierry has an interesting perspective on life. He has been surrounded by beautiful people all his years, but he gives the impression that he prefers to be surrounded by beautiful things. We thoroughly enjoyed our conversations about life, style, fashion and art. Not to mention the fabulous breakfast: fresh orange juice, tea, coffee, ripe apricots and blackberries, fresh baguettes and croissants with butter and jam. Very French, very lovely.

We decided to pop into the tourist office in Vence to pick up a map of the walking trail to St-Paul-de-Vence. We set off in shorts and trainers, fearing we looked like cartoon tourists. Map in hand, we still didn't get it quite right, and went a little off-piste. It was a beautiful sunny day, though, and the walk through pine trees looked and smelled wonderful. We knew ↓

St-Paul-de-Vence was an idyllic place, all winding streets and steep inclines; what we didn't expect was the quality of art for sale in this little hilltop town: from original Dalí sculptures at €425,000 to vintage fashion ads for €25. We stopped for a lovely lunch on a terrace, and admired the pretty streets, although we did get the impression that it is a bit of a Disneyland village intended for British, American and Japanese tourists. We certainly weren't the only people looking in confusion at a map in the middle of the street.

Back in Vence, we went for a wander around the irresistible galleries and met Brett Rhodes-Neal, a painter and sculptor who trained with Hockney and who is one of the artists whose work is represented in La Maison du Frêne. My husband is a completely obsessive canine-lover, and he fell head-over-heels in love with Brett's *Beagle in Boots*, a carbon-fibre dog wearing trainers, painted in tribute to Lichtenstein. We commissioned our own

Picasso-inspired hound, which will shortly appear in a Taschen book. Most importantly, I had found the perfect 40th-birthday present for my husband, and there was no disputing it was an original one.

Not content with spending a small fortune on the four-legged artwork, we then made our way to Galerie de l'Evêché to look at some new Dalibert oils, and to meet the man himself – artistic temptation seems to wait around every corner in Vence. Suffice to say, we ended up buying five paintings for our new house. We don't have a sofa, a bed or a table, but never mind: we can sit on the floor and be inspired by our first experience of buying art as a couple. There was no denying that La Maison du Frêne had certainly had a profound effect upon us. More than that, we can say we returned from our stay in Vence inspired by *l'art de vivre*, aka the art of living.

Reviewed by Kirsten McNally

NEED TO KNOW
Rooms Four.
Rates €160–€200, including breakfast.
Check-out 13h.
Room service There is no room service available.
Facilities TV, DVD.
Poolside There is no pool.
Children The hotel's art collection makes the hotel unsuitable for under-12s. One of the suites can accommodate three people.
Also The hotel is perfect for art-lovers, filled with the owner's personal art collection and an extensive library of original art books.

IN THE KNOW
Our favourite rooms The Chapel Suite is lovely, light and airy, and the balcony of the Pop Art Suite has a view of the Matisse-designed Chapel of the Rosary.
Hotel bar Guests can enjoy drinks throughout the house.
Hotel restaurant Complimentary tea is served in the afternoon. Evening meals are available on request, made from the best fresh produce from the local market.
Top table In the intimate dining room.
Dress code Artistic flair.

LOCAL EATING AND DRINKING
With two Michelin stars, **Restaurant Le Moulin de Mougins** on Quartier Notre Dame-de-Vie in Mougins (04 93 75 78 24) has suitably excellent cuisine. Book a table in their sculpture garden. **Le Crabe Enragé**, on Avenue Marcellin Maurel in Vence (04 93 24 61 50), specialises in tasty crab and seafood dishes. The **Colombe d'Or** in Saint-Paul-de-Vence (04 93 32 80 02) is as famous for its fabulous art collection as it is for its fine food. Le Château du Domaine St Martin on Avenue des Templiers in Vence (04 93 58 02 02) has a Michelin-starred restaurant, **La Commanderie**, with fantastic panoramic views across the Côte d'Azur, as well as an excellent, less formal grill restaurant in an olive grove. **La Farigoule** on Rue Henri-Isnard (04 93 58 01 27) has rich, comforting Provençal dishes and a beautiful rose garden.

 Smith members get a presentation box of locally produced handmade soap.

GET A ROOM!
Use our online booking service at www.mrandmrssmith.com to check availability and make reservations. Register your Smithcard to find out about current member offers for this hotel.

La Maison du Frêne
1 Place du Frêne, Vence
+33 (0)4 93 24 37 83
contact@lamaisondufrene.com; www.lamaisondufrene.com

PACK THE
PERFECT
PICNIC

HOW TO... PACK THE PERFECT PICNIC

Here, top chef and restaurateur Sally Clarke and the Smith team offer tips for on-the-hoof haute cuisine. And remember, once you've got your beautiful food, find a peaceful pitch with a view and a comfortable sitting surface. Avoid lakes or stagnant water because they attract bugs – gently flowing rivers are better. One rug for each pair of picnickers offers optimum comfort, and grab cushions too if you can. It's smart to have a big umbrella at hand for shade or rain, and take two plastic bags: one with a clean damp cloth for wiping fingers and faces; one for rubbish – a picnic spot should be left looking as beautiful as it was when you arrived.

France This land of food-lovers is full of perfect picnic fare. Every town offers different shops for breads, cheeses, ripe fruits and vegetables (if you ask nicely in your best French, the grocer will wash them for you), and a delicatessen for terrines, salamis and hams, which you can have sliced to your specifications while you wait. You'll also be able to get chilled water and wine. The only downside is that you will need to visit each shop separately while you compile the feast, leaving a hot, cross spouse (or worse: hot, cross children) in the car outside.

Greece Pick up ingredients for a classic Greek salad on market day: lettuce, tomato, cucumber, red onion, capers, Kalamata olives, feta and oregano. You will also find soft pitta breads for dipping into taramasalata and tzatziki. Every other street boasts a *zaharoplastio* – a patisserie selling freshly ground coffee. The best ones will offer not only baklava but also custard pies called *galaktoboureko*, which should not be missed. If the local wine is not to your taste, ouzo, well-chilled with ice and kept in a Thermos flask, is very refreshing. Don't forget you will need lots of cool Loutraki water to counteract the heat (and the ouzo).

Italy Another country to get full marks for ease of picnic foraging, Italy has wonderful weekly *mercati*, so get up early and select the best of each season's fresh produce: vines of ripe tomatoes, bitter salad leaves, glistening cherries, soft figs, heavy grapes, sun-warmed peaches – you can easily find a *fontana* (fountain of spring water) in most villages to wash your finds. Most markets also have a couple of must-visit stands selling snacks to add sparkle to any spread. These might include *porchetta* (spit-roast pig with salty, crunchy crackling, filled with a scented stuffing of wild herbs) which can be crammed into crusty rolls; *piadine* (flatbreads filled with ham and cheese); and crisp *fritto misto* (tiny fish in light batter) sold in paper cones. If you're in a rush, most supermarkets have excellent deli counters that slice hams and salamis and offer a range of cheeses, as well as delicacies such as roasted peppers, sweet baked onions, roasted artichokes and olives. Get the best breads from the *panificio* (bakery) – where you can also look out for fresh pizza and home-made breadsticks. *Pasticcerie* sell fancy cakes and fruit tarts for an added 'ta-da!' factor at the end of the meal. There's no shortage of fantastic regional wines: dry, fizzy prosecco is excellent value and will make your picnic feel extra-special.

Spain Start by opening a chilled bottle of La Guita manzanilla – and follow it swiftly with slices of potato tortilla and Manchego cheese (preferably a young one, as the mature cheeses are often too salty for uninitiated palates). For salami lovers, a pure *salchichón ibérico* will be the best choice, alongside the chorizo sausage, of course. Drop into a tapas bar for some chicken or ham *croquetas*, which will have been made fresh the night before – delicious eaten cold, perhaps with a jar of manzanilla olives. Look out, too, for freshly fried potato crisps, and maybe rice salad with apples, peas, pine nuts and sultanas. For pudding you cannot do better than simply serving some fresh fruit – peaches and apricots – and the strange-looking but very tasty cherries called *picotas*, which are sold without their stems.

And finally... Lie back with a satisfied stomach, gaze up at the clouds while listening to birdsong, with another bottle chilling in a stream or in a cooler by your elbow, and wonder to yourself why it is you don't plan a picnic a little more often.

● SOUTHWEST PROVENCE

Southwest Provence

COUNTRYSIDE   SCENES FROM VAN GOGH
COUNTRY LIFE   WHOLE LOTTA ROSÉ

MTWTFSSMTWTFSSMTWTFSSMTWTFSSMTWTFSSMTWT
FRANCE

SOUTHWEST PROVENCE

This area of Provence is a land of light and colour, where the languid river Rhône winds its way through fruit orchards and fields of lavender before melting into the watery maze of the Camargue. The wild dunes and marshes of the Med coast are the domain of cowboys, white horses and neon-pink flamingos. Inland, Arles, and its laidback neighbour Nîmes, are a beguiling blend of Roman amphitheatres, Provençal cuisine, café culture and sun-dappled boulevards. From the dramatic clifftop village of Les Baux, set among the olive groves, vines and craggy uplands of the Alpilles, you can look out across a land of Van Gogh, sunflowers and starry, starry nights.

GETTING THERE

Planes There are regular flights to Aix-en-Provence, Marseille, Montpellier and Nîmes.

Trains The TGV from Paris to Avignon and Nîmes takes three hours.

Automobiles A car is only necessary if you want to explore the countryside. Inter-city transport is good and town centres are often pedestrianised.

DO GO / DON'T GO

Spring and autumn are perfect: the weather is warm and there are fewer crowds. May is a riot of flowers, and September sees the grape harvest.

PERFECTLY PROVENCE

The Camargue is a coastal wilderness of marshes, dunes and flamingo-specked salt flats, with whitewashed houses and gypsy villages. *Gardians* (cowboys) watch over the region's famous herds of black bulls and white horses.

LOCAL KNOWLEDGE

Taxis Use a taxi rank or have your hotel order a cab. Prices are cheaper than on the Côte d'Azur, but there may be a charge for luggage.

Tipping culture A 15 per cent service charge is included in French restaurant and café bills by law; it's usual to round up the bill or leave a few euros, as well.

Siesta and fiesta Businesses are normally open 09h–12h, and 14h–18h. Banks close at 16h30. Restaurants get busy after 21h and are often closed on Mondays and Tuesdays.

Packing tips Take cobble-friendly sandals rather than stilettos, and pack binoculars and mosquito repellent for the Camargue.

Recommended reads *The Yellow House: Van Gogh, Gauguin, and Nine Turbulent Weeks in Arles* by Martin Gayford; *Caesar's Vast Ghost: Aspects of Provence* by Lawrence Durrell.

Cuisine Provence's *cuisine du soleil* is bursting with sun-ripened fruit and vegetables. Local specialities include bouillabaisse and red-wine stews known as daubes. There are excellent tapas in Spanish-influenced Nîmes. Seek out the refreshing rosé wines of Provence.

Currency Euro.

Dialling codes Country code for France: 33. Provence: 04.

DIARY

Mid-May Feria de Pentecôte celebrations in Nîmes include bullfights in the amphitheatre. **24–26 May** Gypsies from all over Europe gather in Saintes-Maries-de-la-Mer to pay their respects to St Sarah, the Black Madonna. **July** The Festival d'Aix-en-Provence is an opera festival in the grounds of the 14th-century palace (www.festival-aix.com). **Early September** With paella, sangria and bull-running, the Rice Festival in Arles feels decidedly Spanish.

WORTH GETTING OUT OF BED FOR

Viewpoint There's a wonderful view towards the Camargue from the battlements of the fortress in Les Baux-de-Provence. In summer, go early in the morning to avoid the crowds.

Arts and culture The 20,000-seat Roman amphitheatre in Nîmes doubles as a bullring and theatre venue. Nîmes' beautiful Maison Carrée temple occupies the site of the old Roman forum. Arles has an equally impressive amphitheatre, also used for hosting cultural events. Just outside Les Baux-de-Provence, Cathédrale d'Images is a huge cave in which famous artworks related to the area are projected onto its stone walls (www.cathedrale-images.com).

Activities The best way to see the Camargue is *gardian*-style, on horseback: go to www.promenadedesrieges.com for details. Kayak down the Gardon river to the towering Roman aqueduct of Le Pont du Gard, with Kayak Vert in Collias (04 66 22 80 76).

Daytripper Montpellier is one of the most energetic and prosperous cities of Mediterranean France. The vast Place de la Comédie is a good starting point for an exploration.

Perfect picnic Find a spot among the sunflower fields, vineyards and olive groves on the slopes of the Alpilles (little Alps) and enjoy the landscapes that inspired Cézanne and Van Gogh.

Something for nothing Vincent Van Gogh painted almost 200 paintings during the year or so he spent in Arles. Many of the spots where he worked are marked by a series of panels dotted around the city.

Shopping Uzès, north of Nîmes, has a Saturday market selling home-making goodies, from honey to linen quilts. Rue de la Madeleine in Nîmes is great for window-shopping. Buy slabs of nougat, almond-paste *callisons* and pastries from Maison Villaret and costume jewellery from Météorite. Aix-en-Provence has a wide range of design boutiques on Rue Fabrot, and a fantastic food market every day on Place Richelme.

CAFES

Right next to Nîmes' ancient temple, **Café Carrée** is the place to watch the performers and general bustle in the square over a coffee. There are plenty of cafés on Place aux Herbes next to the cathedral. **Le Napoléon** on Boulevard Victor Hugo is great for watching the world go by.

BARS AND RESTAURANTS

Deep in the Camargue, **La Chassagnette**, Domaine de L'Armellière on Route du Sambuc (04 90 97 26 96) is unmissable. Sit in the kitchen garden at lunchtime and enjoy their modern organic cuisine. The restaurant even supplies diners with straw hats on sunny days. In Nîmes, **Le Lisita**, next to the amphitheatre (04 66 67 29 15), is a stylish option with a fine seasonal menu. **Le Magister** on Rue Nationale (04 66 76 11 00) is an intimate restaurant with an extensive menu of Provençal specialities. In Eygalières, near Baux-de-Provence, **Chez Bru**, aka Le Bistrot d'Eygalières, on Rue de la République (04 90 90 60 34) is a Michelin-starred place of pilgrimage for gourmets. Their salt-marsh lamb is perfection. **Le Petit Bru** on Avenue Jean Jaurès (04 90 95 98 89; closed on Thursdays) is Bru's excellent bistro. In Arles, **Le Cilantro** on Rue Porte-de-Laure (04 90 18 25 05) does a fantastic blend of traditional and fusion dishes.

NIGHTLIFE

The region has nothing as glitzy or as noisy as the clubs of the Côte d'Azur. In southwest Provence, the best nightlife involves sipping pastis outside a local café on a balmy evening.

Jardins Secrets

DESTINATION	SOUTHWEST PROVENCE
STYLE	OPULENT CLASSIC
SETTING	ROMAN NIMES

MTWTFSSMTWTFSSMTWTFSSMTWTFSSMTWTFSSMTWT
FRANCE

'The communal areas
are littered with books,
photographs, musical
paraphernalia and aviaries
full of tiny singing birds'

Jardins Secrets, Southwest Provence, France

We reach a nondescript sidestreet in a nondescript part of town. There's a dreary grey door in a dreary stone wall. An impersonal sign sits next to an impersonal buzzer-and-speaker system. We are greeted by a rather sharp, disembodied French voice. The omens certainly aren't promising as this Monsieur et Madame Smith approach their refuge for the next 48 hours, seeking relief from stressful work, draining parenthood and sometimes-burdensome responsibilities. We don't mind admitting that, as we entered Jardins Secrets, were feeling thoroughly nondescript and dreary ourselves.

Then we are buzzed in and those indicators prove to be wildly misleading. What greets us feels little short of magical – it feels rather like we're entering an entirely new world through that Narnian wardrobe of a grey door. Jardins Secrets is not so much a hotel as a beautiful private house that, since 2005, has allowed members of the public to pay for the privilege

of staying there. And it really is a privilege. Boutique-hotel lovers everywhere should salute Christophe and Annabelle Valentin for opening up their family home and garden. On the edge of the ancient town centre of Nîmes in southern France, this pink-hued 17th-century city villa has just four guest rooms. There are more, we are happy to reveal, on the way – although not *too* many, of course.

The garden is what blows us away first. It banishes our mental cobwebs and ignites our enthusiasm (and even our travel-dampened ardour) from the moment we enter through that unremarkable gate. Rich, lush, colourful, it is full of olive trees, giant palms and bougainvillea. There is a soft, dappled light, and wooden loungers are here and there, in areas of inviting shade. The water gently laps the sides of the small but beautifully formed stone swimming pool, which is partly shaded by more olive trees. In this garden, we will have breakfast, read, swim, talk, doze, drink wine, debate whether to return to bed, eat olives, drink more wine, and genuinely relax for the first time in months.

On our arrival, a smiling maid appears as if from nowhere and guides us straight to our *chambre*. There is no checking in here, no reception area, no handing over of passports or credit cards – you get the impression that your hosts just want you to enjoy the absolutely enormous bed, and everything else this lovely house has to offer, as soon as possible. The rooms are large, luxurious and decorated with impeccably chic French taste. Elegantly shabby antiques sit alongside polished modern pieces. There are thick, heavy drapes hanging next to delicate, decorative writing tables; we have a shiny new widescreen TV and a stunning, spacious old-fashioned bathroom. Each room is individually decorated and furnished, and all have double doors which open out onto the garden. The attention to detail gives a clue to Christophe

and Annabelle's own professional backgrounds: he is an interiors and food photographer; she is a stylist. Together they have created what we suspect is their dream come true.

Later, Annabel approaches and introduces herself, checking that we are happy with everything. The low-key, 'nothing is too much trouble' level of service is consistently excellent. For example, in the morning we get an unexpected copy of *The Times* laid next to our breakfast of fresh croissants and home-made conserves, and a plate of fresh charcuterie appeared with some aperitifs in the early evening.

The communal areas of the house are littered with books, photographs, musical paraphernalia and aviaries full of tiny singing birds. We stumble across other guests intermittently, at most. Even as we lie in the garden (and we do a fair amount of this), the occasional sonic intrusions from over the walls – a nearby school, trains, a van rumbling down the ↓

street – only reminded us of how pleasant it was to be separated from the outside world.

Thankfully, there is no restaurant at Jardins Secrets (though they offer one or two special dishes), otherwise we might never venture beyond our cosseting cocoon. We manage to poke our noses around Nîmes itself, heading for the Old City, a five-minute walk from the hotel. It is studded with Roman relics, including the huge and intact Les Arènes amphitheatre and La Maison Carrée – a grand first-century temple. There is a distinctly Spanish-tinged feel to this Mediterranean region – in its food, its fondness for flamenco and bullfighting, its relaxed but upbeat air.

We wander the pedestrianised streets that connect a series of little squares, with cafés, restaurants, boutiques and often live music, before dining on simple-but-superb *plats du jour*. Both evenings we sit outside on secluded terraces, consuming three courses, coffee and a more-than-decent bottle of Costières de Nîmes, all for less than €100. On our return to Jardins Secrets, we find two slices of divine chocolate cake, left in our room for late-night nibbling. The cake – already building an international reputation all of its own – is much like the place as a whole: personal, unexpected, romantic and delicious.

Jardins Secrets is a hush-hush hideaway where we are made to feel welcome, but are left undisturbed. And thanks to low-cost flights from London, and Christophe happily shuttling us to the airport in less than 15 minutes, a two-day break really has been a two-day break. How grateful we've been for every extra second that we can add to our demanding itinerary of commuting between bed and garden, interspersed with the occasional meal out. Having enjoyed such a special stay there, the temptation is to let Jardins Secrets remain our secret – consider yourself let in on it.

Reviewed by William Drew

NEED TO KNOW
Rooms Four (with more planned).
Rates €190–€260, excluding breakfast.
Check-out 13h.
Room service Available between 18h and 23h.
Facilities TV and wireless Internet.
Poolside The outdoor pool is set in a walled garden.
Children It's not suitable for small children – the hotel is filled with highly breakable *objets d'art*.
Also The beautiful walled garden makes a tranquil retreat in the heart of Nîmes with its palms, bougainvillea and birdcages.

IN THE KNOW
Our favourite rooms All four rooms are individually styled, and have views over the garden. They are all beautiful: Room 1 is exquisite, with antique turquoise paintwork; Room 2 has lofty ceilings and bold black and white prints.
Hotel bar There is an honesty bar serving wine, beer, spirits, and so on.
Hotel restaurant Only breakfast is served, but it's exceptional.
Top table On the terrace in the garden.
Dress code Refined but relaxed.

LOCAL EATING AND DRINKING
The courtyard restaurant of **Le 9** on Rue de L'Etoile (04 66 21 80 77) has a romantic and relaxed atmosphere, and serves excellent fish dishes. **Le Grain de Soleil** on Rue des Greffes (04 66 38 97 94) is a top choice for organic and vegetarian food. **Aux Plaisirs des Halles** on Rue Littré (04 66 36 01 02; closed Sundays and Mondays) serves delicious Provençal cooking on a beautiful terrace. The bistro-style **Jardin d'Hadrien**, on Rue Enclos Rey (04 66 21 86 65), has a lovely shaded garden and does fine local beef and lamb dishes. Slinky **L'Exaequo** on Rue Bigot (04 66 21 71 96) is perfect for late-night mojitos and flamenco.

 Smith members receive a free bottle of wine.

GET A ROOM!
Use our online booking service at www.mrandmrssmith.com to check availability and make reservations. Register your Smithcard to find out about current member offers for this hotel.

Jardins Secrets
3 rue Gaston Maruejols, Nîmes
+33 (0)4 66 84 82 64
contact@jardinssecrets.net; www.jardinssecrets.net

L'Hôtel Particulier

DESTINATION   SOUTHWEST PROVENCE
STYLE   URBAN MANSION
SETTING   ARISTOCRATIC ARLES

MTWTFSSMTWTFSSMTWTFSSMTWTFSSMTWTFSSMTWT
FRANCE

'The enormous, crisp-linened bed and Provençal furniture in our whitewashed boudoir were enlivened by a turquoise *lit de repos*'

TWTFSSMTWTFSSMTWTFSSMTWTFSSMTWTFSS

As I sat in the Hôtel Particulier's sun-dappled courtyard, scooping fresh raspberry jam onto delicate little pastries and listening to the soft coos of the somnolent doves perched plumply on the roof, I marvelled at how the Arlésiens' hospitality has improved in the 120 or so years since they petitioned for the removal of their most famous guest. In their defence, this uncongenial reaction to the hard-drinking and prickly artist would have probably gone unnoticed had Vincent Van Gogh not later become a household name, forever associated with twinkling Provençal scenes. Since then, the locals have been trying to patch things up with the Dutch master by memorialising a café in the main square and creating a museum in his name – although, tellingly, it doesn't actually contain any of his paintings. They've also definitely been working on how to treat outsiders, a skill that's been honed to a fine art at the Hôtel Particulier.

Having abandoned satnav in favour of the tried and tested method of sticking his head out the window and asking a local, our genial taxi driver eventually deposited us at the Hôtel Particulier. Down a side street a five-minute stroll from the centre of Arles, the location is not glamorous, but the 18th-century splendour of the courtyard through the front door makes up for that.

Each of the rooms is individually designed in the classic French style, with diverting pieces here and there: the enormous, crisp-linened bed and Provençal furniture in our huge whitewashed boudoir were enlivened by a turquoise *lit de repos*. After two minutes of rummaging and many appreciative squeals, Mrs Smith was on the phone to her best friend, itemising our room's delights: the pair of ornate writing desks, the vast gilt-edged mirrors, the freestanding bath groaning under the weight of a chemist's worth of Gilchrist & Soames products. I was most impressed by the hotel's disdain for the television set. Ours was perched in the corner, discreetly hooded like a kestrel. The implication was clear: the hotel recognises that it should supply a TV, but it would rather you didn't watch it, thank you very much.

After we'd decided the room was to our liking, we slipped into our swimmers, donned our fluffy robes, and headed outside to soak up the last of the afternoon sun. The Particulier's pool sits within the courtyard's tall walls, surrounded by even taller trees, so privacy is guaranteed, but loungers must be strategically placed in order to make the most of the sun. We settled in among our chic fellow guests, ordered drinks and toasted Arles for being so gloriously different to our exuberant but exhausting home in the London Borough of Hackney.

Outside the bedrooms, the hotel has a strong Moroccan streak, with rugs and incense-burners dotted around its halls, and it was at a distinctly north African table on the terrace that we dined, with just one other couple for company. Like all the guests, the staff at the hotel are impeccably discreet – it's such a pleasure to be able to enjoy a meal without having your glass topped up every 30 seconds – and the courtyard at night is serene and charming. The food is good rather than exceptional, but that does little to detract from the pleasure of staying here: there is an almost Moroccan feel to the super-stylish courtyard, and the interiors are further proof of our hosts' knack for effortless-feeling glamour.

On Saturday, after a leisurely breakfast and long baths, we wandered to the square for lunch. As well as the Van Gogh Café, there are four or five other restaurants serving trad bistro fare. We went for that holiday staple: steak frites and pichets of rosé. By the time we were on our exhilaratingly bitter coffees, I had come to terms with the fact that Mrs Smith was ready to elope with our elfin 18-year-old waiter, who blushed so disarmingly every time he spoke to her that I had actually started to sympathise with her Shirley Valentine-like longings.

When we got up to leave, the Place du Forum was washed in the soft, creamy late-afternoon light that makes Provence so beautiful at that time of day. Emboldened by the heady mix of wine and caffeine, I saw an opportunity to take back the initiative from my new love rival and whisked Mrs Smith off on a romantic tour of Arles. We started at the magnificent arena ↓

where, rousing myself with thoughts of my own ongoing gladiatorial conflict, I expounded lengthily on blood sports, reality television and civilisations in decline. Mrs Smith, who has forgotten more history than I have ever known, rolled her eyes, took my arm and told me that all I needed to do was buy her a poster and she'd definitely be accompanying me on the flight home.

The poster in question was a beautifully designed Seventies advert for a bullfight. For, unlike me, the city hasn't let its history become a millstone. The Arlésiens revel in their ancient buildings as vibrant living spaces: in addition to the matadors thrilling the 20,000 fans that pack into the arena, the Roman theatre still hosts concerts, two millennia after the builders packed up their hods and left.

After a couple of hours soaking up the antiquity, we felt culturally enriched and quite entitled to another drink and more food. For our Saturday night splurge, we picked the Nord Pinus on Place du Forum – a hotel and restaurant considerably smarter than its neighbours. We walked through the modern dining room and headed straight to the livelier terrace, where we settled down with another bottle of excellent rosé and crisped breads with tapenade. I'm a sucker for any course that arrives without being advertised, and was suitably impressed by the wild-mushroom cappuccino that appeared immediately after we'd ordered. Afterwards, we drank cognacs in the Nord Pinus bar, an atmospheric little place once frequented by Graham Greene and Picasso.

Strolling along the river, full of good food and drink with our enormous bed enticingly near, I realised that we'd seen most of Arles' attractions and that next time we visit, we'll have nothing to do but lounge around at the Hôtel Particulier, perhaps devoting an entire day to its atmospheric spa – a thought that filled us with a great deal of good cheer.

Reviewed by David Annand

NEED TO KNOW

Rooms Eight, with a handful more to come.
Rates €190–€290.
Check-out 11h.
Room service A selection from the main menu is available from 08h until 21h.
Facilities TV, wireless Internet access.
Poolside The outdoor pool is slim but elegant.
Children Are welcome; an extra bed is €30.
Also The hotel's Space Spa has massage, sauna and a hammam. A range of health and beauty treatments is available.

IN THE KNOW

Our favourite rooms The Suite Luxe is decorated with white drapes and antique furniture. It's on the ground floor with a private terrace and view of the gardens and swimming pool. The suites in the old stables have private terraces.
Hotel bar Drinks are served in the salon or on the terrace until 23h.
Hotel restaurant The kitchen uses the freshest local produce, and the menu changes daily. There is one menu and one price: €50. A reservation is required.
Top table The best tables, next to the fireplace or out on the terrace, are reserved for guests.
Dress code Elegant, comfortable Med style.

LOCAL EATING AND DRINKING

At the dignified Hôtel Jules César on Boulevard des Lices, **Lou Marquès** (04 90 52 52 52) serves excellent traditional French cuisine. Rising star Jérôme Laurent's **Le Cilantro** on Rue Porte-de-Laure (04 90 18 25 05) is equally good but more modern and adventurous. **L'Entrevue** on Place Nina Berberova is a fashionable riverside bar with a north African vibe, attracting a relaxed bohemian crowd. **Café Van Gogh** in Place du Forum is where the great artist painted Terrasse de Café la Nuit. The café has been cashing in for over a century, but the atmosphere, evening light and general hubbub in the square are still very special.

 Smith cardholders receive a free upgrade when possible, and a complimentary cocktail.

GET A ROOM!

Use our online booking service at www.mrandmrssmith.com to check availability and make reservations. Register your Smithcard to find out about current member offers for this hotel.

L'Hôtel Particulier
4 rue de la Monnaie, Arles
+ 33 (0)4 90 52 51 40
contact@hotel-particulier.com; www.hotel-particulier.com

Oustau de Baumanière

DESTINATION   SOUTHWEST PROVENCE
STYLE   CHIC COUNTRY RETREAT
SETTING   ROCKS AND RUINS OF LES BAUX

MTWTFSSMTWTFSSMTWTFSSMTWTFSSMTWTFSSMTWT
FRANCE

'Spacious, lofty and slightly
asymmetrical, it matched
17th-century origins with
modern-day surround-sound'

With a song in my heart, I met Mrs Smith at the airport and off we soared to Marseille. In my pocket were five lines of spider-scrawl directions I'd taken down on the phone to the hotel that early and bleary morning. The weather was spectacular, so at the airport we coughed up the extra few euros and upgraded from a rental car that looked like it should have been reserved for Noddy and Big Ears to a sporty convertible Mégane. Now, be warned: Oustau de Baumanière is hidden away in an obscure spot. It's a good hour's drive from Marseille if you know where you're going, and an infinite puzzle if you don't. So, lost and tetchy, somewhere between Nice and Barcelona, we bought a map ('la carte' *en Français* – something I discovered it was worth knowing). Having thrown away my smudged scribblings and given Mrs Smith

a speed lesson in navigating, I made steady progress towards l'Oustau de Baumanière. When you peel off the highway, the world changes. The drive takes you between Salon and Arles, and every town looks like it's out of one of the Stella Artois idents that pop up during films on Channel 4. We resisted the temptation to join in a communal summer party at a village along the way, and continued towards our destination, the hot, moist air making a giant herbal humidor of olive, garlic and rosemary. We wound our way up a small mountain, crossing the castle ruins of Château des Baux. Rolling down to our final target was like descending into Shangri-La, but without those annoying singing children.

I find carparks give a fair indication of a hotel's calibre, and Oustau de Baumanière's screamed

'understated' and 'high-end'. The pristine gravel path crunched beneath our tyres as we slid in between our car's rich relations. There is a huge emblem projected onto the rocks above Baumanière that looks Egyptian or Masonic. The light flattered the exquisite architecture of this ten-roomed hotel and the majestic cliffs behind. It might just as well have read 'class'.

A *garçon* appeared from nowhere, welcoming us by name. This exquisite cordiality continued into the tiny high-polished hardwood and limestone check-in, and as we travelled in the crocodile-skin lift up the single floor to our bedroom. Our room looked just superb: gave us a warm glow that lingered for days. Spacious, lofty and slightly asymmetrical, it matched 17th-century origins with modern-day surround-sound extras. The creative lighting design supplied switches ready to match any mood. Handmade wood-block furniture and a ten-foot satin chaise longue were pure design-museum pieces. The dull stuff (minibar, safe) was hidden behind a false wall. French doors opened out on to a view of the verdant grounds, then olive groves and vineyards. The bathroom held its own, too. I spent a foolish few seconds pressing a jade pebble on the wall in an effort to turn the lights on, only to discover that the walls were embossed with seashells and stones. The bath was bigger than the car we nearly hired.

A patio in front, protected from any light drizzle by a canopy of fig trees, is where Baumanière guests eat some of the best food in France. A glance at the prices might shave the edges off your appetite: ↓

we opted for just the one course, while I kept an eye on everything served around me as it either burst into flames or was cut from its bone with the hiss of Sabatier. The wine list arrived, the size of a pantomime fairy-tale book, and after struggling like a nine-year-old with the Sunday papers, I let our waiter select something with the decimal point nearer the front end of the price. The chef meekly approached us and asked our opinion; I told him it was excellent and with reassured strides he bowled back to a hot kitchen. We ended on a shared crêpe Suzette and some crystallised local fruits, and retired to bed trying to pretend this was the sort of place we come to all the time.

The next day we took a little sun in the small but beautiful grounds and a dip in the icy-cold Twenties pool, then walked up to the castle carved into the mountain. The Château des Baux is touristy without being tacky; the ancient

alleyways are lined with shops full of local products, and the bars and cafés are cheap and friendly. A steep walk up to the remains of the fortifications rewarded us with a wondrous view; I wondered whether it was that great artists were drawn here or if reasonable artists were just blessed with great things to paint. Down the hill, on the way back to the hotel, we came across Cathédrale d'Images, a huge cave that hosts sound-and-light shows, with locally inspired masterpieces projected onto its walls.

As our farewell to this fine land, we took the car on a burn around some of the local towns; then, after getting utterly lost for a final time, we headed back for a few nightcaps at the hotel. Now I can safely say I know exactly where in the South of France Oustau de Baumanière is. It's *en Provence*, in the village of Exquisite, near Perfection, just above Timeless, in the state of Class.

Reviewed by Nick Moran

NEED TO KNOW

Rooms 30, including three junior suites and 11 apartments.
Rates €225–€490; breakfast is €20.
Check-out Midday.
Room service A room-service menu is available 12h–15h and 19h–22h.
Facilities TV, wireless Internet access. In-room massages can be arranged.
Poolside There's an outdoor pool in front of the main terrace.
Children Are welcome. An extra bed can be added in the apartments for €23.
Also There is a tennis court, and guests have access to the grounds of the whole estate.

IN THE KNOW

Our favourite rooms The junior suites at the front of the house enjoy views over the terrace and the swimming pool.
Hotel bar Drinks are available from the restaurant, 09h–00h. Try the estate's own wine, L'Affectif.
Hotel restaurant With two Michelin stars, the restaurant at Oustau de Baumanière is world-renowned. The menu features caviar, foie gras and a dazzling array of premiers grands crus. Lunch is 12h30–14h; dinner 17h30–21h30.
Top table Near the window overlooking the terrace and garden.
Dress code Refined sophistication.

LOCAL EATING AND DRINKING

La Cabro d'Or is also located on the Baumanière estate (04 90 54 33 21), with dining on the wonderful patio under the trees during the warmer months. Most ingredients among the fish, shellfish and meat dishes are sourced locally, including vegetables and olive oil from the estate. Nearby in Eygalières, **Chez Bru** aka Le Bistrot d'Eygalières (04 90 90 60 34) is another Michelin-starred honeypot for gourmets. In Maussane-les-Alpilles, **La Place** on Avenue Vallée des Baux (04 90 54 23 31) is an excellent bistrot run by the same people as Oustau de Baumanière, and does wonderful Alpilles lamb dishes. For lighter snacks and drinking, head to alleyways around the **Château des Baux** in nearby Les Baux de Provence and see which of the little bars and cafés takes your fancy. Many have terraces wonderful views over the surrounding countryside.

A recipe book by the Michelin-starred owner and chef Jean-Andre Charial.

GET A ROOM!

Use our online booking service at www.mrandmrssmith.com to check availability and make reservations. Register your Smithcard to find out about current member offers for this hotel.

Oustau de Baumanière
Les Baux de Provence
+33 (0)4 90 54 33 07
contact@oustaudebaumaniere.com; www.oustaudebaumaniere.com

Tarn

COUNTRYSIDE   OLD TOWNS, OLDER HILLS
COUNTRY LIFE   TASTING AND TOURING

MTWTFSSMTWTFSSMTWTFSSMTWTFSSMTWTFSSMTWT
FRANCE

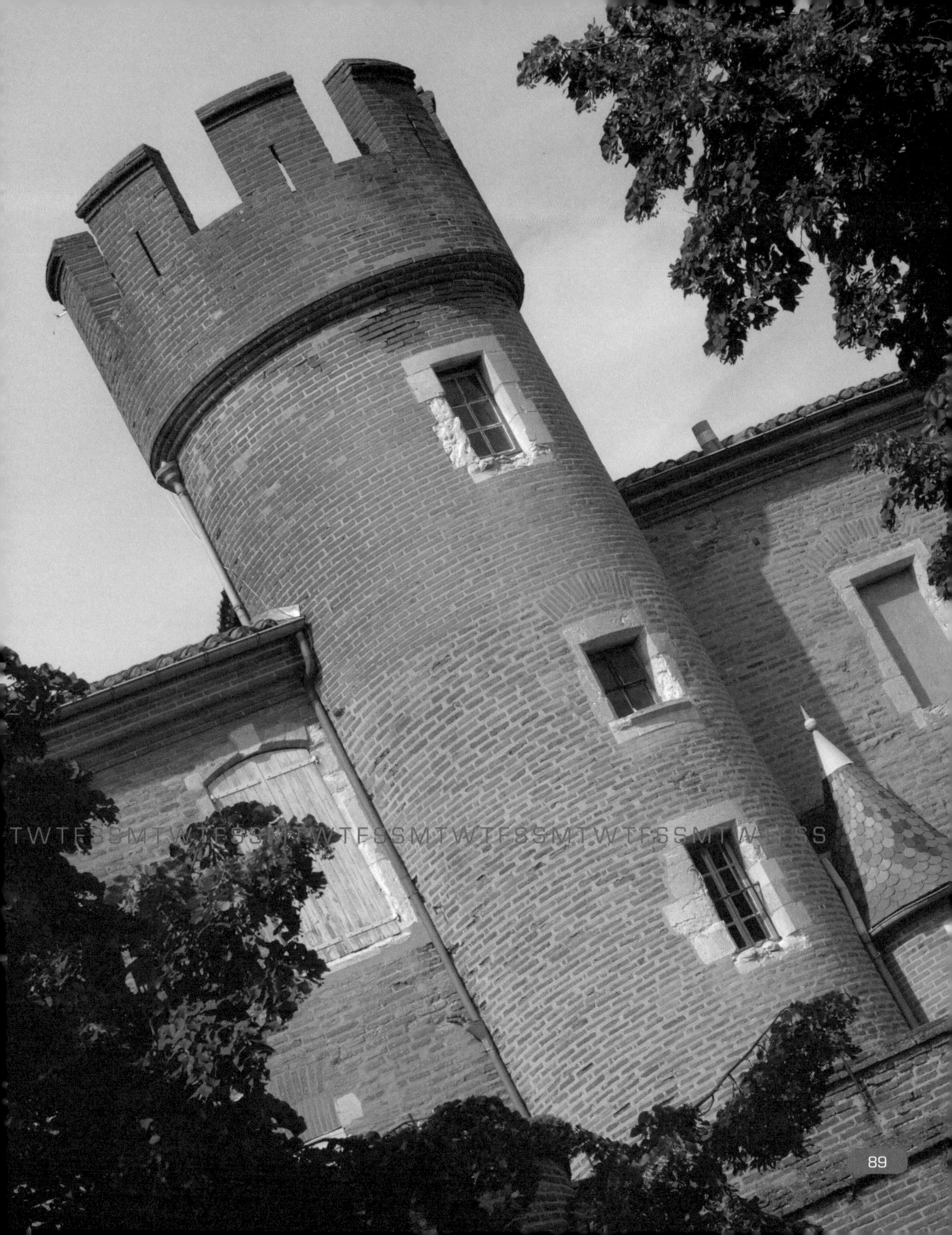

TARN

Among the deepest-green depths of rural France, life is as unhurried as a game of boules in the village square, and stress is an alien concept to all except the local geese. For centuries the Tarn's rolling hills and fortified mediaeval towns have represented the stoutly defended heartland of Gallic culture, where the French first discovered their passion for wine, and where they continue to nurture their genius for foie gras and potent cheeses. As you drift down the plunging Tarn and Aveyron gorges, carved over time by the rivers that flow graciously through the region, you might ask yourself if the rocks change faster than local ways.

GETTING THERE

Planes There are regular flights to Toulouse and Rodez airports. Both airports are two hours from Albi.
Trains The TGV from Paris to Toulouse takes five hours. Local trains can be infrequent and slow.
Automobiles It takes six hours to drive from Paris. A car is essential if you want to explore the bastide towns and the countryside.

DO GO/DON'T GO

The climate of the region is essentially Mediterranean, with warm spring and autumn months and hot summers. In May, the flowers bloom. The region can get a dusting of snow in the winter.

TYPICALLY TARN

The mediaeval Cathar religious sect built over 40 heavily fortified villages, often on hilltops, known as bastide towns. Cordes-sur-Ciel, Najac, Penne, Castelnau-de-Montmirail and Bruniquel are typical, with winding cobbled streets, ruined castles and massive ramparts.

LOCAL KNOWLEDGE

Taxis There are plenty of taxi ranks in the towns but cabs are hard to come by out in the countryside – book ahead.
Tipping culture By law, service charges are added to all restaurant bills, but it's nice to leave a euro or two.
Siesta and fiesta Businesses are generally open between 9h–13h, and 15h–19h Monday to Saturday. Banks close at 16h30.
Packing tips A fishing rod and an encyclopaedia of wine.
Recommended reads *Le Petit Prince* by Antoine de Saint-Exupéry; *Chocolat* by Joanne Harris; *Labyrinth* by Kate Mosse.
Cuisine Regional, or *terroir*, cooking, featuring local produce: *lait de brebis* (sheep's-milk), Rocamadour and Roquefort cheeses, plums from Agen, wind-dried ham from Lacaune. Duck dishes and foie gras are particularly good. The region is also famous for cassoulet, a casserole of white beans, herbs, meat and vegetables. Gaillac is France's oldest wine-making region and a treasure trove for connoisseurs.
Currency Euro.
Dialling codes Country code for France: 33. Toulouse, Albi 05.

DIARY

Mid-May The four-day Gaillac Wine Contest, when the New Year's vintages are debuted, tasted and judged. **Mid-July** Inhabitants of Cordes-sur-Ciel celebrate their Mediaeval Festival by dressing up in silly costumes and challenging each other to duels. **Late July** Cordes-sur-Ciel's inhabitants pack away their jester's outfits and enjoy the classical programme of the town's Music Festival (www.festivalmusiquesurciel.com).
First weekend of August Gaillac's second Wine Festival coincides with the start of the wine harvest, with yet more thorough and thoughtful analysis of the local tipple. See www.tourisme-tarn.com for details of events.

WORTH GETTING OUT OF BED FOR

Viewpoint Hilltop Cordes-sur-Ciel is the finest of the region's fortified *bastide* towns. There are sweeping views from the ramparts across the surrounding countryside.

Arts and culture Visit the Musée Toulouse-Lautrec in Albi, home town of the absinthe-soaked artist. The museum is housed in the old archbishop's palace next to the cathedral and contains a range of the artist's work, including the cabaret posters that made him so famous.

Activities The Aveyron gorge has spectacular scenery and excellent canoeing and rafting. St-Antonin is a good starting point but some stretches are challenging, so check conditions in advance (www.variation82.eu). There's also canoeing on the upper reaches of the Tarn. Horse riding is popular; contact Les Juliannes Riding Centre in Paulinet (www.lesjuliannes.com). Take the opportunity to indulge in wine tasting in the Gaillac area (www.vins-gaillac.com).

Daytripper The confident city of Toulouse is both a historic city of grandiose squares, leafy boulevards and sleepy barge-lined canals, and the centre of the European Space Programme, which you can explore at the sprawling Cité de l'Espace (www.cite-espace.com).

Perfect picnic There are perfect picnic spots with views over the Tarn near the ancient priory at Ambialet, east of Albi. Doze in the sun with a bottle of inky-black Cahors wine.

Something for nothing Sir Norman Foster's awe-inspiring bridge over the Tarn gorge at Millau is an engineering marvel, higher than the Eiffel Tower. Crossing it feels more like flying than driving. Nearby in Roquefort-sur-Soulzon, it's possible to visit the labyrinthine Roquefort cheese caves where the pungent cheese is left to 'ripen'. Take a jacket; the caves never get warmer than eight degrees (www.roquefort-societe.com).

Shopping Many local villages have excellent food markets, such as the wonderful Sunday market in the mediaeval village of St-Antonin in the Aveyron gorge. Cordes-sur-Ciel is a warren of artists' studios and craftsmen's workshops. Gaillac is the centre of the local wine industry, and the place to pick up a case or two.

CAFES

Salon de Thé Herytage, on Place Sainte-Cécile in Albi, is a pretty tearoom with delicious cakes and great views of the imposing cathedral. Try the almond croissants at **Varen** in the little mediaeval village of St-Antonin-Noble-Val in the Aveyron gorge.

BARS AND RESTAURANTS

Michelin-starred **Le Grand Ecuyer** in the Haut de la Cité in Cordes-sur-Ciel (05 63 53 79 50) is housed in the 800-year-old palace of Count Raymond, and has excellent foie gras. Or try the less-expensive sister restaurant **Tonin'Ty** on Rue St-Michel (05 63 53 79 20), which has a lovely terrace and is more 'terroir'. **L'Epicurien** at 42 Place Jean-Jaurès in Albi (05 63 53 10 70) has sleek design and great food. Also in Albi, **Le Clos de Ste-Cécile** on Rue du Castelviel (05 63 38 19 74) is set in a converted schoolhouse behind the cathedral, and serves fine French country cooking on the terrace.

NIGHTLIFE

Out in the depths of the Tarn countryside, nightlife options are restricted to trying to decipher the local *langue d'oc* dialect over a few glasses of pastis with the locals. Toulouse has a big student population and a livelier bar and club scene, centred on Place St Pierre.

Le Manoir de Raynaudes

DESTINATION   TARN
STYLE   GASTRO ECO-MANOIR
SETTING   ORGANIC MEADOWS

MTWTFSSMTWTFSSMTWTFSSMTWTFSSMTWTFSSMTWT
FRANCE

'Our room is huge, with lots of natural light, cream walls, wood floors, classical French bedlinen and views of the distant Pyrenees'

Having never been on particularly good terms with early-morning starts, I must confess I did not anticipate the city of Toulouse or Le Manoir de Raynaudes, an hour's drive away, with obvious enthusiasm. But inwardly I was happy in the knowledge I had gleaned from the hotel website, which invited us to imagine 'a tiny French hamlet where life goes on as it has done for centuries, interrupted only by the tolling of the church bell and the occasional bray or quack.' Although I might recognise the quack of a modern-day duck, I was intrigued about what a 'bray' might sound like, and what type of animal might make it. Perhaps I don't get out of London as often as I should.

As our plane lurched away from the stifling streets of heatwave London, the prospect of kicking off my boots and relaxing in a sun-drenched garden teeming with fruits, flowers, herbs and vegetables, and falling on exquisite meals created from all this natural goodness, began to make me feel very pure.

We ignored Toulouse – the mighty capital of the Midi-Pyrénées region, Haute-Garonne département and the former province of Languedoc – and headed for the hills in search of our rustic retreat. Tower blocks and offices gave way to grand suburban townhouses, which in turn thinned out to reveal the magnificent open spaces of the French countryside. Thoughts of home evaporated. We drove through a parade of unspoilt villages until, just as the lunch hour fell, we crossed a moat (with a wooden birdhouse for those ducks) and arrived at Le Manoir de Raynaudes. We are offered a warm greeting by Peter, one of the two English owners, who proudly gave us a guided tour. It is a simple 19th-century property, built around a traditional courtyard, with a converted barn providing more accommodation.

Set in 13 acres of Tarn meadows, with no TV or radio apparent, Le Manoir de Raynaudes gives you a delightful feeling of living in a world free of mayhem and complication. Peter and his partner,

Orlando, have updated the building with a great deal of love and affection; their attention to detail is immediately apparent. Everything has been done with respect for the original architecture and colours. Peter says we can help ourselves to refreshments from the fridge, and any of the books in their extensive collection. Generous hosts and an ice-cold beer can do wonderful things for your soul.

Each of the four rooms is named after a past female owner of the house (the apartments take their surnames). We stay in Mauricette: spectacularly huge with lots of natural light, and furnished tastefully and simply, with cream walls, wood floors and classical French bedlinen. The views from the open windows are of the distant Pyrenees, all wild green peaks. We walk through to the bathroom, to find a large freestanding bathtub in the centre of the room. Plump white towels, an oversize mirror and cream-painted floorboards complete the French country feel.

With no connection to the outside world, we spend the afternoon in peaceful relaxation, allowing our minds to tune in to the calm rhythms of the countryside. We bypass Le Manoir's lake and amble along to the tiny hamlet of Raynaudes, which fails to trouble most maps, and briefly swell its population to an impressive 16. Returning to the hotel, we enjoy a glass of fine Bordeaux before Mr Smith takes a refreshing early-evening swim in the perfectly natural, chlorine-free swimming pool.

Fresh and natural is the Raynaudes philosophy. Their food is obviously something that they take great pride in: Orlando, a food writer and superb chef, has promised us an eight-course feast on the Saturday evening. (As a vegetarian, I have learnt that we are a breed often frowned upon by our Gallic cousins. As far as I am aware, there are only ten vegetarian dishes in existence in France, so for dinner I know I will be trying eight of them.) Orlando manages to hide his shock at my ↓

95

unfortunate persuasion admirably, and we settle down to dinner with the other guests on the beautiful terrace. Orlando does us proud. The produce is almost exclusively sourced from Le Manoir's gardens and thereabouts, and seemed to have been picked just hours before: you could taste the freshness and vitality. Our incredible meal was finished off with the finest cheeses of the region, served with quince jam and just-picked figs. Delicious, and all set to an aristocratic view, soundtrack of Handel, and the odd bray of a… donkey. Aha.

Le Manoir's style and pace make it the perfect rural retreat. It soothes busy minds and calms tense shoulders. If you can drag yourself away from it, you will discover sleepy hilltop villages with thriving markets. The market at St Antonin sells all sorts of simple and practical things for the house and garden, as well as the usual excellent comestibles. And the Tarn Gorge is a spectacular canyon where you can swim and go canoeing.

This is a hotel that delivers exactly what it promises. It is rustic and organic, yet supremely comfortable. It transports you back to an age when life was lived much more slowly, sidestepping technological progress and instead offering simple pleasures: beautiful views, a comfortable bed, a warm welcome and divine food.

Reviewed by Hus Mozaffar

NEED TO KNOW

Rooms Five double bedrooms and two apartments.
Rates €95–€170, including breakfast.
Check-out 11h.
Room service Fresh fruit is available in the rooms; for anything else, simply ask Peter or Orlando.
Facilities Bedrooms have L'Occitane toiletries. Apartments have TV, DVD, CD players and fully equipped kitchens.
Poolside Secluded pool and suntrap decking area.
Children Le Manoir de Raynaudes is not suitable for children. Although the pool has a safety-alarm system, the small lake and pond do not.
Also Guests can help themselves to seasonal vegetables from the kitchen garden. There is fishing at a small lake within the grounds. The hotel has a boulodrome and boules sets.

IN THE KNOW

Our favourite rooms Mauricette is light and airy, with a free-standing rolltop bath and views all the way to the Pyrenees. Maison Bonné is a spacious apartment with its own private patio garden, perfect for a late breakfast. Maison Montfort also has its own patio garden next to the swimming pool.
Hotel bar Apéritifs are served at 19h30 with home-made amuses-bouches.
Hotel restaurant Dinner is at 20h every evening except Mondays and Thursdays. Reservation essential. The gastronomic menu (€45) and Saturday's eight-course dégustation menu (€55) are based on seasonal local produce and the cooking of southwest France.
Top table Dinner is served on the terrace in summer. A maximum of 12 guests can dine à deux or share a single communal table.
Dress code Relaxed house party.

LOCAL EATING AND DRINKING

Aux Berges du Cérou in Salles (05 63 76 40 42) has a beautiful village setting, a pretty terrace and an imaginative menu. **Au Chapon Tarnais** in Carmaux (05 63 36 60 10) serves excellent modern French cuisine. **La Falaise** in Cahuzac-sur-Vère (05 63 33 96 31) has a small menu of well-prepared local dishes.

Stay for one night, and you'll receive one of the house cookbooks; stay two nights, and you get two; there's a glossy hardback cookbook for Smith guests who book three nights or more.

GET A ROOM!

Use our online booking service at www.mrandmrssmith.com to check availability and make reservations. Register your Smithcard to find out about current member offers for this hotel.

Le Manoir de Raynaudes
Monestiès, Tarn
+33 (0)5 63 36 91 90
peter@raynaudes.com; www.raynaudes.com

MTWTFSSMTWTFSSMTWTFSSMTWTFSSMTWTFSSMTWT

SANTORINI ●

GREECE

SANTORINI
Astra Apartments and Suites
Perivolas Traditional Houses

TWTFSSMTWTFSSMTWTFSSMTWTFSSMTWTFSSMTWTFSS
HELLAS

Santorini

| COASTLINE | AZURE AEGEAN WATERS |
| COAST LIFE | LAZY DAYS, CANDLELIT DINNERS |

MTWTF**SS**MTWTF**SS**MTWTF**SS**MTWTF**SS**MTWTF**SS**MTWT

HELLAS

TWTFSSMTWTFSSMTWTFSSMTWTFSSMTWTFSS

101

SANTORINI
From its birth in the apocalyptic volcanic explosion of 1450BC to the snow-white cubist villas hugging its sheer cliffs, Santorini (also known as Thira) is arguably the most dramatic of the Greek islands. This rugged beauty is famed for its sunsets, wine and turquoise seas. Barhoppers and gourmets will love its lively tavernas and outstanding restaurants, where just-landed fish is always on the menu. Take a hotel room facing the vast volcanic bay, or *caldera*, and as you watch ships criss-cross below, you'll realise that you're looking at one of the most awe-inspiring, and romantic, views on the planet.

GETTING THERE

Planes The airport is ten minutes from Fira, the island's capital. There are regular flights in summer via Athens but fewer services in winter. Taxis cost around €6 from the airport.

Boats There are regular ferry services to Naxos (three hours), Paros (four hours), Mykonos (four hours) and Piraeus (nine hours; €28) as well as other islands.

Automobiles You'll need a car or scooter if you feel like spending a day or two touring the island. There are free parking zones outside the towns of Oia and Fira.

DO GO / DON'T GO

The high season is April to October, but even in early spring and late autumn the weather is normally fine, and bars and restaurants are busy enough to have a good buzz.

SUITABLY SANTORINI

Santorini has the oldest vineyards in Europe, producing mostly white wine – and very good it is, too. At the welcoming Santo winery, close to Pyrgos, a few euros gets you a tour and a tasting of some choice bottles.

LOCAL KNOWLEDGE

Taxis Cabs are inexpensive. You can order one by phone or pick one up at a designated rank in town.

Tipping culture Tipping isn't required, but ten per cent is always nice. Cab drivers don't expect a tip.

Siesta and fiesta Most shops are open until elevenish, but almost all stop for a siesta (this starts at 14h and can last anything between two and four hours). Banks and post offices close at 13h.

Packing tips Comfy shoes. An oxygen mask for smokers – your hotel is likely to be on the side of a steep cliff, which makes for lots of marching up and down stairs. In midsummer, it cools down considerably come the evening; bring something to throw over your shoulders.

Recommended reads *Captain Corelli's Mandolin* or *Birds Without Wings* by Louis de Bernières; *The Republic* by Plato; *Zorba* by Nikos Kazantzakis.

Cuisine Classic Greek food such as tyropita (cheese pie), tzatziki, barbecued meat, dips made from fava beans, white aubergines or cherry tomatoes and, especially in these parts, lots of fresh seafood. Santorini capers are delicious. Don't miss out on the island's excellent dry white wine from Asyrtiko, Athiri and Aïdani Aspro.

Currency Euro.

Dialling codes Code for Greece: 30. Santorini: 22860.

DIARY

There are religious feast days almost every month. For visitors, the two best are probably the following. **15 August** The Feast of Panagia Episkopis in Mesa Gonia, the biggest celebration of the year, with great food and dancing. If you're lucky enough to get invited along, it's a great way to meet the islanders. **22 October** The Feast of Agios Averkios in Emborio celebrates the protector-saint of wine, so everyone is encouraged to drink their fill of the excellent local tipple. It would be rude not to join in.

WORTH GETTING OUT OF BED FOR
Viewpoint Anywhere on the caldera will have you reaching for your camera.
Arts and culture Santorini is dotted with white chapels, decorated with cobalt-blue domes. The island is a contender for the location of the lost city of Atlantis, so keep your eyes peeled…
Activities There's fantastic scuba diving in the caldera. Try Santorini Dive Center on Perivolos Beach (www.divecenter.gr). The best dive site is Taxiarhes Bay, where there's the wreck of a small passenger ship and underwater deposits of volcanic sulphur. The Open Air Cinema (31974) in Kamari has screenings throughout the summer in a lovely garden setting.
Daytripper Sail out to the neighbouring islands: tranquil Thirassía for the views; volcanically active Paléa Kamméni and Néa Kamméni with their sulphurous mud pools. Hire a *kaïki* (wooden fishing boat) for a trip across the caldera, or get Captain Ted to take you out in his catamaran (www.santorinisailing.com).
Best beach Santorini has volcanic black-sand beaches. Red Beach, on the south coast, lies beneath towering red cliffs near the site of ancient Akrotiri. Perivolos Beach is quieter (turn right when you reach the beach and walk down as far as Seaside Lounge).
Something for nothing Windowshop at the dozens of jewellery stores in smart Oia. Stroll the cliffside of the caldera and take in the view.
Shopping In Fira and Oia, shopping is based around mazy central streets. You'll find some clothes shops, and lovely silver and amber jewellery. Many local artists have their own shops.
And… Watching the sun set over the caldera is as popular as it is unforgettable. If you want the best spot, you have to arrive early and, whatever you do don't forget your camera.

CAFÉS

Café Classico, in the heart of Fira's huddle of streets, is a lovely spot, with a view out to the islands. It's perfect for breakfast or a quick coffee or ice cream.

BARS AND RESTAURANTS

The contemporary **Sea Side Lounge** in Perivolos (22806 82801), at the far right-hand side of the beach, is great for lunch or dinner. Nearby **Wet** (22806 82990) holds Mykonos-style parties all day in summer. **Kokkino Podilato** in Oia (22806 71918) is one of the island's swishest wine bars. **Archipelagos** (22806 23673) has great views looking out to the surrounding islands. It is one of Fira's best restaurants, serving up tasty Greek/Mediterranean food (tables 1–6 are on the upper level with a sea view). A Mr & Mrs Smith romantic favourite is **Vanilia** (22806 25631), high on the cliff, opposite the church in Firostefani. Choose a table downstairs for intimacy, or upstairs for an ocean view. Do try a local wine from the carefully put-together lists (Nikteri was our favourite). Highly respected **1800** (22806 71485), on one of Oia's quieter streets, has a great roof terrace. Rustic **Nikolas** (22806 24750) is a family-run place on one of Fira's back lanes, next to the Enigma club. It serves fantastic home-cooked food, but be prepared to queue for the privilege of eating with the locals.

NIGHTLIFE

Follow the signs from Fira's pedestrianised square and you will find two fun and lively nightclubs, **Enigma** and **Koo**, together with some decent bars. Casual dress is fine, although some of the locals do get glammed up of a weekend.

Astra Apartments and Suites

DESTINATION   SANTORINI
STYLE   CANDLELIT APHRODISIAC
SETTING   CALDERA PANORAMA

S S
HELLAS

'Hugging the postcard-perfect
cliffs, Astra provides satisfaction
that would be surprising in
a five-star city hotel, let alone
a Greek island hideaway'

TWTFSSMTWTFSSMTWTFSSMTWTFSSMTWTFSS

There's more than a little magic about the island of Santorini, the biggest of the Cyclades. Ancient Greek philosopher Plato reckoned its lava-baked mass to be a result of the volcano eruption that destroyed the mythical civilisation of Atlantis. Another legend says it was once infested with vampires. Whatever the Ancients say, for us Moderns the incredible view is more than exciting enough without lost cities and otherworldly stalkers.

Mrs Smith and I are also rather enchanted by Santorinian wine. Let's face it: when a free bottle is left in your hotel room, it is often only suitable for clearing troublesome plugholes. Yet when we opened our complimentary Assirtyko, we found nectar in a bottle. As introductions to accommodation go, it was a good one. Super-luxe hotels can keep their personal butlers, hot-towel assistants, sunglass-cleaning technicians and other nannying. What we want is a stylish room with a world-class view and a seriously good bottle of wine to help us enjoy it.

If you're of a like mind, you'll love this boutique abode. Hugging the island's postcard-perfect cliffs like a particularly pretty limpet, Astra's apartments provide a level of satisfaction that would be surprising in a five-star big-city hotel, let alone a hideaway perched on a quiet corner of a Greek island. Any attempt to be blasé about it falls flat. Let's try: the view from the balcony is of your standard volcanic islands, surrounded by the requisite turquoise-blue bay and flanked by the usual twinkling lights of nearby villages sitting flush on the cliffs. See, it just doesn't work.

With its high white ceilings, arty ornaments and candles – so many candles – on every available surface, this is a room to spend some time in. Add to this the giant his 'n' hers whole-body shower, a four-poster bed and an outrageously comfortable sofa in the separate lounge area and you have a ready-made excuse for permanent room service. Call it record-breakingly unadventurous but, so entranced were we with this room that on our first night we

foresook the fish restaurants of Oia and the tavernas of Imerovigli and Fira and called out for a delivery. Hummus, pitta, skewered meat and all manner of meze appeared a short while later, along with another bottle of that fine Santorinian wine.

At this point, we made a unfortunate mistake. Just outside the bedroom is a private pool: in the daytime, a locus of luxurious joy. The sun is beating down, your skinny white body is crying out for respite, and right there in front of you is a cool, clean waterworld all of your own. Perfect. At one o'clock in the morning, however, it's the coldest plunge pool you could ever be foolish enough to jump into. Take my advice and do the baby-bathing elbow-dip first. If nothing else, it'll save you waking up the neighbours with your wussy yelps.

Our equilibrium was restored by a fine breakfast delivered to our room at no extra charge. While laying down yoghurt, breads, cheeses and fruit juice out on the private terrace, our waiter tactfully ignored the mezze remains and glasses sitting around the edge of the pool. Clearly, slightly sozzled guests who fancy a bracing midnight dip were nothing new to him. A hefty tip recognised his Jeeves-like aplomb. Thanks again, my friend, and sorry about the floating wine bottle.

Although gazing from our terrace at the beauty of the deep-blue caldera (underwater volcano crater, to those without geology degrees) held us entranced for some time, it was worth taking the 20-minute walk into the town of Fira. There's a fair bit of nightlife in high season, and excellent seafood to be had at Skaros restaurant. If you manage to push the night on long enough, as we did, you'll find that Corner Crêpes can provide for all your late-night munchy needs.

Like a siren call, though, Astra begs you to come home, offering you a midnight view of the three facing volcanic isles of Thirasia, Paléa Kamméni and Néa Kamméni. ↓

107

To complete the picture, you'll see ships cruising slowly across the caldera and pulling into dock, their onboard lights throwing the massive cliffs of the nearby islands into sharp relief.

Like all the best holidays, Astra has us wondering how we can possibly wangle staying here longer. Could there possibly be a gap in the market for event-organising experts? What about penniless writers – do they have enough of them? In truth, though, Santorini and the Astra apartments should remain a place for temporary visitors, because no one could live with this level of spiritual uplift all the time: perfect happiness can only be savoured in small doses.

Reviewed by Scott Manson

NEED TO KNOW

Rooms 22.

Rates €200–€700, including breakfast.

Check-out Midday, but the hotel has a hospitality suite which can be used by guests who arrive early or check out late.

Room service Light meals available until midnight.

Facilities Book exchange, free Internet access. Massages can be arranged.

Poolside There is an infinity pool with a bar and spectacular view of the caldera. Several of the suites have their own Jacuzzi or small pool.

Children Welcome.

Hotel closed November to March inclusive.

Also Wedding planner available.

IN THE KNOW

Our favourite rooms 302 and 304 are the most private suites, each with its own Jacuzzi or private pool; 5 and 9 are the best superior apartments.

Hotel bar Poolside drinks available 15h–23h.

Hotel restaurant There isn't a restaurant as such, but private dining can be arranged on request. Breakfast is served on your balcony or by the pool.

Top table Every private balcony has a jaw-dropping view of the caldera.

Dress code Blissfully blasé.

LOCAL EATING AND DRINKING

The hotel provides guests with a guide to eating and drinking all over the island. Otherwise, our advice is to head down to the wharfside at Oia where there are several fantastic fish restaurants, perfect for lunch or dinner. **Dimitri's** (22860 71606) has delicious seafood, and its view of the sunset over the caldera is unobstructed by the rocks. If you want a traditional Greek taverna serving a range of excellent local specialities, both **Imerovigli** (22860 24190) and **Skaros** (22860 23616) are only five minutes' walk from the hotel. Both have outside seating and are highly recommended by the hotel – especially Skaros if you fancy seafood.

 Smith members receive a bottle of champagne; book a suite, and ladies also receive a silk sarong, and gentlemen receive a gift of some toiletries.

GET A ROOM!

Use our online booking service at www.mrandmrssmith.com to check availability and make reservations. Register your Smithcard to find out about current member offers for this hotel.

Astra Apartments and Suites

Imerovigli, Santorini
+30 22860 23641
astra-ae@otenet.gr; www.astra.gr

Perivolas Traditional Houses

DESTINATION   SANTORINI
STYLE   GAUDI-CONTOURED CAVES
SETTING   DREAM LAVA

M T W T F S S M T W T F S S M T W T F S S M T W T F S S M T W T F S S M T W T
HELLAS

'Anyone who has experienced childlike pleasure at
climbing into a cave will be in seventh heaven'

TWTFSSMTWTFSSMTWTFSSMTWTFSSMTWTFSS

My good lady's mind was already made up. 'Now this,' she said, 'is where we're going on our honeymoon.' It's a phrase that normally strikes terror into the heart of the uncommitted but, although this reviewer's Mrs Smith was a relatively new arrival, I had to admit I could see exactly what she meant. Perivolas is perfect. Perched high on the cliffs of Santorini above the Aegean Sea, it's the sort of place that inspires spontaneous marriage proposals. Indeed, if top scientists were to analyse this splendid luxury inn from top to bottom, it's likely that they'd find that it sits on top of the world's most powerful love ley line.

Ancient history plays an important part in Santorini, arguably the most impressive of all the Greek islands. Formed entirely from volcanic rock, it is the result of the massive Minoan eruption of 1450BC which, legend has it, destroyed the lost city of Atlantis. It now sits in a circle with its neighbouring islands, surrounding the mile-deep undersea trench like disciples patiently awaiting the return of a deity.

It's this connection to Mother Earth that makes Perivolas such a find. Before owners Manos and Nadia took the property on, the site was actually a set of disused fishermen's cottages, which had been painstakingly carved out of the hillside itself. Anyone who has ever experienced childlike pleasure at climbing into a cave will be in seventh heaven here. The rooms are all whitewashed walls, with no hard edges. Santorini's fishing folk, it seems, had a thing for curves, and the effect it has on visitors is rather astounding. Instantly welcoming, even womb-like, our room felt like home from the moment we walked in.

A view from every room over the caldera, (the proper name for the sea-filled volcanic crater, we learnt), saw us sitting in stunned silence for some time. (The wonderfully fragrant Korres natural toiletries also helped woo Mrs Smith.) Our terrace, with its comfy sunloungers, continued the relaxation theme, making any decision incredibly tricky. 'Shall we go for lunch or do another ten minutes watching ships criss-cross the caldera?' After a few hours, it became more basic still. 'Shall I scratch my nose now, or later?' Such is the lethargic power of Perivolas.

A quick swim in the infinity pool, followed by a Jacuzzi and cocktails from the surprisingly clued-up bar staff (well, would you know how to make a raspberry martini without a cocktail crib sheet?) saw us ready to enjoy the famous Santorini sunset. Without prompting, some olives arrived at our table but, delicious though they undoubtedly were, all superlatives were overshadowed by this merging of sun and sea. Hundreds of feet below us were dozens of boats bobbing on the water, all sunset-seekers whose captains knew that this particular point was the place to see the big sky fires. Sitting above them on the cliff's edge, we were realising just why the ancient Greeks worshipped such dramatic, powerful gods. Santorini is drama itself. Drinks in the charming town of Oia are walking distance away, and we enjoyed a spectacular cliffside dinner at Ambrosia, a well-judged suggestion from our Perivolas concierge. Although the restaurant occasionally overreached itself in terms of trendy food fusion, the quality of the produce shone through. Indeed, if the swordfish had been any fresher it would probably have leapt off my plate, making a bid for freedom towards the crashing waves below.

The walk back to the hotel passes all sorts of cute Greek shops and tavernas; dropping in for a shot of the extremely potent local vinsanto seems almost mandatory. Drinking an age-old recipe before returning to ancient traditional houses provided a beautiful synchronicity, which we found incredibly profound. At least until the wine had worn off. The next day saw us cutting through ↓

the water on a catamaran as guests of Blue Lagoon Cruises. Captain Ted, a Brooklyn-born Greek chap who has been settled in Santorini for more than ten years, took us on a gentle cruise around the island's dramatic coastline before dropping anchor for a sunset dinner. Like culinary David Blaines, he and his sidekick produced some fresh Greek salad, roasted vegetables and on-board barbecued lamb and steak that had been marinated in – well, he's keeping schtum about the ingredients. Despite my best efforts, the coy captain refused to give up the recipe, so give Mr & Mrs Smith HQ a call if you manage to extract it from him.

The meditative silence of Perivolas greeted us on our return. With no television in the room, and only the distant lapping of the waves as a soundtrack, one thing became clear. We had to book this place for next year. Granted, Mrs Smith may not be in line for anything resembling a marriage proposal but hey, for this reviewer at least, planning a whole year ahead represents some serious long-term commitment. Such is the ancient power of Perivolas and its love ley lines.

Reviewed by Scott Manson

NEED TO KNOW

Rooms 19, all with sea view.
Rates €368–€1,400.
Check-out Midday.
Room service Food and drinks are available until 23h.
Facilities Spa, hamman, sauna, pool, full gym.
Poolside Infinity pool with sweeping views over the caldera.
Children This is a haven for grown-ups.
Hotel closed November–March inclusive.

IN THE KNOW

Our favourite rooms Studio 8 is cosy and bright, with a balcony. Suite 15 has a big, secluded outdoor terrace. The new deluxe suite has its own Jacuzzi tub and hammam. The Perivolas Suite is extremely spacious, with a hot tub big enough for ten and a private pool.
Hotel bar In high season, it closes when the last person leaves.
Hotel restaurant Only residents can enjoy the Mediterranean cuisine here. Tables are candlelit with views out to sea.
Top table The outside terrace has just six tables; book one by the pool. Inside, the best are those nearest the entrance.
Dress code Carefree.

LOCAL EATING AND DRINKING

On the road into Oia you will find a few small tavernas that serve up great traditional food. Housed in a traditional sea captain's abode in one of the town's little streets is the acclaimed **1800** (22860 71485). Its roof terrace is perfect for watching the sun set. Also in Oia, **Ambrosia** (22860 71413) clings dramatically to the cliff edge, high above the caldera, and serves equally impressive seafood. On the road to Kamari, you'll find barbecue heaven at **Taverna Kritikos**, famous for its lamb chops; don't expect any frills. Depending on what time you visit, you'll be surrounded by large Greek families, local farmers and their wives, or glamorous professionals. **Katina's Taverna** (22860 71280) in tiny Port Amoudi is recommended for its fresh fish dishes.

A bottle of local Santorini white wine, from one of the island's excellent wineries.

GET A ROOM!

Use our online booking service at www.mrandmrssmith.com to check availability and make reservations. Register your Smithcard to find out about current member offers for this hotel.

Perivolas Traditional Houses
Oia, Santorini
+30 22860 71308
info@perivolas.gr; www.perivolas.gr

REYKJAVIK

MTWTFSSMTWTFSSMTWTFSSMTWTFSSMTWTFSSMTWTFSSMTWT

ICELAND

TWTFSSMTWTFSSMTWTFSSMTWTFSSMTWTFSSMTWTFSS

ÍSLAND

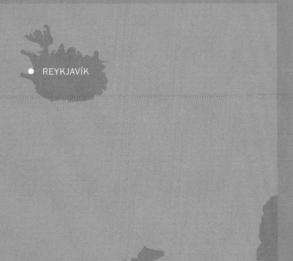

REYKJAVÍK

Reykjavík

COASTLINE   FIRE AND ICE
COAST LIFE   WILDLIFE AND WILD LIVING

MTWTFSSMTWTFSSMTWTFSSMTWTFSSMTW
ÍSLAND

REYKJAVIK

On the edge of the Arctic Circle, surrounded by an otherworldly volcanic landscape, Reykjavík has developed its own fantastically idiosyncratic character. Far from being a remote and frozen outpost, Iceland's capital has nightlife every bit as hot as the city's geothermally heated pools. The locals are also some of the warmest people you'll ever meet (and many of them believe in the existence of elves and trolls, which we find weirdly charming). With its unique combination of glaciers, volcanoes, hip clubs and stylish bars, there's ample opportunity to explore the wild and untamed. If you're looking for something a little different, then Reykjavík is most definitely it.

GETTING THERE

Planes Keflavík airport is 35 miles from the city centre. The 50-minute Flybus costs ISK 1,150 and will take you to your hotel. A taxi costs a painful ISK 7,500.
Trains There are no rail services at all in Iceland.
Automobiles Hire cars are expensive. Remote dirt roads, limited mobile phone coverage and sudden weather changes can turn a drive into a drama: it's best to go with a local tour company.

DO GO/DON'T GO

In the height of summer, the sun barely sets; some locals play golf in the middle of the night. Winter is the opposite, with long hours of darkness, but that means that daylight conditions are perfect for snowmobiling and dog-sledding.

REMARKABLY REYKJAVÍK

Reykjavík's Whale Watching Centre has tours out into Faxaflói Bay, where you're likely to see minke whales and, if you're lucky, a humpback or two. The excursion also takes you to the tiny island of Lundey which is home to around 20,000 puffins (www.whalewatching.is).

LOCAL KNOWLEDGE

Taxis Taxis are fairly inexpensive for short journeys, but they can be hard to find in the small hours. There are taxi ranks on Lækjargata and opposite Hallgrímskirkja church.
Tipping culture Tipping is practically unheard of in Iceland. A service charge is automatically added to most bills.
Siesta and fiesta Clubs and bars don't get busy until well after midnight. It only takes a few hours to party till dawn in summer – and empty the average bank account – so best to pace yourself.
Packing tips Iceland's weather is notoriously unpredictable, but you can always warm up in one of the geothermally heated pools. Pack a thick jumper and some swimwear.
Recommended reads *101 Reykjavík* by Hallgrímur Helgason; *Independent People* by Halldór Laxness; the anonymous mediaeval epic *Egil's Saga*.
Cuisine The seafood is so good that Iceland fought the Cod War against Britain in the Seventies to protect its fishing grounds. The langoustine, herring and salmon are delicious. Hákarl (putrefied shark meat) is strictly for gastro adventurers only.
Currency Icelandic króna.
Dialling codes Country code for Iceland: 354. No city code.

DIARY

February The Winter Lights Festival perks up those long, dark nights. **21 June** The Summer Solstice Festival has bonfires, picnics and a strong Viking flavour. **August** Gay Pride is a whole weekend of celebration. Cultural Night sees bars, galleries and churches open all night. **September–October** The Reykjavík International Film Festival (www.filmfest.is) screens the best of local and international film. **October** Iceland Airwaves is a supercool music festival (www.icelandairwaves.com).

WORTH GETTING OUT OF BED FOR

Viewpoint Take the lift up the tower of Hallgrímskirkja church for a great view of the city.

Arts and culture Kjarvalsstaðir Art Gallery on Flókagata displays the collection of Jóhannes Kjarval, Iceland's most celebrated landscape artist. 101 Hotel on Hverfisgata, a few doors down the street, has its own excellent gallery.

Activities The Activity Group (580 9900) can take you horse riding and river-rafting in the summer, or snowmobiling in the winter (www.activity.is).

Daytripper About 40 miles from Reykjavík, on the Hvítá River, is the thundering waterfall of Gullfoss. Nearby, the bubbling hot pools of Geysir include Strokkur ('The Churn'), which blasts a column of boiling water 30 metres into the air every few minutes.

Best beach Perhaps unexpectedly, there's a gorgeous beach here. Hot springs flowing into the sea at Nauthólsvík make the water warm enough for a pleasant dip.

Something for nothing Reykjavík's light pollution can make it hard to see the ghostly Northern Lights, so head out of town for the best views.

Shopping Kisan on Laugavegur is a charming French-Icelandic boutique with homewares, books and children's clothes. Next door, Trilogia stocks fabulous clothes from Icelandic and international designers. For music shopping, try 12 Tónar on Skólavörðustígur, where the staff will be happy to recommend their favourites.

And… The Blue Lagoon is Iceland's most-visited attraction: it's touristy, but it's definitely worth a visit. This warm, milky-blue lake is between Reykjavík and the airport so it's a good place to relax before your flight home (www.bluelagoon.com).

CAFES

Get yourself a coffee, some delicious carrot cake and a window seat at the cosy **Te Og Kaffi** on Laugavegur, a busy street perfect for people-watching. You can easily spend an entire afternoon upstairs at the **IÐA** bookshop on Lækjargata, browsing the books and magazines, and eating their hot soup served in a hollowed-out loaf of bread. If it's sunny, sip coffee outside at **Segafredo** on Lækjartorg. Blankets are provided in case the wind picks up.

BARS AND RESTAURANTS

Vox on Suðurlandsbraut (444 5050) is a treat for gourmets, with a strong emphasis on seasonal and local ingredients. **b5** on Bankastræti (552 9600) serves the best mojitos in town. It's a stylish lounge bar, dominated by two enormous Philippe Starck lampshades. **Skólabrú**, in the street of the same name (562 4455), has an intimate, homely feel – try their flambéed langoustine tails. **Siggi Hall** on Thorsgata (511 6677) is an acclaimed restaurant run by Iceland's most famous celebrity chef. It's an informal affair, with Siggi himself often making an appearance. The organic lamb and the bacalao (salt cod) are extremely tasty.

NIGHTLIFE

Go downtown to Laugavegur to sample the best of Reykjavík's celebrated nightlife. The Bohemian **Kaffibarinn** on Bergstaðarstræti is a long-time favourite with artists, musicians and students. **Café Oliver** on Laugavegur and the stylish **Pravda** on Austurstræti are currently attracting the crowds. Also on Austurstræti, **Rex** is an upscale club where Quentin Tarantino holds his parties when he's in town.

'A huge bed draped
in white linen and
a monogrammed rug
added cosiness to
the modern decor'

101 Hotel

REYKJAVIK
METROPOLITAN, MONOCHROME
HIP HARBOURSIDE

S S
ÍSLAND

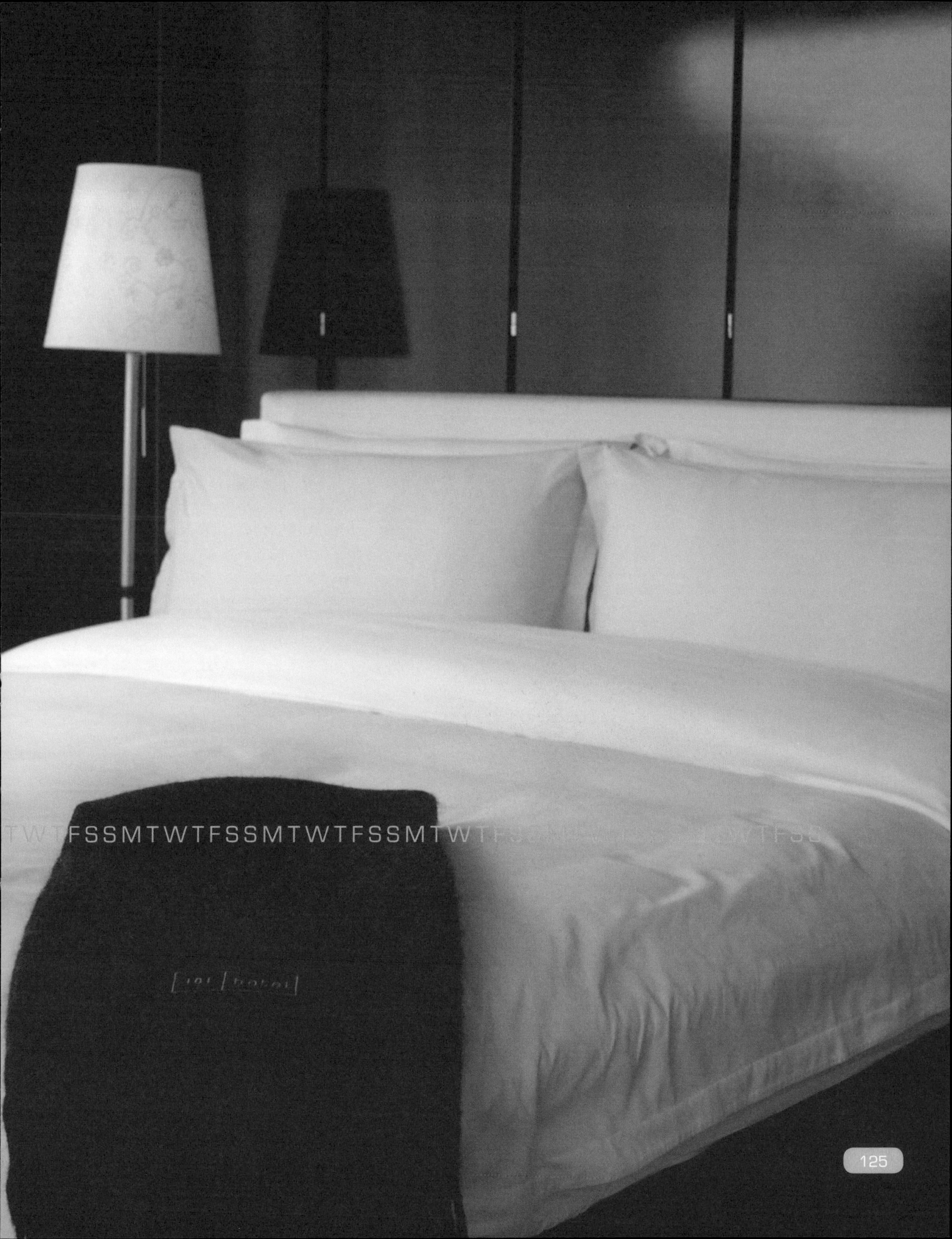
TWTFSSMTWTFSSMTWTFSSMTW

We were overjoyed to be asked, at the end of another long British winter, to review a slick new coastal hotel. Immediately we thought of alfresco dining and chirping cicadas. We were not expecting to be handed tickets to the world's northernmost capital, Reykjavik. Our knowledge of Iceland included Björk, 24-hour daylight in the summer, lots of snow, and not much else. We were assured that 101 Hotel, near the ocean's edge, promised an alternative designer 'beach' experience, and that there was no need to take the trunks and bikinis out of our suitcases. With its own gallery and a wealth of cutting-edge contemporary art, this also sounded like the most cultural seaside accommodation we'd heard of.

As we touched down on the icy runway, we tried to imagine our plane had skis rather than wheels, as snow stretched as far as the eye could see. Outside the airport (the only one we know with underfloor heating), the cold took our breath away, so we leapt into a taxi and learned our first lesson: like most things here, cabs are costly. If we'd been more frugal, we'd have taken the Flybus, but then we'd have missed the entertaining and informative introduction to the country from our driver. On our way to 101, we learned that: water is to Iceland what oil is to Texas – it erupts almost boiling straight from the earth, and in winter this geothermal energy heats some of the pavements, as well as that airport floor; Icelanders are keen golfers, playing round the clock during summer; they can give the Inuits a run for their lexical money, with 17 different words for snow; and beer was prohibited here until 1989.

We arrived at the understated façade of 101 Hotel a little unsure whether to check in or find a local quiz night, so that we might make use of our new encyclopedic knowledge. We got a very friendly welcome in a reception that proves that, when it's done well, minimalism is anything but sterile, and were shown to our black and white boudoir. It was as contemporary as can be, and attention had been paid to every detail. A silver-clawed freestanding bath, blanched-oak floors,

a huge bed draped in white linen and a monogrammed rug added cosiness to the thoroughly modern decor. Resisting the urge to coo for long over the luxurious bathroom products and covet the sleek silver alarm clock, we headed down for something to eat in 101's restaurant.

After some bistro-style favourites (including a perfectly executed burger and chips and fresh fish) from a menu that's spot-on for the travel-weary, we flopped by the fireplace in the lounge bar. We ordered nightcaps from the long, black, glass bar, where white leather stools lined up like soldiers on parade, raided the magazine library and settled into black leather banquettes, feeling like extras in a Scandinavian arthouse movie. The next morning, our guide Ozzy (a foreign-friendly nickname – Icelandic names can be tough on the uninitiated tongue) picked us up in a huge snow-truck that made us feel as though we were in the A-Team, and casually remarked that it was the worst weather he'd seen in years. Despite eight snow tyres and our very experienced guide at the wheel, we soon skidded off the road, satisfying our hunger for adventure before we'd even got anywhere.

The day's outing took us to see geysers, the second-largest waterfall in Europe, and a volcanic crater. Our ultimate goal, though, was a hut in a snow-filled valley, where a team of beautiful Newfoundland dogs and fleet of Skidoos were waiting. (The huge huskies looked a smidge jaded – perhaps, having starred in *Tomb Raider* and a few Bond films, they no longer get excited about pulling lowly tourists around.)

We put on *Barbarella*-ish jumpsuits – to protect us from the cold and the wind, we thought, though we soon found they were more valuable in keeping us safe from a pack of pups determined to mark their territory. The dog-sledding did not give us the adrenalin surge we'd hoped for (maybe Angelina Jolie was a little lighter or Hollywood just paid a little better), so after our ride with the furry fellows we had a go on the Skidoos. They're only snowmobiles, but they felt like Ferraris. ↓

Exhausted but exhilarated, we were deposited back at 101, where we took a dip in the hotel's basement Jacuzzi – just what we needed after our chilly, high-speed adventure – and had a laze on our supremely comfortable bed before heading out to sample Reykjavik's legendary nightlife.

We ate beautiful fresh fish as well as Icelandic lamb at the Seafood Cellar on Aðalstræti, and indulged into the small hours at Pravda, knowing the next day would consist of pampering at the Blue Lagoon, the hot, milky spring waters where Icelanders go to relax and detox. Salt-rub massages, taken floating on lilos, pummelled away all traces of the previous night's vodkas, and left us refreshed for our final excursion: a 4x4 search for the Northern Lights. A blizzard put paid to any hopes of a sighting, so our driver, Inkie, took us off-road for some late-night exploring. In the pitch black, we suddenly came to a standstill. Headlights revealed a black lava beach, waves crashing in, bringing small icebergs ashore. A surrealist monochrome landscape,

it was the coolest black and white movie set – perfect, considering the surprise geology display that this Mr Smith had planned. Sure, it was well below freezing in the driving snow, but an amazing beach, all the same. And a twinkling rock for a now Mrs-Smith-to-be provided a very happy ending to our Icelandic adventure.

Reviewed by Mr & Mrs Smith

NEED TO KNOW

Rooms 38.

Rates ISK27,900–ISK69,900.

Check-out Midday.

Room service The restaurant menu is available until 23h.

Facilities DVD, wireless Internet access, small Jacuzzi, steam bath and gym. Massages can be arranged in your room.

Poolside There's a small plunge pool and sauna in the basement.

Children Are welcome. An extra bed is ISK8,900; a cot is ISK7,100.

Also The 101 Gallery hosts art exhibitions, and has an impressive permanent collection of works by local artists, which spill out into the communal spaces of the hotel itself.

IN THE KNOW

Our favourite rooms One side of the hotel faces over the harbour, so ask for a sea view. Junior suites have two-way views of the harbour and the old town. Suite 516 has particularly good views; we also like junior suite 501, apartment 101, and corner rooms 201, 301, 401 and 501.

Hotel bar Open 07h–00h (01h at weekends), the bar is modern but very cosy, with huge leather sofas around an open fireplace.

Hotel restaurant Modern Icelandic and European cuisine is served in the comfortable surroundings of the chic monochrome restaurant, which is filled with modern art. Last orders for food is at 23h.

Top table They're all good.

Dress code Elegant Euro-chic.

LOCAL EATING AND DRINKING

For a fresh fish supper with Asian flavours, try the **Seafood Cellar** on Aðalstræti (511 1212). It's glam, with a vibrant atmosphere. Ask for a table at the back, not too close to the kitchen door. **La Primavera** on Austurstræti (561 8555) offers northern Italian food with a great wine list. Dine at the fashionable **Apotek** on Austurstræti (575 7900) for a huge variety of Euro-Asian food in lively, dynamic surroundings.

 Smith members receive a free copy of the 101 Hotel CD and a room upgrade subject to availability.

GET A ROOM!

Use our online booking service at www.mrandmrssmith to check availability and make reservations. Register your Smithcard to find out about current member offers for this hotel.

101 Hotel
10 Hverfisgata, Reykjavík
+354 5800 101
reservation@101hotel.is; www.101hotel.is

spot

stars

your

Leo

Orion

How to...

HOW TO... STARGAZE

Look up at the night sky from a city and all you see is the orange glow of urban light pollution. Escape to the countryside or a beach, and you'll find the heavens filled with countless constellations to ooh and aah over. Firstly, to stargaze properly, the need to find somewhere dark and secluded is a scientific necessity. (Or so you tell your other half.) Piers Sellers was the first Brit to spacewalk from a shuttle; his first words as he floated 200 miles above the Earth's surface? 'Yippee! Oh boy! Wow... Where am I?' Once you've lured your Mr or Mrs Smith to the right romantic spot, don't be at a loss for words – let your astronomical nous be the added aphrodisiac.

Scintillating conversation The scientific name for the twinkling of stars is stellar scintillation, which even Mozart would agree was a bit of a mouthful for his legendary nursery rhyme. It occurs because we view the stars through layers of turbulent air; not so magical, but it's one for the fact fans among you. Now, with so many stars up there it's difficult for would-be stargazers to tell our Arcturus from our elbow. Luckily there are 'skymarks' to guide us...

Not just a pretty space One of the most familiar shapes in the sky is the PLOUGH or BIG DIPPER. Just to be difficult though, it looks more like a Philippe Starck angle-poise lamp or a huge cooking pot than a farm- or fairground-related object. The two stars in the saucepan's bowl, furthest from the handle, point towards the POLE STAR or POLARIS. This is also the NORTH STAR, the one beloved by navigators, and one that can help you find your way back to the hotel if you get lost. The curving handle of the Plough points to bright ARCTURUS. The stars change gradually through the year: the reappearance of this daffodil-yellow star signals the approach of spring. On summer evenings, the first star to start its sparkling is blue-white VEGA. If you're sitting outside by candlelight, follow the flame upwards and you'll find Vega almost directly overhead, forming a triangle with DENEB, also high up, and ALTAIR, closer to the southern horizon. (If it's starting to feel like a double science lesson and this is blurring into a bunch of possible pop-band names, bear with us: after a few glasses of wine, it will all make sense.)

Deneb marks the tail of the constellation CYGNUS, imagined as a swan flying along the stardust trail of the MILKY WAY. Autumn sees the appearance of a W-shaped constellation, CASSIOPEIA, the mythical queen who regarded herself as more beautiful than the sea nymphs. (Mr Smith's cue to come in with a killer line to his Mrs.) The centrepiece of the winter sky is ORION, the hunter, recognisable by a line of three stars that stud his belt. To his upper left is giant BETELGEUSE, a ruddy-coloured star some 500 times larger than our Sun. (Due to a frequent mistranslation from the original Arabic its name is often thought to mean 'the armpit of the central one'. Not so romantic, admittedly, and hopefully not one to inspire Mrs Smith to direct a quip back at Mr Smith.) As you wish upon a star, consider how far away that apparently tiny twinkler actually is. SIRIUS is the nearest and brightest to be visible from the northern hemisphere. It glimmers when low on the horizon and is often mistaken for a UFO (keep an eye out for these, too).

The glow you see from Sirius, a mere 80 trillion kilometres away, was light that left it more than eight and a half years ago. But that's nothing in stargazing terms. Polaris and Betelgeuse are both about 430 light years away. (Which should cue a remark about how long you hope to stay together; cynics, resist the gag about that being how long it feels like you have been.) And finally, for those really momentous wishes, seek out the ANDROMEDA galaxy, known by some modern astronomers as M31. (When it comes to any special-occasion aspirations, the image of a Greek goddess rather than a defunct Berkshire motorway tends to sound sexier.) You can find it by drawing an imaginary line from Polaris through the W of Cassiopeia; it's the furthest object visible from Earth with the naked eye – a staggering 2.5 million light years off.

MTWTFSSMTWTFSSMTWTFSSMTWTFSSMTWTFSSMTW

SOUTH TYROL

● PIEDMONT

● TUSCANY

● SARDINIA

● SORRENTO ● PUGLIA

● AEOLIAN ISLANDS

ITALY

AEOLIAN ISLANDS
Hotel Raya
Hotel Signum
PIEDMONT
La Villa
PUGLIA
La Sommità
Masseria Torre Coccaro
SARDINIA
La Coluccia
SORRENTO
La Minervetta
SOUTH TYROL
Vigilius Mountain Resort
TUSCANY
Villa Bordoni
Villa Fontelunga
Villa Sassolini

T W T F S S M T W T F S S M T W T F S S M T W T F S S M T W T F S S M T W T F S S
ITALIA

AEOLIAN ISLANDS

Aeolian Islands

COASTLINE   EARTH, WIND, FIRE AND WATER
COAST LIFE   IDLE PLEASURES, ACTIVE VOLCANOES

MTWTFSSMTWTFSSMTWTFSSMTWTFSSMTWTFSSMTWT

ITALIA

TWTFSSMTWTFSSMTWTFSSMTWTFSSMTWTFSS

AEOLIAN ISLANDS

The 'seven sisters' of the volcanic Aeolian Islands are scattered like stars across the deep blue Tyrrhenian Sea, north of Sicily. Once believed to be the home of Aeolus and Vulcan, the god of the winds and the god of fire, they are now worshipped by island-lovers drawn to the cobalt waters, secret coves, rumbling volcanoes and windswept mountainsides. The islands mix elemental forces in extraordinary variety: the fiery volcano of Stromboli; black-sand beaches of sulphurous Vulcano; glamorous bougainvillea-framed hideaways on Panarea; the lush vineyards of Salina. Serene and peaceful and yet volatile and capricious – a playground fit for the gods.

GETTING THERE

Planes The nearest airports are Palermo and Catania. You can reach the islands by five-seater helicopter: Air Panarea flies from Rome, Palermo, Reggio Calabria and Naples (www.airpanarea.com), as does Dedalus Helicopters (+39 090 983 333).
Boats Hydrofoils run from Milazzo and Reggio di Calabria, as well as Messina, Palermo and Naples (summer only). See www.siremare.it or www.snav.it for details. The ferries are much slower.
Automobiles A car is unnecessary, and Panarea is car-free. Scooters can be hired on the larger islands.

DO GO/DON'T GO

Spring and autumn are warm and tranquil. July and August can be very busy and prices soar. Ferry and hydrofoil are sometimes cancelled due to heavy seas, particularly in winter.

ABSOLUTELY AEOLIAN ISLANDS

Hire a boat to reach the secluded coves and grottoes that line the coasts of this archipelago. The harbours are full of local operators and colourful characters ready to charter. Your hotel can also arrange vessels.

LOCAL KNOWLEDGE

Taxis Golf buggies on Panarea (hold on tight!); three-wheeled Vespa pick-ups on Vulcano. Taxis can be scarce and somewhat undependable. Get your hotel to order one for you.
Tipping culture A service charge is often added to restaurant bills, but an additional tip of ten per cent is usual for good service.
Siesta and fiesta The most active aspect of the islands are the volcanoes; otherwise the pace of life is very relaxed.
Packing tips Only Lipari has good banking facilities, so make sure you arrive with enough cash in your pocket. Salina is very popular with mosquitoes; pack some repellent.
Recommended read *The Leopard* by Giuseppe di Lampedusa.
Cuisine Dishes make extensive use of fragrant herbs and locally produced capers; the liberal use of these little pickled green buds is said to give Aeolian cooking an aphrodisiac quality. There is a big focus on fresh fish and squid; the Aeolian speciality of scorpion fish is fantastic. Don't miss the sweet Malvasia wine.
Currency Euro.
Dialling codes Country code for Italy: 39. Aeolian Islands: 090.

DIARY

First weekend of June The bizarre Caper Festival in Pollara, Salina, is a fiesta of food, music and street games in the main square, all in honour of the humble caper. **23 July** Pious pilgrims visit the Santuario della Madonna del Terzito, south of Malfa, on Salina on the day it is claimed that the Madonna appeared in 1622. **21–24 August** Lipari's Feast of St Bartholomew, with processions and fireworks. **First week of October** Food and Wine Week in Salina showcases the island's excellent cuisine with a series of island-wide events and demonstrations.

WORTH GETTING OUT OF BED FOR

Viewpoint The summit of Fossa delle Felci, on Salina, has super views over the neighbouring islands. Head to the prehistoric ruins of Punta Milazzese on Panarea for a view over the picture-perfect cove of Cala Junco.

Arts and culture The Greeks and Romans, whose ruins dot the archipelago, believed the islands to be the home of the fire god Vulcan. Volcanic activity has influenced life here for millennia and created dramatic rock formations, from soft silvery pumice to black obsidian.

Activities The crystal-clear waters make diving and snorkelling extremely popular. Rinella, on Salina, is popular for speargun fishing. There's excellent diving at Lisca Bianca off Panarea, and Malfa on Salina. Nautica Ondaeoliana in Malfa hires out boats (www.ondaeoliana.com).

Daytripper Rumbling Stromboli is wisely appreciated from a distance. The island of Vulcano is a lunar landscape of sulphurous fumaroles, steaming craters and bubbling hot springs. Try the therapeutic mud baths at Laghetto di Fanghi, but don't wear silver jewellery or your best bikini as the mud will ruin them.

Best beach Pretty Cala degli Zimmari is Panarea's only sandy stretch. Our favourites on Lipari are the secret coves on the east coast between Cala Fico and Punta Palmeto. The beautiful beach at Pollara on Salina is the setting for *Il Postino*.

Something for nothing The neighbouring islands will have a grandstand view when Stromboli stops rumbling and smoking and finally blows its top. If you're lucky you can see lava jet from the crater from the safety of a boat offshore. Organised night-time trips and boat rental are available from the appropriately named village of Scari.

Shopping Opportunities to shop on the islands are largely limited to beachwear and the occasional jewellery shop. Make sure you stock up on the islands' capers and deliciously sweet Malvasia wine, particularly in Salina.

CAFES

You'll find the harbours of the Aeolian Islands abuzz with activity as the day's catch of fish or boatload of tourists is unloaded. The **Tartana Club** on Stromboli and **Bar del Porto** on Panarea are among the best places to sit and watch the spectacle.

BARS AND RESTAURANTS

Bar La Precchia on Corso Vittorio Emanuele on Lipari is the spot to head to watch the world go by and enjoy cocktails and live music. **Filippino** on the bustling Piazza Mazzini, also on Lipari (090 981 1002; www.filippino.it), is perhaps the islands' most famous restaurant, serving an antipasto of capers and pecorino cheese or paddlefish turbans with basil. It's also the perfect place to try stromboli – delicious black squid-ink risotto with fish, chillies and tomatoes.

Albergo Ristorante Da Pina on via San Pietro Panarea (090 983 032) tempts the jet set to lava-rock tables with specialities such as gnocchi with aubergine. **Trattoria Maniaci Pino** in Gelso on Vulcano (368 668 555) is great for a lunch of fresh fish, or spaghetti with cuttlefish ink.

NIGHTLIFE

The islanders' idea of nightlife is their pleasant evening stroll, or *passeggiata*, when they catch up with island gossip and watch the sunset. Alternatively, **La Raya** nightclub on Panarea (see Hotel Raya review, page 140) attracts a chic party crowd from across the islands.

Hotel Raya

DESTINATION   AEOLIAN ISLANDS
STYLE   SICILIAN SIMPLICITY
SETTING   HOTSPOT BY NIGHT

MTWTFSSMTWTFSSMTWTFSSMTWTFSSMTWTFSSMTWT

ITALIA

'The room itself is pure Med heaven: a good size for two, with ample balcony space, and simple, tasteful furnishings in Raya's signature colours of blue and white'

What a debate there is over deciding on the world's greatest work of fiction. Some claim one of Shakespeare's should be number one; others point to the enduring appeal of Tolkien. But I can now reveal that the most inventive body of fiction ever written is the timetable for the hydrofoils, hovercraft and ferries that run between Sicily and the Aeolian Islands. It is quite staggeringly useless. Our initial error was to foolishly believe it had some vague connection with reality.

Once we were over the confusion of figuring out which boat went where, we realised that a sea voyage was the best way of clearing our frustrations and preparing ourselves for the full splendour of what lay ahead. Thanks to its relative remoteness, the island of Panarea has a magical quality, attracting those in the know,

rather than the tourist masses that descend on the Amalfi coast or Capri in high summer. Just over three kilometres in length, it's scattered with whitewashed buildings carved into the hillside. Somewhere up on those red and black rocks was our weekend home – the beautiful Hotel Raya.

We were met at the dockside by the lovely Giuseppe, and two minutes later his golf buggy had deposited us at the hotel reception. It was all I could do to stifle a squeal: the views from this hotel redefine the word 'panoramic'. It's as though you've suddenly gone from watching a portable TV to having an IMAX cinema in your lounge. The cone of the Stromboli volcano rises in the distance, a thin wisp of smoke trailing from the summit. Closer to shore, super-yachts deposit their glossy cargo in the seclusion of the island's more low-key islets.

The hotel is split into three levels – Raya Alto, Raya Basso and Raya-Peppe Maria. Raya Basso contains the reception, bar, restaurant and sundeck; Raya-Peppe Maria houses the island's hippest shopping boutique, together with a few small rooms; and Raya Alto, with its mesmerising views, is the level to choose your accommodation on. After a ten-minute walk uphill from reception, through the easily navigable maze of streets, we arrived at the cosy, hilltop Raya Alto bar. Its two or three tables face the sea and are located, rather conveniently, a few steps from our room.

The room itself is pure Med heaven: a good size for two, with ample balcony space, and simple, tasteful furnishings. Decorated in Raya's signature colours of blue and white, it didn't feel like a luxury room, and was all the better for that. We loved our very private island boudoir, and settled in nicely with a glass of prosecco from the bar – followed by a fat siesta.

Dinner that evening was the highlight of the trip. We booked a table at the rooftop restaurant for 23h, Italian-style. It's a place custom-designed for love, with lanterns and candles lighting each of the intimate tables that sit on different levels, every place setting cleverly positioned to look out to sea. Glamorous yet casually dressed guests mingled at the rooftop bar while jazz played lightly in the background. We dined on fresh tuna carpaccio and king prawns, followed by the fish of the day – lightly marinated, simple and delicious.

Over coffee and limoncello, we met the elegant Miriam Beltrami, owner of Hotel Raya since 1960. The property initially served as a guesthouse for her friends, and a sense of personal service and inclusiveness is what now makes it a favourite among clued-up weekenders. Miriam insisted we accompany her down to the hotel's open-air nightclub, where she left us partying with some of her friends, more glasses of prosecco in hand. This is the only nightspot in Panarea, and its remoteness gives it an electric atmosphere. The free-spirited danceteria entices people from their yachts moored in the bay, plus night-trippers from nearby islands who want to party. We danced for hours, before struggling up the hill to our room, managing to break the torch on the way. A word to the wise – carry two torches between you, as Panarea is pitch-black and potentially treacherous if you've enjoyed several glasses of wine. ↓

The next day was spent checking out the island's stylish boutiques and lazing on Hotel Raya's sundeck. We hadn't a clue that the weather was due for a dramatic change, and that all hovercraft and boats had been cancelled. The idea of being stranded on this tiny island had a spontaneous, romantic appeal but, sadly, just as we'd resigned ourselves to starring in our own private and very glamorous version of *Robinson Crusoe*, rescue was on hand. Panarea's only helicopter firm had two spare seats on the last flight of the day. Damn.

Still, as we pulled on the headphones and listened to the chatter of Italian air-traffic control, we reflected that there are worse ways to leave an island hideaway. Flying low over the deep blue sea, all Mr Smith's James Bond fantasies fulfilled, we waved to the passengers on the boats below. They, like us, may have spent hours travelling to the paradise of Panarea but, as they say, all good things come to those who wait.

Reviewed by Mr & Mrs Smith

NEED TO KNOW

Rooms 36: two suites, one junior suite.
Rates €195–€480, including breakfast.
Check-out 11h, or later if possible.
Room service Food and drinks are available between 08h30 and midnight.
Facilities Luggage service from the port or helipad. Solarium with steps down to the sea.
Massages can be arranged in your room. Internet connection in the downstairs bar, and
comfortable TV room.
Poolside There is no pool at the hotel, but you're never far from the sea on this tiny island.
Children Not good for small children, since there are lots of steps, and no protection on
the terraces.
Also No TV or music systems. Discount in the hotel boutique for guests.

IN THE KNOW

Our favourite rooms Rooms 41 and 42 are located at the top of the cliff and are the most private,
with the best views. 38 and 39 also have great views, 36 has a private terrace, and 32 an
enormous private patio. Number 14 is the best suite and has two bathrooms.
Hotel bar The open-air bar on the lower level opens for drinks at 14h. From 18h everyone moves
to the higher terrace (Raya Alto) for the *aperitivo* and to watch the sunset. Then from 01h,
downstairs becomes a fabulous open-air club.
Hotel restaurant Coffee and croissants are served in the small bar by the Raya Alto. Dinner is
served from 20h30 on the lower level. In August, you can dine on fantastic fish or organic meat
on the candlelit roof terrace, enjoying incredible sea views.
Top table Reserve a table on the lower level, directly overlooking the water; or, for a more
romantic setting, book a table on the roof terrace at 23h (August only).
Dress Bellissimo.

LOCAL EATING AND DRINKING

Everybody heads down to **Bar del Porto** for the traditional *aperitivo* (18h–21h). Lunch or dine
on fresh fish at **Hycesia** (090 983 041). The menu changes daily, based on that day's catch.
Cala Junco (090 983 032) is also great, especially for grouper and tuna steaks. Go to the
terrace of **Da Pina** (090 983 032) for the fresh pasta with aubergines by candlelight. After
dinner, go drinking at **Bridge** on Via Porto before hitting **La Raya** nightclub at the hotel.

Smith members receive a five per cent discount off a helicopter transfer.

GET A ROOM!

Use our online booking service at www.mrandmrssmith.com to check availability and make
reservations. Register your Smithcard to find out about current member offers for this hotel.

Hotel Raya
Via San Pietro, Panarea, Aeolian Islands
+39 090 983 013
info@hotelraya.it; www.hotelraya.it

'A series of tiled, landscaped terraces are bursting with scented lime-trees, bougainvillea and honeysuckle'

Hotel Signum

DESTINATION   AEOLIAN ISLANDS
STYLE   FAMILY-RUN FARMHOUSE
SETTING   *IL POSTINO* COUNTRY

MTWTFSSMTWTFSSMTWTFSSMTWTFSSMTWTFSSMTW

ITALIA

145

Scan any literature on this part of the world and you wince at warnings of hectic summer months, when the Aeolian Islands are said to be overrun with holidaymakers from Sicily and beyond. So, as our hydrofoil pulled away from the mainland port of Milazzo, we prepared for elbows at dawn and swinging hand luggage come disembarkation. We engineered ourselves a pole-position place by the exit so that we'd be first to alight, the better to dive straight into one of the island's few taxis. We arrived and, with a deep breath, a big push and a few squashed toes, we were thrust forth. We found ourselves dazed, and strangely alone, at Salina's main port of Santa Marina.

The few other people who had arrived on the boat with us disappeared in 10 seconds flat, all whisked off by Vespa to the holiday homes that lightly pepper this greenest and most fertile of the seven islands of the Aeolian archipelago. So much for the silly season – instead, we were beginning to sense the *dopo* ('later') sentiment that lies at the heart of the Sicilian lifestyle. The equivalent of the Spanish *mañana, mañana* approach to life, it is one we can certainly relate to. In next to no time, our usually frantic pace of life had decelerated to a suitably lethargic one.

Given our usual orientation skills, it's a small miracle that we found Hotel Signum without drama, but there are only two roads on the entire island, so the odds were very much stacked in our favour. A discreet tile on the white-painted clay wall told us we were at the right address, and we followed our noses down a honeysuckled path to reception.

Now, as seasoned travellers we realise that, to get the best out of the locals, it helps to try and speak the language. There I was, about to launch into some considered Italian, when Mr Smith ventured forth with his own Euro patois – a unique combination of French and Spanish vocabulary with an Italian inflection, accompanied by a wild flurry of gesticulations. This was met with what most would recognise to be

incredulous stares, but what Mr Smith read as encouragement. He continued to herald our arrival with great theatre while I ventured off to explore.

The house style is, well, house style, with an informal reception containing an antique table and a few simple lamps, surrounded by beautiful old cabinets housing objets d'art and vintage books. There is a library and sitting room furnished with the same understated elegance, and throughout the hotel are scattered a number of interesting bookcases, backgammon sets and paintings to distract from the main attraction of the hotel – the spectacular views.

Set around a series of tiled and landscaped terraces, bursting with scented lime-trees and tumbles of bougainvillea and honeysuckle, the rooms are each named after an indigenous flower. They are dotted throughout the grounds: some above the main house, others to the rear in the gardens. (Signum's foliage-filled spaces also house speakers, cunningly

disguised as rocks, as we inadvertently discovered when discarding a particularly challenging after-dinner grappa in a flower bed.) Almost all of the rooms have their own tiny piece of private outside space where guests can dawdle away sunset with a G&T and a game of backgammon while comparing brown feet. If you're smart, you'll earmark an ocean view so that you get a gulp of the gardens right down to the Tyrrhenian Sea and to the horizon, with only Stromboli (an active volcano) and its stylish sister island, Panarea, to punctuate the vista.

It didn't take us long to figure out that hours can be whiled away dangling from the edge of the infinity pool, gazing into the far distance. Here, we spent most mornings sipping glasses of home-made lemonade and deliberating over which pasta dish to try later on. It took a great deal of focus to decide on the pressing issues of the day: should I venture out in my new Miu Miu heels that night, and would it be wise to get a bit of practice walking in them first? ↓

Hotel Signum is very relaxed indeed; however, our self-imposed Smith-holiday protocol was observed at all times. At least two bikini changes a day to justify the multiples purchased; mandatory cigarette smoking even if one gave up one's dirty habit last summer; a daily excursion via motorbike; and saying yes to everything offered. So as soon as the dashingly handsome receptionist with the flirty eyes recommended the massage service, I was sold. Off I skipped to the all-white treatment room with floating muslin curtains, and doors that open onto the garden and a view of the ocean. Bar the whale music, it felt like my own self-conjured heaven.

The hotel encourages guests to let it be known by lunchtime if they wish to have supper that evening at the restaurant: we were quick to learn that you should also reserve a sea view, to guarantee a breeze and for the star-gazing. Also worthy of note: when you are offered a medium-sized whole fish, be prepared to tackle something more like an average-sized whale. It can be a bit embarrassing for a Mrs Smith when it takes two struggling waiters to ferry a dish to her table and then a third to plate it, while Mr Smith tucks into a more modestly proportioned aubergine pasta. Even Captain Ahab would have blushed. It is easy to be the last up and the last to bed at Signum, but staff are always around to pour just one more almond wine or recommend another delicious Sicilian red. They are true holiday-enhancers, able to organise all manner of excursions, from diving or sailing on a fisherman's boat to Vespa hire. Which is just as well. Otherwise Mr Smith and I would have stayed put, happy exactly where we were.

Reviewed by Mr & Mrs Smith

NEED TO KNOW

Rooms 30.

Rates €110–€320, including breakfast.

Check-out 11h.

Room service Food and drinks are available 07h–00h.

Facilities Solarium, massage, library. Vespa hire can be easily arranged at the hotel. The staff are also happy to organise sailing and diving trips.

Poolside There is an infinity pool.

Children Welcome, although the atmosphere is one of quiet relaxation.

Hotel closed Mid-November to mid-March.

IN THE KNOW

Our favourite rooms Rooms 11 and 12 both have terraces with sea views, and are located slightly away from the rest of the rooms, offering a bit more privacy and seclusion. Room 34 is the most spacious in the hotel.

Hotel bar Open until midnight.

Hotel restaurant Mediterranean food with a international twist; we love the four-course tasting menus of Aeolian specialities. You are encouraged to let the hotel know by lunchtime if you plan to dine in the restaurant.

Top table On the terrace or, if it's a chilly evening, by the window.

Dress code Dress up for dinner.

LOCAL EATING AND DRINKING

For lazy lunches, **Portobello** in Santa Marina (090 984 3125) serves up fine seafood and classic Italian dishes. A stunning all-white outdoor bar, **Santa Isobel Lounge** is a two-minute stroll from Hotel Signum, and great for sunset G&Ts to chilled-out beats. In Lingua, also within walking distance of the hotel, **A Cannata** on Via Umberto (090 984 3161) has a sunny terrace where you can try fantastic penne alla salinara with peppers, pine nuts, capers and olives. Nearby **Da Alfredo** serves the best granitas on the island. When you want a change from delectably fresh fish, head round the corner to **Pizzeria a' Lumeredda'** on Via San Lorenzo (090 984 4130) for a simpler supper.

Smith members receive a picnic lunch and ten per cent off boat hire at Onda Eoliana (www.ondaeoliana.com).

GET A ROOM!

Use our online booking service at www.mrandmrssmith.com to check availability and make reservations. Register your Smithcard to find out about current member offers for this hotel.

Hotel Signum
15 Via Scalo, Malfa, Salina
+39 090 984 4222
salina@hotelsignum.it; www.hotelsignum.it

PIEDMONT

Piedmont

COUNTRYSIDE   PROSPEROUS FOOTHILLS
COUNTRY LIFE   FARMING AND FEASTING

MTWTFSSMTWTFSSMTWTFSSMTWTFSSMTWTFSSMTWT
ITALIA

PIEDMONT

This northwestern region is a reminder that until just over a hundred years ago, Italy wasn't a country, but a collection of states, each with its own distinct identity. Until the 19th century, folk in this aristocratic province spoke French and, geographically, it has a multiple personality too, with its rolling farmland punctuated by perfectly preserved mediaeval villages and energetic industrial towns. This neighbour of the Swiss and French Alps may be landlocked, but it's only a drive from some of Europe's favourite lakes and beaches. And this is a part of the world that takes its consumption very seriously, so if you like your feeding-time to be formal, or your fashion labels designer, you'll find that, in Piemonte, you've hit the jackpot.

GETTING THERE

Planes Milan Malpensa airport is just east of Piedmont, and easily reached by car. Turin-Caselle airport is to the west; Genoa, to the south, completes the triangle of accessible airports.
Trains Turin is the capital of Piedmont, and gateway to other regions of Italy and abroad, particularly nearby France. For more info, go to www.trenitalia.com.
Boats The ports of Savona-Vado and Genoa are linked by road and rail.
Automobiles Take advantage of the efficient motorway and road network, and rent a car to explore. This is the birthplace of Fiat, after all.

DO GO/DON'T GO

Every season has its own allure. This Alpine-fringe region is ideal for winter sports in January and February. After the heat of summer, October to December sees the wine and truffle harvest.

PERFECTLY PIEDMONT

Go *funghi* hunting during the autumn, and whet your appetite for delicious local cuisine, particularly dishes using the prized local white truffle.

LOCAL KNOWLEDGE

Taxis Towns have taxi ranks but you should book ahead in rural areas.
Tipping culture In restaurants, the cover charge represents your tip.
Siesta and fiesta Small shops tend to close 12h30–13h and 15h–15h30; shopping malls and supermarkets don't close at lunchtime.
Packing tips It's less about what you take than the space you should leave to cart home edible and drinkable delicacies.
Recommended reads *A Long Finish* by Michael Dibdin; *Italian Hours* by Henry James; *The Devil in the Hills* by Cesare Pavese.
Cuisine Ditch diet thoughts and revel in a serving of Castelmagno cheese melted over gnocchi, washed down with a full-bodied Barbera, Barbaresco or Barolo, or the ubiquitous Asti Spumante. Try *bônet*, a local pud using amaretti biscuits.
Currency Euro.
Dialling codes Country code for Italy: 39.

DIARY

February The three-day orange fight is reason enough in itself to visit the Ivrea Carnival (www.carnevalediivrea.it). **August** For dazzling art in the sky, head to Lake Orta's World Fireworks Championship (www.parente.it).
September Turin's Settembre Musica treats your ears to jazz, world and classical music (www.settembremusica.it); the food-fanatical Festival Delle Sagre in Asti will make your tastebuds happy (www.doujador.it).
Third Sunday in September The streets of Asti come alive with banquets and horse riding for its annual Palio (www.palio.asti.it). **Mid-September to mid-November** Alba and the surrounding area celebrate the riches brought home by the *trifulau*, or truffle hunters, during their annual truffle festival. **Mid-November** Torino Film Festival takes place in the birthplace of the Italian film industry (www.torinofilmfest.org).

WORTH GETTING OUT OF BED FOR

Viewpoint Wending your way through the countryside, it's hard to find anywhere in Piedmont that *doesn't* have a view. In the Roman spa town of Acqui Terme, a bird's-eye spot is from the panoramic terrace next to Castello dei Paleologi.

Arts and culture For museums, and an eyeful of baroque at its best, head to the centre of Turin. You'll also get a glimpse of modern-day architecture from the likes of Renzo Piano. Asti is replete with cobbles, churches and charm; we loved the unique venue where Diavolo Rosso hosts a wide range of music concerts (www.diavolorosso.it).

Activities All the great-outdoors adventures are available, such as walking, cycling, horse riding and golf. In the winter, skiing is possible around Turin and Cuneo. Those not feeling very sporty might prefer visiting the many vineyards, and cheese or chocolate factories, where tasting is, naturally, a highlight.

Daytripper If you seek water-related thrills, head north to the lakes – Orta, Maggiore and Como – or south to Liguria and Italy's prime Riviera destination, Portofino.

Something for nothing A driving tour of the winelands, stopping off in the beautiful villages of Nieve, Barbaresco, La Morra and Serralunga d'Alba. Another scenic route might take in any of Carròsio, Voltaggio, Capanne di Marcarolo natural park, Bòsio, Tornese, Lerma, Tagliolo Monferrato, Castelletto d'Orba and Gavi.

Shopping Serravalle Designer Outlet is open Monday to Friday 10h–19h; Saturday and Sunday 10h–20h. Here you can find Prada, Versace, Diesel, Bulgari and Dolce & Gabbana goods at up to 70 per cent off (www.mcarthurglen.it). The local food markets in the mornings are fun, plus, on Sundays, antiques markets; ask your hotel to steer you to the nearest one.

CAFES

Mombaruzzo is the birthplace of those magnificent macaroons, so head to any café off the main square of the quaint town and treat yourself to a couple of amaretti with your espresso (www.amarettidimombaruzzo.com). And remember, they'll know you're a tourist if you order a cappuccino any time other than breakfast; Italians look down their nose at milky coffees after 11h as it's deemed bad for the digestion.

BARS AND RESTAURANTS

Locanda del Sant'Uffizio is a charming spot in the heart of Monferrato (0141 91 62 92) if you fancy a special affair; the gardens and the sage-green 17th-century building make a magical setting, even if the service isn't the most smiley. The cuisine is geared to the gourmands that flock here for fancy fodder. **La Gallina** at the Monterotondo di Gavi (0143 685 132) is hard to beat for style and service; book a table out on the terrace, loosen your waistband and go the whole four-course hog. If you're smart you'll do it the tasting way when it comes to the acclaimed local white wines. **Enoteca del Roero** in Canale (0173 978228) is one of the dons of fine dining for this region; closed Wednesday and Thursday lunchtimes.

NIGHTLIFE

Night owls should head to the bigger towns such as nearby Milan for the liveliest late-night excitements. If you fancy a wine-bar crawl, head to Turin. Our favourite though is **Vineria Tastè Vin** on Via Vassallo in Asti (0141 320017), an excellent wine bar.

'Our ground-floor
boudoir was charming,
with its soothing
simplicity, handful
of antiques and slick
travertine wet room'

La Villa

DESTINATION   PIEDMONT
STYLE   SIMPLE-CHIC PALAZZO
SETTING   MONFERRATO VINEYARDS

MTWTFSSMTWTFSSMTWTFSSMTWTFSSMTWTFSSMTWT
ITALIA

TWTFSSMTWTFSSMTWTFSSMTWTFSSMTWTFSSMTWTFSS

All our concentration was required not miss the turning to La Villa, off a winding country lane. One impressive right-angled swerve into the foliage-framed driveway and there it was: a handsome butter-coloured property with sage-green shutters came into view. We'd barely made a crunch on the gravel when one half of the English couple behind this converted palazzo spotted us across the garden and cheerily indicated that a glass of prosecco awaited us inside. What, no queuing at reception? No bellboy to tip? *This* is what we call arriving.

The hotel – originally 17th-century – has undergone some impressive anti-ageing procedures. You can't tell it is such an oldie, and I intend this as a salute to its English owners, who have given the three-storey building a fantastic new lease of life as a country hideaway. That said, it is far from bereft of classic charm: the vaulted ceilings have been preserved, the flooring is original, and the render is perfectly sympathetic, but neutral colours and unfussy, comfortable furnishings give it a modern-day freshness. We'd missed out on doing the serious Mr & Mrs Smith thing, since the two honeymoon-worthy suites were booked, but our ground-floor boudoir was charming, with its soothing simplicity, handful of antiques and slick travertine wet room.

As I was sniffing the White Company bathroom products, I was alerted to the fact that sunset was upon us by Mr Smith wielding his camera. His manly non-verbal communication skills lured me away from the handmade olive-oil soap and out onto the terrace, to make the most of this gorgeous dusky time of day. A tip for the vain: don't turn down a snapshot at twilight. Forget Vaseline on the lens, or having to fool around in Photoshop when you get home – this flattering half-light is like cracking open a tin of insto-airbrush, so there's no better hour to agree to pose for some holiday snaps.

As darkness fell outside, we picked up our welcome drinks from the bar in the living-room area, and wandered up to the pool. Our feet dipped in the water, a chilled glass of the local fizz in our hands, we savoured every second. It's moments like these you yearn for again – anything for just a quick trip in a Tardis – when you're back in front of your computer at work. 'I've always been a fan of wine with holes in it,' remarks Mr Smith, swirling his aperitif like the cat that got the cream. I was too busy snaffling another crumbly amaretto biscuit to dignify his quip with a smile.

The pool is of the intimate kind, rather than some monumental infinity affair. Having the spot all to ourselves, looking out across that countryside, was heavenly. And it wasn't simply a case of the bubbles in the local fizz enhancing our view of undulating hills and terracotta-roofed farmhouses. As we headed back to the house for supper, we were already looking forward to soaking up the Piedmont tableau in the morning sun.

The following morning, the bright Italian sunshine roused us wonderfully early – we had big plans for the day and were grateful for the wake-up call. The husband and wife who run La Villa were on hand at breakfast on the terrace to offer suggestions of where to go sightseeing, where they could book us a table for supper, and to give us a hand with directions. After greedily sampling enough conserves, cheeses and cold meats to rival a tasting tour of Borough Market, washed down with impeccable cappuccino, we set off for a fix of culture and consumerism.

If typing in 'Asti' into your brain's Google brings up images of hen-night shenanigans, then it's time to update your mental search engine. As well as being the producer of the famous *spumante*, it's a charming town, and refreshingly untouristy. We strolled its cobbled streets through the bustling food market, our grazing broken up by a whirl around some pretty churches. Duly impressed by the craftsmanship of Italian designers of centuries past, we were also quite keen to check out some more contemporary creations at the Serravalle Designer Outlet, an hour's drive back in the direction of Milan. With Prada, Dolce & Gabbana and Versace up to 70 per cent cheaper than in the shops, by the time we were ready ↓

for our dinner, this Mrs Smith was struggling under the weight of enough bags to rival even the most dedicated WAG.

From one indulgence to another: our next pilgrimage was in honour of the grape. La Gallina restaurant in the stylish Monterotondo di Gavi resort made a rewarding destination. The cossetting cluster of L'Ostelliere hotel, its eatery and Villa Sparina farm were created by the original champion of this vintage, so we resigned ourselves to the duty of having to sample as many variations of the fine white wine as possible. Mr Smith pointed out that our first glugs out in the open-air bar, overlooking endless vines, amid a fragrant herb garden, must have represented one of the finest tipple/terrain combos going.

Out on the terrace of La Gallina, a parade of culinary treats occupied the rest of our evening, along with a little eavesdropping – irresistible among such interesting-looking glamorous guests. But it was

hard to make use of our ears when our mouths were getting so much attention – we ate mouthwatering salads, risotto, lamb cutlets and fresh fruit. Piedmont is a destination to please refined sensualists, with its epicurean delights, shopping fit for a footballer's wife, sightseeing to sate the keenest amateur art historian… We experienced more in one day, by exploring in each direction from La Villa, than some holidaymakers do in a fortnight. So much so that we were quite prepared to spend the next day – and, quite possibly, the one after that – snoozing by the pool.

Reviewed by Mr & Mrs Smith

NEED TO KNOW

Rooms 12: five suites, seven doubles.

Rates €165–€215, including breakfast.

Check-out 11h; if guests want to stay by the pool, changing facilities are possible.

Room service Light snacks for late-arriving guests, but otherwise no room service.

Facilities Air-conditioning, minibar, Internet; flatscreen TVs and DVD/CD player on request.

Poolside Outdoor pool (no diving: adults' feet can always touch the bottom).

Children Very welcome. There's a games room with satellite TV. All suites have large sofa beds, suitable for families of up to four; there's a charge of €10 a night for family use. Cots can be provided at no extra charge. Babysitting available at €8 an hour.

Hotel closed From 5 January until March, although groups are accepted, by prior agreement.

Also Small, well-behaved dogs are allowed, one at a time. Smoking is allowed outside.

IN THE KNOW

Our favourite rooms The Honeymoon suite is huge, has original terracotta floors, arched ceilings, a four-poster bed and a bath overlooking the vineyards. If you're a sucker for a vista, the Terrace Suite and the peaceful Moroccan room share a fabulous private patio. The view from the claw-footed bath in the Romeo and Juliet room is also lovely.

Hotel bar This little enclave is the hub of the hotel. In winter, they light a wood fire; in summer, it opens onto the courtyard. Guests can drink as late as they like on an honesty-bar basis.

Hotel restaurant Opening spring 2007, serving local produce and great Piemontese wines.

Dress code *Completamente casuale*; unless you're off to a Michelin-starred eatery, when you might want to plump for Prada.

LOCAL EATING AND DRINKING

The hotel is proud of the fact that it has the largest concentration of gourmet chefs in Italy within a 30km radius. If you just fancy a quick bite, **Mistral** in Bazzana (0141 702967) is ideal for a steak and chips or a simple pasta. **Alla Locanda** in Mombaruzzo is a local trattoria with a sweet courtyard; closed Mondays. If you want a formal Piedmont experience, **Bardon del Belbo** in San Marzano Oliveto (0141 831340) will regale you with a set menu, and let you choose from their dazzling wine list. In summer, earmark a table on the terrace; closed Wednesdays and Thursdays. Family-run **San Marco** in Canelli (0141 823544) has a Michelin star, and it's elegant but friendly; closed Tuesday evenings and Wednesdays.

 Smith members will get a bottle of prosecco in their room and an upgrade subject to availability.

GET A ROOM!

Use our online booking service at www.mrandmrssmith.com to check availability and make reservations. Register your Smithcard to find out about current member offers for this hotel.

La Villa
7 Via Torino, Mombaruzzo, Piedmont
+39 0141 793 890
info@lavillahotel.net; www.lavillahotel.net

Puglia

COASTLINE   THE SHAPELY HEEL OF ITALY
COAST LIFE   TRULLI, MADLY, DEEPLY

MTWTFSSMTWTFSSMTWTFSSMTWTFSSMTWTFSSMTWT

ITALIA

PUGLIA

Located in Italy's sunny south, Puglia has a unique character and charm, little known to outsiders; the Italians who flock here in the summer keep this laidback playground of blue sea, golden sands and olive groves strictly a family affair. As at all good Italian get-togethers, food takes centre stage: fresh fish, melons, figs, olive oils and wines. Puglia produces almost all of the country's – in fact Europe's – pasta. Yet although the region may appear Italian down to its boots, the heel of Italy has a very cosmopolitan past; the Greeks, Spanish and Normans all paid visits, leaving a quirky mishmash of architectural heirlooms, from Baroque churches and Romanesque cathedrals to whitewashed villages and the traditional conical dwellings called *trulli*.

GETTING THERE

Planes There are airports at Brindisi and Bari, both with regular flights.

Trains Puglia's main towns and cities are connected by train, though local services are often scenic and slow. Remoter areas, such as the 13th-century Castel del Monte, require a car.

Automobiles Car hire is essential if you really want to explore. Chancing upon remote villages as you drive along is all part of the fun.

DO GO/DON'T GO

If you don't fancy sweltering-hot weather and busy beaches, visit in early or late summer for milder conditions and the chance to bag a decent spot on the sand. Fine, sunny weather starts in spring and lasts well into autumn this far south, and sees the region at its best.

PERFECTLY PUGLIA

Puglia produces 70 per cent of Italy's olive oil. There are many different varieties, each with its own unique flavour. The olive press of Il Frantolio di D'Amico Pietro near Cisternino offers tours and tastings – great for wine buffs looking for a new challenge.

LOCAL KNOWLEDGE

Taxis Trying to hail a cab on the street won't get you anywhere; go to a taxi rank or ask your hotel to order one for you. They are metered and levy small extra charges for luggage and for travelling after 22h.

Tipping culture A service charge is usually added to restaurant bills, but it is customary to tip an extra five or ten per cent.

Siesta and fiesta Shops open early and close late, with long lunch breaks. Most close on Sundays and Monday mornings, except in resort areas. Banks also break for lunch, reopening at 15h for an hour. Restaurants only start to fill at 21h; nightclubs hot up around midnight.

Packing tips Summer wardrobe staples – think laidback southern style, not chi-chi Capri.

Recommended reads *Casa Rossa* by Francesca Marciano; *Heel to Toe* by Charles Lister.

Cuisine Enjoy an abundance of sun-ripened fruit and vegetables and delicious olive oil. Definitely try the local pasta orecchiette or 'little ears'. The region produces huge amounts of wine, too: Salice Salentino, a full-bodied red, is one of the best.

Currency Euro.

Dialling codes Country code for Italy: 39. Local area codes: Foggia: 0881; Bari: 080; Brindisi: 0831; Lecce: 0832; Taranto: 099. Remember, with Italy you need to leave in the 0, even when dialling from abroad.

DIARY

June One of the oldest motorcar races in the world, the Rally del Salento, takes place in Lecce – a nail-biting event characterised by its sharp turns (www.rallydelsalento.com). **20 July** The start of the Festival della Valle d'Itria – a three-week event in the town of Martina Franca, with opera, classical and jazz performances (www.festivaldellavalleditria.it).

WORTH GETTING OUT OF BED FOR

Viewpoint The hilltop mediaeval town of Locorotondo on the Murge plateau gives panoramic views of the surrounding Itria Valley.

Arts and culture Don't go to Puglia without seeing the *trulli*. The Itria Valley is home to thousands of these circular dwellings, with beehive-shaped roofs and whitewashed walls, particularly around Alberobello.

Activities The region's flat terrain is ideal for cycling. The gentle coastal route from Bari to Monopoli offers a taste of Puglia's varied scenery. In the fishing village Polignano a Mare, which sits on the clifftop, stop for an ice cream at Il Super Mago del Gelo on Piazza Garibaldi.

Daytripper The Parco Nazionale del Gargano, in the north of Puglia, contains the Foresta Umbra (Forest of Shadows). The 1,000 hectares of pine, oak and beech is the last remnant of an ancient forest, which once spread over most of Puglia.

Best beach The fishing village of Torre Canne has a long stretch of soft sand and shallow water for cooling off your toes after working on the tan.

Something for nothing The shopkeepers in the trulli-town of Alberobello pride themselves on their hospitality and their wares. Many offer free wine tasting in their shops.

Shopping Bari's Via Sparano is the place to go for fashionable boutiques. Bari also has some excellent delicatessens. De Carne, on Via Calefati, is popular for local meats and cheeses. Almost every town in Puglia has its market day where, in addition to the fruit and vegetables, you can find handicrafts, such as terracotta and embroidery. Ostuni's market is on Saturday.

And… Puglia was once a Greek colony, and nowhere suggests this heritage better than Ostuni's gorgeous whitewashed houses. Go along later to join the locals on their evening *passeggiata* – the see-and-be-seen stroll.

CAFES

Lecce has a great café culture – the picturesque Piazza Sant' Oronzo is a great place to watch the world go by. Try **Caffè Alvino**, which serves fabulous cream cakes. **Caffè Ronchi** in Altamura is a 100 year-old establishment, famous for its bitter walnut liqueur.

BARS AND RESTAURANTS

Ostuni's untouristy restaurants are some of the best in the region. **Osteria del Tempo Perso** on Via Gaetano Tanzarella Vitale (083 130 3320) serves traditional Pugliese fare. One part of the restaurant is set inside a cave, the other is adorned with farm tools – bizarre but charming. On the same street, the romantic **Taverna della Gelosia** (083 133 4736) does some unusual and tasty dishes, such as black pasta and barley with bitter herbs and nettles. For great seafood and stunning views of the Adriatic, go to Monopoli's **La Peschiera** on Contrada Losciale, Località Capitolo (080 801066). Bari's most stylish citizens can be found enjoying martinis in **Barcollo** in Piazza Mercantile (080 521 3889).

NIGHTLIFE

Lecce's Via Gusti is a good place to work off those pasta calories. **Corto Maltese** is open from Wednesday to Monday 21h until late. The town of Cisternino has open-air cafes that stay open late in summer. **Bar Fod** in Piazza Vittorio Emanuele plays live jazz until 02h. Ostuni's sophisticated lounge bar **Riccardo Caffè** on Via Gaetano Tanzarella serves lethal mojitos and super antipasti.

La Sommità

DESTINATION   PUGLIA
STYLE   DESIGNER DEN
SETTING   UP-AND-COMING OSTUNI

MTWTFSSMTWTFSSMTWTFSSMTWTFSSMTWTFSSMTWT
ITALIA

'Slick stone interiors and low-slung, contemporary furnishings enhance the beauty of the ancient walls, stone lintels and vaulted ceilings'

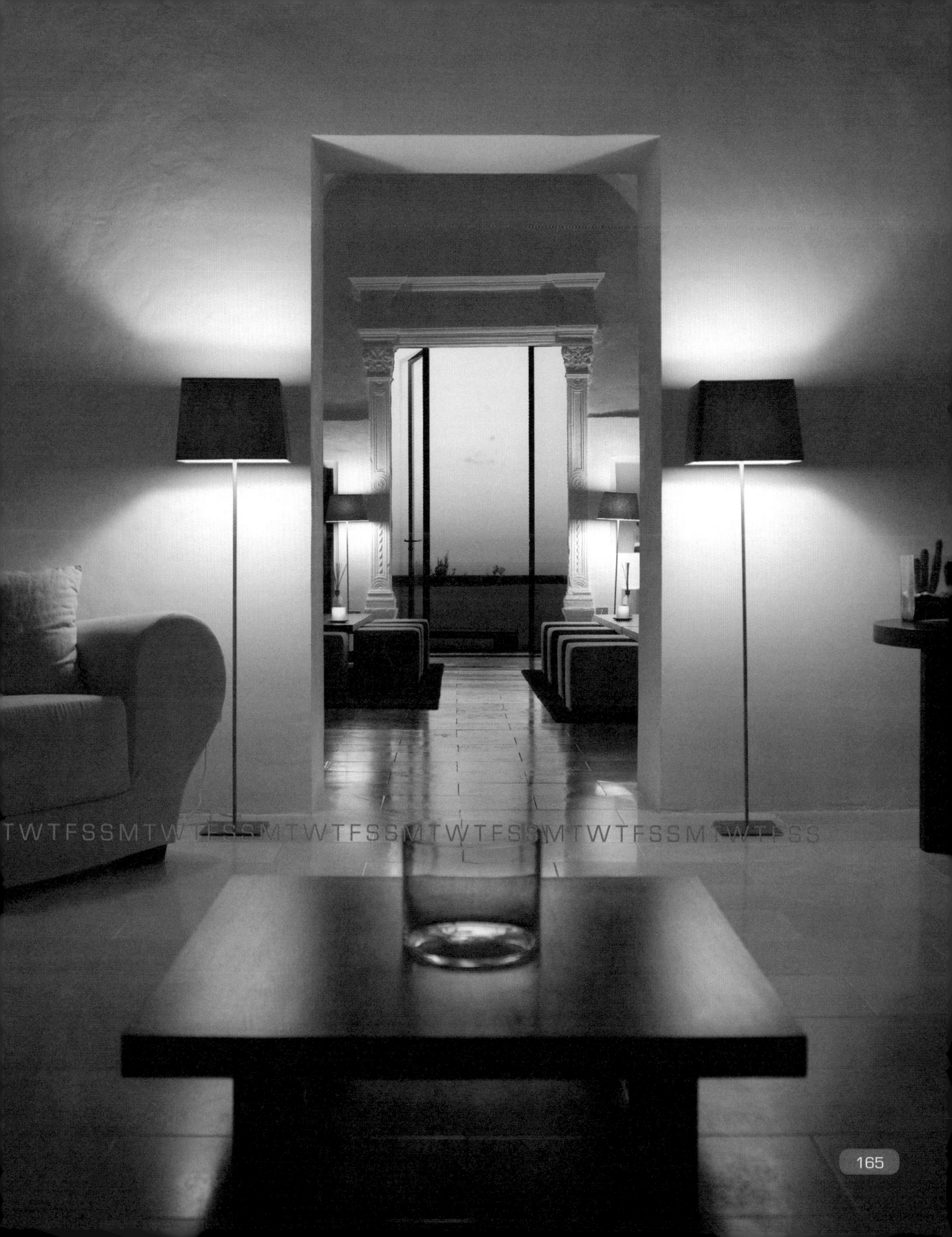

For a while now I've been hearing that Puglia, a sleepy, sun-baked province in the heel of Italy, is the new Tuscany. (Then again, I read something the other day that tried to peddle the Channel Islands as the new Caribbean – nice try.) The baroque jewel of Lecce has been rebranded the Florence of the South, and fashionisti from Milan have been snapping up the traditional, conical-roofed, white-washed *trulli* (limestone abodes) and *masserie* (fortified farmhouses) for a song and parading, Prada-clad, across deserted beaches, much to the bemusement of locals.

As we zoomed past gleaming, two-storey villas along the immaculate motorway from Bari airport to Ostuni, it dawned on me that regeneration and development happen quickly these days, and that the Italians are clearly as much of a dab hand with not-quite-dry concrete as the Spanish. La Sommità, luckily for us, is hidden well away from these new developments. Despite my terrible map reading, we found our turn-off after an hour and wove through ancient olive groves before spotting the mediaeval hilltop town glowing golden against a clear night sky. Neat, provincial streets gave way to a warren which took us to the pretty, baroque centre, and after a couple of directions-begging calls to the chirpy hotel receptionist, we finally parked next to Ostuni's 16th-century cathedral.

The designer of La Sommità, Alessandro Agrati, kindly helped us with our bags and led us down a tiny alley to the chic, discreet retreat we'd call home for the next two days. (He used to be a designer at Culti, the contemporary Italian lifestyle brand which has a stake in the hotel.) It was late and the kitchen was about to

close, so we headed straight for the dining room and ordered from the mercifully short menu (rabbit for him, steak for me) before unwinding with a fragrant bottle of local wine and taking in our elegant surroundings.

La Sommità has all the elements that a contemporary hideaway needs. There are just ten rooms, and so the handful of guests have the potential to remind you of characters from an Agatha Christie novel. Except that most of them are chic young couples who have left urban stress and the kids at home; they don't tend to suck seductively on cigarettes in holders plotting their next murder. Instead, they spend their precious hours of freedom flicking through glossy magazines in the sleek lounge or on the extensive patio overlooking the town, they canoodle in sunloungers on private balconies, or sneak off for a pummel and a preen in the little spa.

The architects of this exquisite place, a converted 16th-century palace, have been smart to keep the charm of the original structure. They've added slick stone interiors and low-slung, contemporary furnishings in off-whites and earth tones, which enhance the beauty of the ancient walls, centuries-old stone door lintels and vaulted, arched ceilings. Unlike the sterile, minimalist hotels that have reached epidemic levels around the world, La Sommità has a palpable sense of history and, thanks to subtle, sympathetic lighting and friendly service, it offers a relaxed sense of intimacy that allows you to unwind from the very moment you arrive.

Having said that, don't think the hotel doesn't celebrate some of the delights of modern hospitality. Dinner consisted of the kind of dishes that are set to become the new big fad in fine dining. I don't mean any silly fusion-related gimmickry – simply healthy, beautifully presented, super-fresh, organic ingredients that still give a nod to traditional local cuisine. After admiring the views from the massive terrace over post-prandial ciggies (smoking inside is illegal in Italy – although unlike so many other places, here you don't feel like a social pariah when you nip out for your nicotine ↓

fix), we savoured a smooth Amaretto each and, inevitably, contented as can be, succumbed to travel fatigue. We staggered up the stairs to our room, passing elegant potted aloes and lavenders, to our generously sized, white-on-white junior suite.

The following morning, as we made our way to breakfast, after spending ages in the shower indulging in the organic products laid out for us, I was very pleased to see that you can snap up some of the discreetly packaged branded lotions and potions on sale. After pouncing on black plates of bacon and eggs, bowls of fresh fruit and creamy cappuccinos, we were most definitely set up for a quick tour of the sites of Ostuni. Our €6 bilingual local guidebook turned out to be an admirable exercise in spin: the town's tiny list of notable buildings (the main square, Piazza della Libertà, an 18th-century column, La Colonna di Sant' Oronzo and a handful of churches) was stretched out to fill 144 pages. Ostuni is no Rome or Florence, but I confess this came as a relief, as we really weren't up for a cultural steeplechase. Don't fret, though, souvenir and second-home seekers: there's still the usual dose of tourist shops and holiday-house estate agents.

We abandoned culture in favour of La Sommità's recommended beach club, down the coast at Torre Canne. Unfortunately, it simply didn't match the sophistication of the hotel, so I dragged my reluctant *compadre* back to base camp, as happy as he was ogling the Speedo-clad kite-surfers. As we lolled about on the terrace with a bottle of crisp white wine, I asked the smiley waiter why there was no pool at the hotel. Apparently the local bureaucrats wouldn't let them build one, despite the fact that temperatures here soar to 50°C in August. I guess that just gives credence to the adage that nothing's perfect. Still, when it comes to boutique boltholes, La Sommità comes pretty close.

Reviewed by Jeroen Bergmans

NEED TO KNOW

Rooms Ten, including three suites.
Rates €250–€600, including breakfast.
Check-out Midday, but flexible.
Room service Restaurant menu available until 22h30.
Facilities Modern spa under vaulted stone celings, in-room Internet access.
Poolside There is no pool at La Sommità, but guests can ask reception for a pass to a nearby beach.
Children Are welcome, although the building isn't really suitable for very young children.
Also Horse riding, cycling and cookery courses can be arranged. Small pets are welcome.

IN THE KNOW

Our favourite rooms Ask for a room with a terrace and a view out to sea. The suites are much larger and have big windows with great views.
Hotel bar The subterranean wine bar has a good selection of regional and international wines. You can sip a drink anywhere you choose here. The castle ramparts are the perfect place for a sunset aperitif.
Hotel restaurant Located beneath two massive vaulted stone ceilings, the restaurant also has tables outside in the walled Spanish garden. Fresh local produce is served, including fish cooked to perfection, great pasta and wines.
Top table In the garden, among the orange blossom and olive trees.
Dress code As relaxed as everything else here.

LOCAL EATING AND DRINKING

Watch the *passeggiata* with an aperitif at **Café Centrale** in Ostuni's Piazza della Libertà. A two-minute walk from the hotel, **Osteria del Tempo Perso** on Via Gaetano Tanzarella Vitale (0831 303 320) offers traditional Puglian cuisine and wine in its grotto-like dining rooms decked with traditional farming implements. There's a modern flair to the traditional dishes at **Osteria Piazzetta Cattedrale** (0831 335 026), set in a whitewashed former monastery just by the cathedral. The restaurant prides itself on its selection of excellent and unusual cheeses that can be matched from the comprehensive wine list.

Smith members receive one 60-minute massage per booking.

GET A ROOM!

Use our online booking service at www.mrandmrssmith.com to check availability and make reservations. Register your Smithcard to find out about current member offers for this hotel.

La Sommità
7 Via Scipione Petrarolo, Ostuni
+39 0831 305 925
info@lasommita.it; www.lasommita.it

Masseria Torre Coccaro

DESTINATION	PUGLIA
STYLE	REFINED FORTRESS
SETTING	SEA-SCENTED OLIVE GROVES

MTWTFSSMTWTFSSMTWTFSSMTWTFSSMTWTFSSMTW

ITALIA

'Our room, an old hayloft, was exquisitely furnished with linen bedding, silky sofas, large baroque mirrors and antique furniture from local markets'

TWTFSSMTWTFSSMTWTFSSMTWTFSSMTWTFSS

Masseria Torre Coccaro, Puglia, Italy

The night sky sparkled with stars as we watched the massive electric entrance gates to Masseria Torre Coccaro swing open. A long drive, flanked by rows of flickering candles in terracotta dishes and lanterns, led us to a carpark containing at least a hundred cars. Having expected a small place with just 30 rooms, we walked timidly towards the warmly welcoming reception area. An open 17th-century chapel beamed out light and revealed crucifixes, while white-tuxedo-clad men and elegantly dressed Italian models crowded around the massive grand piano that dominated a fairy-lit courtyard.

The hotel was hosting a full-scale wedding. Couples whirled rapidly in a clockwise circle around the courtyard, accompanied by the hectic rhythms of tambourines and mandolins. Then they suddenly stopped and whirled anticlockwise for a while, before changing direction again. 'That's the dance they did in *The Godfather*,' said Mrs Smith. 'It must be a Mafia wedding. How exciting!'

There's nothing like letting your imagination run a little wild to kick-start a Smith sojourn. The wedding guests were dancing the tarantella, a dance that originated in the Middle Ages in nearby Taranto as a means of treating the sickness, melancholy and madness brought about by the venomous bite of the tarantula. The spiders were the scourge of the farm workers who spent their days labouring in the fields. Furious frenzied dancing was the only known successful cure.

In a terrace adorned with large wicker baskets and aluminium buckets of red, pink and orange flowers, a team of bustling waiters brought us menus, an amuse-bouche of mango-wrapped salmon mousse, and a dish of fresh organic vegetables served with a bowl of olive oil and balsamic vinegar. I ordered oysters (served with Parmigiano to enhance their taste) and spaghetti with black squid ink, while Mrs Smith settled for carpaccio with slices of deep-red wild strawberry and mango parcels of kiwi and lettuce. As we sat sipping grappa, while seven able-bodied men carried the grand

formal gardens and orchards. Arched windows smiled among trailing plants and fragrant climbing honeysuckle; we were tempted to tarry by caved recesses with padded seating built into the thick whitewashed walls, and wooden benches in the garden. A lake-style pool, superbly integrated into the formal gardens, sloped down from the outdoor restaurant to a subterranean Aveda spa offering a vast selection of massages, and therapies in hot and cold pools. Not suffering from stress or tension, we drove off down the coast in search of Italy's best seafood restaurant, instead.

Extending as far as the heel of the Italian boot (out on a limb, and at the end of the line), Puglia has a relieving lack of tourist-friendly features. The road signs are confusing, and it was proving impossible for either of us to tell if the arrow directing us was pointing down the road or to the right. Whichever option we took, we inevitably arrived at either a *zona industriale* or a forlorn housing project on ↓

piano back to its home in one of the several public lounges (all of which exhibit works of art from the local galleries and contain interesting libraries), we had a rare moment of total agreement: it was the best food we had ever eaten.

Our room (an old hayloft) was exquisitely furnished with linen bedding, silky sofas, large baroque mirrors and antique furniture from the local markets. Much to Mrs Smith's delight, every current English and Italian magazine lay on the wooden desk. In the cave-like bathroom, a giant showerhead presided over a square stone bath surrounded by jars of blue bath salts, indulgent body and hair moisturising creams, lotions, shampoos and conditioners.

Torre Coccaro is a *masseria fortificata*, a family-run working farm and fortress, producing its own vegetables, fruits, olive oil and salami. The next morning saw us strolling for a sumptuous breakfast through the hotel's

the edge of town. We had to weave through a formidable number of one-way streets to get back on to yet another country lane. We got lost, but deliciously so.

Puglia is perplexing. Even the shabby and dishevelled look of the countryside's unkempt olive groves, ruined walls, and scruffy caper and cacti fields is misleading: the region's volcanic soil, reliable sunshine and comfortable winter rain (supplemented by an irrigation system that includes the world's longest aqueduct) produce two-thirds of Italy's olive oil, one-tenth of Europe's wine, and fruit and vegetables that taste as they did when we were children.

Polignano a Mare's Ristorante da Tuccino rises abruptly from the coast. Old men in vests watched their families dive from the rocks or sunbathe like lazy lizards on the

craggy promontories, while posh yachts and speedboats ploughed through the bright-blue mottled sea. A mixed clientele of peasants, yuppies and kids in shorts tucked into enormous platters of fishy and crustacean delights. Wisely, we left the ordering to the head waiter.

Hours later, satisfied, full, but surprisingly refreshed, we drove back along the coast to Torre Coccaro to drink and swim at the hotel's private beach club before being swallowed by our bed. Unless one is a strict dieter, Torre Coccaro provides authentic hospitality at its very best. We left, swamped with reluctance and wishing we weren't already married.

Reviewed by Howard Marks

NEED TO KNOW

Rooms 37.
Rates €242–€1,176, breakfast included.
Check-out Midday.
Room service Provided 07h–02h. A snack menu is available at times when the restaurant kitchen is closed.
Facilities TV/DVD, Internet. The Aveda spa has a small indoor pool, Turkish baths and gym. Shiatsu, ayurvedic and reflexology massage are available.
Poolside Large outdoor pool with a cabana where you can have a light lunch.
Children Welcome. Children under two stay for free. Children between two and 12 are charged at €80. A babysitting service is also available.
Also Torre Coccaro's beach club is five minutes away, with a restaurant, and private 14-metre yacht for guests' use on request. The hotel also runs a cookery school.

IN THE KNOW

Our favourite rooms Room 35 is a junior suite in an ancient tower, with beautiful sea views and cosy fireplace. Room 6 is the Orange Garden suite, set into the bedrock, with large dining area, private garden and Jacuzzi. Room 16 has a private patio and beautiful vaulted ceiling.
Hotel bar Set in one of the towers, with fireplaces, vaulted ceilings and garden terrace.
Hotel restaurant Egnathia restaurant is set under the star-shaped vaults of the old stables and serves organic Puglian cuisine. The beach-club restaurant specialises in sushi and fish dishes.
Top table Under the pergola with a view of the pool.
Dress code Breezy and informal.

LOCAL EATING AND DRINKING

In the neighbouring fishing village of Savelletri, **La Marea** (080 482 9415) has a simple ambience and does excellent seafood, including oysters and sea urchins. Try the gilthead in a salt crust. In the historic centre of Ostuni, **Osteria del Tempo Perso** on Via G Tanzarella Vitale (0831 303 320) serves fine Puglian dishes. **Chichibio** in the pretty village of Polignano a Mare (080 424 0488) offers delicious grilled fish, seafood pasta and home-made lemon ice cream. Nearby **Ristorante da Tuccino** (080 424 1560) does fabulous seafood platters.

 Smith cardholders receive a complimentary massage in the spa.

GET A ROOM!

Use our online booking service at www.mrandmrssmith.com to check availability and make reservations. Register your Smithcard to find out about current member offers for this hotel.

Masseria Torre Coccaro
8 Corso da Coccaro, Savelletri di Fasano, Puglia
+39 080 482 9310
info@masseriatorrecoccaro.com; www.masseriatorrecoccaro.com

SARDINIA

Sardinia

COASTLINE   RUGGED AND MYSTICAL
COAST LIFE   SOPHISTICATED, NATURALLY

MTWTFSSMTWTFSSMTWTFSSMTWTFSSMTWTFSSMTWT
ITALIA

SARDINIA

This Mediterranean island has some of the most beautiful beaches in the world, attracting the super-rich in super-yachts, as well as newcomers ready to be converted. It may be Italian now, but over the centuries Sardinia's shores have seen visits from the Carthaginians, Romans, Genoese and Spanish, and all of them are reflected in the architecture, food and culture here. Venture inland and you'll find the rugged countryside and vibrant folk culture of unconquered Sardinia. Few of the invaders ever got this far – perhaps they couldn't prise themselves away from those white sands and crystal-clear waters…

GETTING THERE

Planes Olbia and Alghero airports serve northern Sardinia. Cabs from the airports are expensive; car hire is a good option.
Trains Sardinian trains can be pretty slow – great for scenic routes but not so good for actually getting anywhere.
Boats There are ferries between Olbia and Civitavecchia, Livorno and Genoa on the mainland, and between Golfo Aranci and Fiumicino.
Automobiles A car is essential if you want to explore the island.

DO GO/DON'T GO

Sardinia can be very wet in the winter, with many hotels and restaurants closed. April to July is ideal, when the flowers are out though warm days and cool evenings last until late October. The mid-August Ferragosto holiday can be pretty crowded.

SECRET SARDINIA

The island's wild and rugged interior is a world away from the coastal resorts and from mainland Italy. The town of Tempio Pausania, perched among vineyards and cork oak forests, has natural thermal spas and panoramic views.

LOCAL KNOWLEDGE

Taxis Cabs can be expensive, and may charge extra for luggage; agree the fare before you get in.
Tipping culture At restaurants, the service charge is included in the bill, although an additional tip of a few euros is usually expected. It is common to tip hotel staff, porters, taxi drivers and tour guides.
Siesta and fiesta Especially in summer, the siesta is strictly observed between 13h and 17h. Restaurants get busy in the evening from 20h.
Packing tips Take good-quality sunglasses if you plan to do any driving. (Of course, they're also useful for posing in Sardinia's more glamorous venues.)
Recommended reads *The Bandit on the Billiard Table* by Alan Ross; *Woman and the Priest* by Grazia Deledda; *Sea and Sardinia* by DH Lawrence.
Cuisine You'll eat superb shellfish, particularly on the north of the island. Other outstanding local specialities include porcheddu arrosto (roast suckling pig), pecorino cheese and zuppa gallurese (baked bread and cheese). The Gallura region produces fruity Vermentino white wine, which is perfect with local seafood. If you're a wine-lover, visit the Cantina del Vermentino vineyard near Monti, west of Olbia (www.vermentinomonti.com).
Currency Euro.
Dialling codes Country code for Italy: 39.

DIARY

13–18 May The Festa di San Simplicio at the beautiful church in Olbia sees a musical procession and fireworks, accompanied by the Mussel Festival, when everyone feasts on the island's 'sea jewels'. **23–24 June** Olbia's Festa della Madonna del Mare is a religious festival with a procession of decorated boats carrying statues of saints. **Early September** The Rolex Cup yacht regatta sails into Porto Cervo. **11 November** The Chestnut Festival in Tempio Pausania has local food and wine, and the island's best polyphonic choirs.

WORTH GETTING OUT OF BED FOR

Viewpoint At Santa Teresa di Gallura, take a stroll up to the church on Piazza San Vittorio and go through the archway on the left. From there you can feast your eyes on Rena Bianca beach and the clear turquoise sea, with Corsica in the distance.

Arts and culture Nicknamed 'Little Barcelona' by Catalan invaders in the 14th century, Alghero, on the northwest coast, is a beguiling mixture of Italian and Catalan culture; many locals speak Catalan. Take a boat tour to the remarkable Grotto di Nettuno caves.

Activities Porto Pollo, near Palau, is a major windsurfing centre and a great place for sailing and kitesurfing (www.portopollo.it). The granite peaks of the Limbara mountains, south of Tempio Pausania, are ideal for hiking. There's excellent diving, too; try Capo Testa (www.capotestadiving.de). Some of the best dive sites are around the French Lavezzi islands in the Straits of Bonifacio between Sardinia and Corsica.

Daytripper Take a trip out to the largely uninhabited Maddalena archipelago off the north coast and enjoy a picnic in one of the many pristine sandy coves. Catch the 15-minute ferry from Palau or ask your hotel to arrange a speedboat for you.

Best beach The area around Punta Capriccioli, north of Olbia, has several secluded white-sand beaches. Liscia Ruja Beach is perhaps the most beautiful. Pevero Beach, a bit further north, is lapped by the sparkling emerald water that made this coast famous.

Something for nothing Around 3,000 years ago, Sardinia was specked with granite watchtowers, called *nuraghi*. Several remain, scattered around the town of Arzachena.

Shopping There are weekly markets in most towns. If you're feeling flash, head to the billionaires' playground of Porto Cervo, where those with yachts shop at Prada and Gucci.

And… Atlantis, the hideaway of Bond villain Stromberg, as featured in *The Spy Who Loved Me*, was at Porto Cervo in Sardinia. There was a pretty good car chase round the island, too, in a fabulous Lotus Esprit.

CAFES

Café Conti in Santa Teresa is a great spot for an *aperitivo*, as are the portside bars in Palau. The beach bar at **Porto Pollo** is a laid-back hangout in a spectacular setting.

BARS AND RESTAURANTS

At **La Gritta** near Palau (0789 708 045), you can dine in the garden overlooking the Maddalena archipelago and enjoy classic Mediterranean food. **Su Gologone** near Oliena outside Nuoro (0784 287 512) is a romantic hotel restaurant with idyllic mountain and sunset views from the terrace. The menu uses only local, fresh produce. **Da Giovanni** in stylish Porto Rotondo (0789 35 280) is an elegant but unfussy choice. Their fresh anglerfish is particularly good. **Gallura** on Corso Umberto, Olbia (0789 24 629) is an unpretentious trattoria with a legendary seafood risotto. **Lu Stazzu** (0789 82 711), in the hills between Arzachena and Porto Cervo, is open in high season, and serves hearty game dishes under a beautiful open-air pergola.

NIGHTLIFE

During the summer, the bars in Santa Teresa stay open all night. In Porto Cervo, slink along to the **Billionaire Club**, owned by Formula One supremo Flavio Briatore and favoured by supermodels, royals and rock stars. The restaurant is fabulous, too.

La Coluccia

DESTINATION SARDINIA
STYLE SIMPLY MODERN
SETTING WOODED WATER'S EDGE

M T W T F S S M T W T F S S M T W T F S S M T W T F S S M T W T F S S M T W T
ITALIA

'Our first impression of the hotel was expansiveness,
as we wandered into its open-to-the-sky atrium'

TWTFSSMTWTFSSMTWTFSSMTWTFSSMTWTFSSMTWTFSS

First, let me explain why our visit to La Coluccia was that extra bit special. When I visited Blanch House in Brighton for the first Mr & Mrs Smith book, three years ago, my co-reviewer was a new girlfriend. We'd known each other for just a few weeks and I was hoping to impress her with a romantic weekend away. Well, it worked – or something did. This time, we were a true Mr and Mrs: our trip to review La Coluccia was also our honeymoon. The desire to find the perfect place was even stronger than it had been on that first brief holiday together.

Getting there was a quick getaway, the scramble for those low-cost seats offset by the convenience of landing in Olbia, an hour's drive from the hotel, on Conca Verde on Sardinia's northeast coast. This is a part of the journey you won't want to rush: the craggy limestone hills and scented scrubland are quintessentially Sardinian.

Our first impression of the hotel was expansiveness, as we wandered into its open-to-the-sky atrium. A tree-lined promenade leads past the lawn to the sea, but before we were drawn, nature-starved city-dwellers, to the water's edge, the very friendly hotel manager directed us to our home for the week. La Coluccia's big selling point is its proximity to world-class beaches, so it's understandable that even its biggest rooms are pretty compact. Maybe most guests don't spend much time in their rooms but, remember, this was our honeymoon… Happily, the sleek design – in minimal blacks, whites and greys – the luxurious bathrooms and our balcony, with its glorious sea view, more than made up for the lack of acreage.

We began our first full day on Sardinia with breakfast on the terrace, looking out over the glittering sea. Others might take this opportunity to thumb through the guidebooks and discover why 5,000 years of turbulent history make Sardinia an ideal destination for archaeology fans, but we were in no mood for such worthy pastimes. We were here to relax after the stress and excitement of our big day. Before we'd finished our coffee, we'd already decided that this would be a holiday of sublime inactivity, spent on some of Sardinia's many hidden beaches.

As well as the sandy spots within walking distance of the hotel, there are tiny, often uninhabited islands scattered in the sea off Conca Verde, ripe for exploring. That first morning, we opted for a speedboat trip, arranged by La Coluccia, and set off for some intrepid adventuring. The €150, plus a little extra for the fuel, was money well spent. We had stop-offs whenever we liked, and saw some of the most incredible beaches. It wasn't all us, us, us, though: we also spent a few hours rescuing another boat, towing it to a nearby bay and enjoying a few drinks with its lovely, chatty owners.

We lunched at the hotel nearly every day, mainly owing to a sense of lazy satisfaction with staying put, but also because the food there was so delicious. During our stay, we had fresh lobster, sea bass and outstanding local sausage from the poolside barbecue. We would sleep off our rosé-tinted lunch, sprawled and satisfied in some semi-sheltered cove, before returning for the four-course tasting menu and some very good cocktails later on. At night, the pool is lit up and La Coluccia feels like the coolest, calmest backdrop you could wish for.

In fact, the whole of Sardinia seemed glamorous yet uncrowded – is this what the Côte d'Azur was like before tourism happened? There are certainly plenty of glamorous types coming here to pose and party. The flagrantly A-list Billionaire Club, owned by Flavio Briatore of Formula One fame, is a short helicopter ride away (or less than an hour's drive along the coast for those not on a billionaire's budget). We did consider heading there to kick back and rub shoulders with a supermodel or two but, as sensible and loved-up newlyweds, we preferred to save our pennies (dinner at Flavio's place can cost as much as our wedding did) and entertain ourselves back in our room, or with late-night walks along the beach. We forgot all about the option of cocktails and clubbing once we'd discovered the quality and range of the local wines. We had no idea ↓

Sardinia had such excellent vineyards. La Coluccia's friendly staff directed us to some robust and delicious reds and, of course, we rounded off most nights with a limoncello or two.

On the final day of our unhurried honeymoon, we were lent a BMW 6 Series (this monster of a car was available for guests to test-drive – obviously, it is hoped that one in a thousand of us will be tempted to buy one). Having expressed a very serious interest in owning such a car, we set off to scare the flip-flops off one another, headlamps on, of course, even in the blazing sunshine, as decreed by Sardinian law. The roads between La Coluccia, on the northernmost tip of Sardinia, and Olbia make for some magnificent driving. This is the Costa Smeralda, or Emerald Coast, and the occasionally scary twists and steep drops (not to mention the less-than-sensible drivers zooming past in cars that they, presumably, didn't borrow from a hotel) only add to the exhilaration. We had never seen more beautiful landscapes or more sparkly, inviting waters.

Sardinia feels like one great big area of outstanding natural beauty, but La Coluccia, one of very few boutique hotels on the island, does everything so well that honeymooners won't regret sticking around there for most of their stay in Sardinia. This is luxury on a medium budget, with superb service. It is not hard to imagine returning for more sun, sea and seclusion further down the line. Anniversary treat, darling?

Reviewed by Ben Sowton

NEED TO KNOW

Rooms 45.

Rates €120–€450 a person, including breakfast and dinner (minimum stay of seven nights June to mid-September, starting either Saturday or Sunday night).

Check-out 10h.

Room service A limited menu is available from 08h to 23h.

Facilities Outdoor swimming pool, beauty centre, Turkish bath, massage room open June to September, small private beach.

Poolside The pool is set in landscaped grounds a few metres from the beach.

Children Are welcome. The hotel has some rooms with a bed for children under six. Cots for under-threes are free; babysitters can be arranged in advance.

Also Complimentary umbrellas, sunloungers and beach towels provided at the beach.

IN THE KNOW

Favourite rooms 53 and 54 have panoramic views out to sea and are not overlooked.

Hotel bar Open until around midnight to one o'clock.

Hotel restaurant Mediterranean food with global influences; we love the four-course tasting menus of Sardinian specialities. Dinner is included in the price of the room.

Top table On the terrace or, if it's a chilly evening, by the window.

Dress code Dress up for dinner.

LOCAL EATING AND DRINKING

Café Conti in Santa Teresa is a great spot for an *aperitivo*, as are the portside bars in Palau. **S'Andira** on Via Orsa Minore (0789 754 273) is only open in high season, and worth finding for seafood under the sky. If you want a relaxed, traditional Sardinian evening meal, head to **Saltara** on Santa Teresa Gallura (0789 755 597). The Michelin-starred **La Gritta** on Località Porto Faro (0789 708 045) is just west of Palau. We loved lunch here, with the sun-drenched garden and ocean vista, but it's just as romantic for supper. Ask for a table on the terrace, or by the window if it's not so warm.

A bottle of wine and a fruit basket on arrival, plus a candlelit dinner for two.

GET A ROOM!

Use our online booking service at www.mrandmrssmith.com to check availability and make reservations. Register your Smithcard to find out about current member offers for this hotel.

La Coluccia
Località Conca Verde, Santa Teresa di Gallura, Sardinia
+39 0789 758 004
lacoluccia@mobygest.it; www.lacoluccia.it

SORRENTO

Sorrento

COASTLINE   PASTEL-PAINTED AMALFI
COAST LIFE   SAILORS AND SIRENS

MTWTFSSMTWTFSSMTWTFSSMTWTFSSMTWTFSSMTWT

ITALIA

SORRENTO

The Ancients believed that mariners were lured to the islands and towering cliffs of the Amalfi Coast by the songs of the Sirens, mythical temptresses who gave their name to the seductive town of Sorrento. The orange and lemon groves, ancient vineyards and perfect climate prove no less irresistible today. Even the sumptuous villas that clamber up the vertiginous mountainsides in pastel ranks of peach, pink and primrose seem to be jostling to get the perfect view of the Bay of Naples and the brooding volcano of Vesuvius. With an elegant palazzo or piazza at every turn, the town bewitches allcomers, and the tiny beaches and family-run restaurants are deservedly bustling in summer.

GETTING THERE

Planes Naples airport, 40 miles from Sorrento, is the most convenient, with regular international flights year round.
Trains Napoli Centrale on Piazza Garibaldi is linked to Sorrento by the Circumvesuviana train which runs twice hourly; See www.vesuviana.it for details.
Boats There are regular hydrofoils from Naples taking 35 minutes and leaving from Molo Beverello off Piazza Municipio.
Automobiles It's worth renting a car to be able to explore, but traffic can be bumper to bumper on the coastal road in summer.

DO GO/DON'T GO

July and August in Sorrento are super-busy, and the narrow beaches and streets get very crowded. Spring and autumn are preferable for sunshine and less elbow action. Winters are rarely cold.

SUPREMELY SORRENTO

Massa Lubrense, at the tip of the Sorrentine peninsula, is an area of hamlets, lemon groves and unrivalled sea views. The groves are criss-crossed by mule paths and marked footpaths – fantastic in spring when the lemon and orange blossom are in bloom.

LOCAL KNOWLEDGE

Taxis Expensive, but most sights in Sorrento are walkable. If you can't do without a driver, call 081 878 2204.
Tipping culture Although restaurant bills include a service charge, an additional ten per cent tip is customary.
Siesta and fiesta Increasingly, there is a trend towards more flexible opening hours. Roughly: Monday to Saturday 09h–13h and 17h–22h, with many shops closing on Saturday afternoons and Monday mornings.
Packing tips Some comfortable shoes for Pompeii and the climb up and down the steep steps to the beach.
Recommended reads *The Last Days of Pompeii* by Edgar Bulwer-Lytton; *The Talented Mr Ripley* by Patricia Highsmith.
Cuisine Fish and crustaceans are the Sorrentine starlets. Specialities include lobster cooked with tomatoes, octopus casserole and sautéed shrimp. Main ingredients include sweet extra-virgin olive oil, tomatoes, *fior di latte* mozzarella (which, in Sorrento, is plaited), and herbs.
Currency Euro.
Dialling codes Country code for Italy: 39. Sorrento: 081.

DIARY

27 June Festa di Sant'Andrea; the statue of Amalfi's patron is taken from the cathedral and hiked about town to commemorate the 'miracle' which saved Amalfi from the fearsome pirate Barbarossa. There's a dashing show of pyrotechnics. **26 July** The Festival of Sant' Anna sees boat processions and fireworks in the bay overlooked by La Minervetta. **July–September** Sorrento Summer of Music takes place in the cloisters of San Francesco monastery and pulls in internationally renowned classical musicians. **November** Sorrento's International Film Festival is Italy's foremost silver-screen shindig. See www.sorrentotourism.com for details.

WORTH GETTING OUT OF BED FOR

Viewpoint There are fantastic coastal views from the Villa Communale park next to the 16th-century church of San Francesco, which also holds regular classical-music concerts.

Arts and culture In 79AD Sorrento had an awesome view of the eruption of Mount Vesuvius and the destruction of Pompeii. It's possible to wander the well-preserved ruins of the doomed city; see www.pompeiisites.org for details. (Wear comfortable shoes – Roman roads are surprisingly ill-suited to sandals.)

Activities The *Sentiero degli Dei* (Path of the Gods) is a spectacularly scenic trek along the cliffs of the Amalfi coast. There are plenty of excellent local scuba-diving sites to explore; contact www.sorrentodivingcenter.it for details.

Best beach A mile west of Sorrento is the Bagni di Regina Giovanna, where the 15th-century Queen Joan II of Anjou reputedly bathed. An opening in the rocks creates a calm natural pool.

Daytripper On the fabulous island of Capri, you can explore dramatic scenery or shop in a miniature Milan of boutiques. The island is a 20-minute journey by hydrofoil; alternatively, you can hire a speedboat in Sorrento, which will allow you to explore the coves and more secluded beaches; contact www.nauticasicsic.com for details.

Something for nothing Try to sneak into one of the wood-inlay workshops and observe the traditional art of intricate mosaic woodwork (Tarsia). Try Gargiulo Salvatore on Via Fuoro.

Shopping Pick up some limoncello liqueur, infused with Sorrentine lemon peel, or *nocino*, made from walnuts and coffee beans. Via San Cesareo is the place to find handicrafts such as ceramics, scented wax, coral or lace. There's also a weekly street market on Tuesdays. It's worth the 20-minute trip over to Capri to join the jet set for some serious boutique spending.

CAFES

Settle down to an alfresco espresso at **Bar Ercolano** or a refined aperitivo on the terrace of **Excelsior Vittoria**, both just off Piazza Tasso. **Sedil Dominova**, on Largo Sedil Dominova, is the place for a shot of limoncello; it's a former meeting-place for the nobility and now a workers' club, consisting of half a dozen tables occupied by card-playing local gents.

BARS AND RESTAURANTS

Il Buco (081 878 2354), the *prima ristorante* on Il Rampa Marina Piccola, has one Michelin star, a superb wine list and a reasonably priced taster menu. Dine outside in the little cobbled area off the square. **Delfino** in Marina Grande (081 878 2038) is great for a leisurely lunch of fresh fish at a table on the jetty. For modern Italian cuisine, show off your boat shoes and dine more formally in the courtyard next door at **L'Antica Trattoria** (081 807 1082) on Via PR Giuliani. **La Lanterna** on Via San Cesareo (081 878 1355) is the place to go for delicious Sorrentine cuisine. Cosied up a pretty alley, it is renowned for its seafood, particularly its wonderful risotto alla pescatore. You'll also find some beautiful Roman mosaics downstairs.

NIGHTLIFE

Dress up and join the locals in their *passeggiata*: a gentle evening stroll around town. It's a good way to walk off your supper and see the town by moonlight. Next, head to **Photo Bar** on Via Correale, a lounge bar where you can drink or dine in the back garden. **Fauno Notte Club**, on Piazza Tasso, is a popular club and open until the wee hours.

La Minervetta

DESTINATION SORRENTO
STYLE QUIRKY NAUTICAL
SETTING NEAPOLITAN CLIFFHANGER

MTWTFSSMTWTFSSMTWTFSSMTWTFSSMTWTFSSMTWT
ITALIA

'The hotel has floor-to-ceiling
windows in every room, and its three
sun terraces are perfect platforms
for admiring the panoramic view'

La Minervetta, Sorrento, Italy

So, we're heading for the Amalfi coast, after a detour to Pompeii, which this Mr Smith (no fan of a crumbling Doric column, me) hopes will be brief. My fellow traveller, however, has other ideas, confessing to a hitherto unrevealed fascination with the Romans. Seems he's hooked on classics, and a whistle-stop tour to tick the history box turns into a marathon expedition.

When we roll up at La Minervetta, all parched and sun-weary, the turquoise-tiled lobby and white walls feel cooling and refreshing. The Fifties villa above Sorrento, which started a restaurant and a small hotel and was reworked by architect Marco da Luca into a boutique hotel, has a prime clifftop position, overlooking the Bay of Naples, that postcard-perfect swathe of the Amalfi Coast immortalised in *The Talented Mr Ripley*. Steadfastly refusing to turn its back on the bay, the hotel has floor-to-ceiling windows in every room, and its three sun terraces (the upper for cocktails, mid-level for chilling and a Jacuzzi pool on the lowest) are perfect platforms for admiring the panoramic view.

And what a view it is: fishing vessels bob prettily, boats carry day-trippers back and forth to Capri – and you've only got Vesuvius in the background to complete the scene. Inside the hotel, the visual impression is of clean contemporary lines. Splashes of navy and red canvas break up the all-over white; freeform eclecticism means European design mags are piled neatly on Indonesian coffee tables; old ships' maps hang alongside flamboyant modern art; and brightly coloured ceramic bowls overflow with lemons. The overall effect is cosy, comfortable and welcoming – stylish, but never styled. Minervetta's homely yet well-travelled feel is ably abetted by the Dornbracht bathroom fittings, Frette robes and Crabtree & Evelyn toiletries – all boutique hotel classics in their own right.

At sundown, we head to the upper terrace, order a Negroni each, and relax on stripy canvas steamer chairs, gazing lazily across the bay at Vesuvius.

Our reverie is briefly interrupted by the faint and very distant sound of raised voices from the harbour below. We strain to hear, and can just about make out that a heated debate seems to have broken out between two fishermen in a single wooden boat. A flame-haired temptress literally wades into the fray to sort them out; eventually, the two hotheads are pulled apart, and retreat to nurse their bruised machismo. We half expect someone to pass the hat round, but this is no show – just a display of Neapolitan fuse-blowing.

It's all peace and harmony in our world and, suitably clad for a summer night, we trip 300 steps down to the harbour for dinner at Delfino, where the Med laps mesmerically beneath our boardwalk table. The staff speaka da kinda Eenglish you'd think confined to amateur dramatics, but the fresh fish, tricolore salad and jugs of rosato they deliver are authentic, down to the last drizzle of locally pressed extra-virgin.

We skip pudding and join the *passeggiata* round the town square, seeking our new passion: lemon granita. It's the ideal street food: refreshing, tasty and low-cal. (Just as well, since over the course of the weekend, we try it from every outlet going.) We can reliably recommend you don't bother with anything from a machine or a gelateria; for the best, visit one of the street vendors, who'll shave off a cupful of fragrant crystals from a barrel set over ice. And don't even think about any of the new-fangled flavours they try to tempt you with. Melon schmelon. Lemon's the only option worth considering. No point messing with a true classic, after all.

The soft tolling of church bells provides our wake-up call on Saturday. Time for buckets of cappuccino and platefuls of fresh fruit on the terrace with all the other Mr & Mrs Smiths: Swedish architects, French designers and, er, us. What a smart, stylish Euro community we make. We decide to grab an early ↓

195

hydrofoil and head for the island of Capri to sate our upmarket-shopping appetites. We're not the only ones... The island's full to bursting with tourists, and MaxMara, Gucci, Prada, Tod's et al already have their autumn/winter collections in stock, which just doesn't seem right in such a spring/summer kind of place. We check out the beach shorts in Vilebrequin (beloved of Hugh Grant). I'm sorely tempted, before deciding that €120 is going it some for a pair of swimming trunks (no matter how tempting fuchsia-pink seahorse print is).

That evening, we dine at Il Buco, which wears its Michelin star proudly on its sleeve, and is the undisputed best restaurant in town, for our money. We're lucky to land one of the sought-after tables outside, and lap up the *amuse-bouches*, obedient service and culinary twists with everything. The chef's signature seems to be a scoop of sorbet. There's a spoonful of iced balsamic with the cuttlefish starter,

and a scoop of delicious prosecco sorbet to cut through the lemon and almond soufflé. Stuffed to the gills, we talk about exploring the town and visiting some of the basement nightclubs, all-hours drinking dens and low-lit piano bars. We're certainly tempted, but there's something that draws us back to La Minervetta. We hunker down with a limoncello nightcap or two and leave the blinds up. It's hard to beat a room with a view of the starlit Bay of Naples and a granita shack just round the corner.

Reviewed by Neil McLennan

NEED TO KNOW

Rooms 12, with one junior suite.

Rates €200–€380, including breakfast.

Check-out 11h30, but flexible.

Room service None as such, but you can always get a coffee.

Facilities Flatscreen TV, Sky TV, wireless Internet. Etro bathroom products, solarium.

Poolside Giant outdoor hydro massage tub, with wooden loungers and towels provided. Reservations on request for private beach La Tonnarella, 200 metres from the hotel. There are stairs direct down to the sea from La Minervetta, but brace yourself for the climb back up.

Children Under-12s can share parents' rooms, with cots provided at no extra charge, and extra beds at €50 a night. Babysitting can be organised.

Also At the main port in Sorrento, where you catch boats to the islands, the hotel can pre-book you a parking space in the underground carpark, which is usually full by 09h.

IN THE KNOW

Our favourite rooms All rooms are sea-facing with fantastic views: some have floor-to-ceiling windows; some balconies. Rooms 7 and 8, 11 and 12 are adjoining pairs, good for families. The junior suite has two balconies and a large walk-in hydro massage shower, though no bath.

Hotel bar Guests can take drinks anywhere they like in the hotel.

Hotel restaurant No restaurant: only buffet breakfast and hot eggs and bacon to order.

Top table On the terrace with a view of the Bay of Naples.

Dress code Insouciant summer cool.

LOCAL EATING AND DRINKING

The Michelin-starred **Il Buco**, on Il Rampa Marina Piccola (081 878 2354), is one of the best restaurants in Sorrento. It's a good idea to reserve one of the tables outside on a warm summer evening. The taster menu is an excellent choice. **Delfino** in Marina Grande (081 878 2038) is the place for a relaxed waterside lunch of wonderfully fresh fish and seafood, just down the steps from the hotel. For a more formal lunch, try next door at **Taverna Azzurra** (081 877 2510). **Da Gigino**, on Via Degli Archi (081 878 1927), is the best place for a pizza, and has great spaghetti with clams.

Smith members receive a bottle of prosecco.

GET A ROOM!

Use our online booking service at www.mrandmrssmith.com to check availability and make reservations. Register your Smithcard to find out about current member offers for this hotel.

La Minervetta
25 Via Capo, Sorrento, Naples
+39 (0)81 877 4455
info@laminervetta.com; www.laminervetta.com

SOUTH TYROL

South Tyrol

COUNTRYSIDE ALPINE OXYGEN
COUNTRY LIFE SKI OR SPA, STROLL OR STRIDE

MTWTFSSMTWTFSSMTWTFSSMTWTFSSMTWTFSSMTWT

ITALIA

TWTFSSMTWTFSSMTWTFSSMTWTFSSMTWTFSSMTWTFSS

SOUTH TYROL

Austrian until 1919, the South Tyrol – or Südtirol – is Italy's most northerly province, with a uniquely Teutonic tone. Two-thirds of the population speak German as their mother tongue, and handsome *schlossen* dot every hillside, but still an Italian sensibility prevails, creating an intriguing cultural mix. The landscape is dominated by the dramatic peaks of the Dolomites mountain range, towering over peaceful valleys of orderly farmland, apple orchards and award-winning vineyards. The spa town of Merano and ancient Bolzano are the South Tyrol's two main towns; their undoubted charms are perhaps eclipsed by the sheer beauty of the natural backdrop, which provides a perfect adventure playground for more open-air activities than you can possibly have time for.

GETTING THERE

Planes Verona and Innsbruck airports are two hours away by car. Lufthansa and Air Alps (www.airalps.com) fly to nearby Bolzano in four hours from London Heathrow. A stopover is required.
Trains It's possible to travel from London to Innsbruck, just over the Austrian border, via Brussels. See www.europeanrail.com for more details.
Automobiles A car is ideal for getting to your next activity appointment on time, and scoping out hillside hamlets, but be prepared for frequent snowfalls and icy road conditions in the winter.

DO GO/DON'T GO

The ski slopes open from December to February. From May through to autumn the upland pastures are popular for walking, biking and riding. The turn-of-season shutdowns are in March and November.

SIMPLY SOUTH TYROL

Cablecars and a network of well-charted walking trails lead you up through deep green pine forests to the lofty peaks of the Dolomites, attracting hi-tech mountaineers and low-tech strollers.

LOCAL KNOWLEDGE

Taxis It's best to book ahead; ask your hotel for details of local firms.
Tipping culture Restaurant cover charges often represent the service charge, but it's customary to round up the bill if the service is to your liking.
Siesta and fiesta Some small shops still close for lunch. Supermarkets usually stay open until 19h.
Packing tips Walking boots, sunscreen, all your usual ski paraphernalia in season. We swear by our CamelBak hands-free hydration systems.
Recommended read *The Magic Mountain* by Thomas Mann.
Cuisine The South Tyrol's Austrian genes mean cricket-ball-sized canederli (dumplings) come drenched in melted butter. Try the hearty schlutzkrapfen – Tyrolean spinach and ricotta-filled ravioli. Vinschgerlen (Rye bread rolls) are chewy and spiked with caraway; smoked speck is tender and delicate. If it all sounds a bit heavy, a wide choice of gourmet restaurants have also sprung up, preparing local fare with a lighter, even Mediterranean touch.
Currency Euro.
Dialling codes Country code for Italy: 39. Merano: 0473.

DIARY

July brings metallers to the mountains at the Badia Rocks open-air music festival (www.badiarocks.com). **Early August** There's a less hairy, more classical tone to the Merano Music Festival (www.meranofest.com).
November The Merano Wine Festival (www.meranowinefestival.com) and Culinaria are twin comestible festivals showcasing local dishes and regional wines. **December** There is a rather Mitteleuropean Christmas market in Bolzano, lasting most of the month. It's a great place to pick up a few last-minute gifts. Check www.suedtirol.info for details of local events.

WORTH GETTING OUT OF BED FOR

Viewpoint Try tandem paragliding for an eagle's-eye view of the scenery. You don't need to be super-fit or highly trained – it's like a flying armchair. Contact Tirolfly (335 67 66 891).

Arts and culture At the South Tyrol Museum of Archaeology in Bolzano, gaze into the face of 4,000-year-old Otzi, found mummified in a glacier by hikers in 1991; see www.iceman.it for more details. South Tyrol's mediaeval castles and monasteries include Muri-Gries Monastery (www.muri-gries.com), which makes and sells red wine, and is open on weekdays.

Activities Summer is perfect for walking, hiking and climbing. The Merano Mountaineering School (www.bergsteigerschule.com) can take you paragliding, Nordic walking, rafting, canyoning, mountain biking and hiking. Or take to the hills on the back of an indigenous Haflinger pony: there's a large stables at the Post Hotel in Olang (0474 49 61 27), or try the excellent Sulfner Stables (0473 279 424) where the breed originates from. In winter, ask at your hotel about skiiing, boarding, bobsleigh, ice-climbing and ice-skating. You may also wish to indulge in post-sporty spa treatments at the Thermal Baths in Merano (www.thermemeran.it).

Daytripper Drive south towards Bolzano and follow the wine route from Appiano to Termeno. Stop in Caldaro for wine-tasting and lunch: Castel Ringberg (www.castel-ringberg.com) overlooks the lake; Manincor is a 21st-century winery with a 300-year-old history. Near Magre is the Vinoteque im Paradeis (0471 818 080) run by renowned wine producers Alois Lageder.

Perfect picnic Pick up artisan bread, hard cheeses and speck from the daily market in the centre of Bolzano. Don't tuck in until you're at the top of a very big hill.

Something for nothing Follow the *waalweg* footpaths along the ancient irrigation channels in the Vinschgau Valley near Merano, through orchards and chestnut woods to Juval Castle.

Shopping Bolzano is home to the usual Italian catwalk suspects including Missoni, Dolce and Prada. You can take home some excellent wines, from perfumed Gewürztraminer to deep reds from the sunny lower slopes of the Dolomites.

CAFES

The mountains are dotted with refuges, all with spectacular views. **Gasthof Sessellift** is at the top of the chairlift near Vigilius, and is perfect for a beer or coffee on the terrace in summer.

BARS AND RESTAURANTS

An award-winning showcase for self-taught chef Anna Matscher, **Zum Löwen** on Via Principale in Tesimo (0473 920 927) is set in an elegant art deco building with views of the Castello Principesco. **Sissi Ristorante Andrea Fenoglio** on Via G Galilei in Merano (0473 231 062) is ultra-innovative, with a super wine list. **Kallmünz** on Piazza Rena (0473 212 917) is built into the palace walls and serves Modern Mediterranean cuisine as a lighter alternative to local dishes. Near Lana, **Trattoria Kuckuck** on Via Palade in Cermes (0473 563 733) serves typically Tyrolean food: smoked sausages and rich cheeses. The restaurant is attached to an excellent winery, and has a tiny terraced garden with a rushing stream.

NIGHTLIFE

Evenings aren't as sleepy as you might imagine, with sessions on the fruit schnapps in tiny bars and a youthful après-ski scene. In Bolzano, **Exil** on Piazza del Grano is good for a relaxing cocktail or two, as is **Parkhotel Laurin** on Via Laurin where Friday night is jaaazz night.

Vigilius Mountain Resort

DESTINATION SOUTH TYROL
STYLE MODERNIST LODGE
SETTING DRAMATIC DOLOMITES

MTWTFSSMTWTFSSMTWTFSSMTWTFSSMTWTFSSMTWT

ITALIA

'Open-plan, but cleverly divided with partitions and simple, functional furniture, it's very design-mag without being cold or uninviting'

TWTFSSMTWTFSSMTWTFSSMTWTFSSMTWTFSS

Vigilius Mountain Resort, South Tyrol, Italy

At the end of an epic race along Italian roads, we spot the cable car: it's the only way to reach our mountaintop retreat. I'm reminded of classic war flick *Where Eagles Dare*, only I don't think Richard Burton and Clint Eastwood arrived at their mountain destination in a Punto. They didn't have accommodation like this, either. Every window of our contemporary cabin frames another spectacular view of velvety mountains. Where land and sky meet, the awesome Dolomites rise. Muscles unknot, features relax, voices hush.

Vigilius Mountain Resort is totally tuned-in. It has not been plonked onto the landscape; it *nestles* there. In fact, Vigilius fits in better than most of the traditional dwellings scattered about these parts. Sleek wooden beams two storeys high stretch horizontally for several hundred metres. At one end, the structure encloses a hillock from which sprouts a cluster of firs, giving the

impression of a green monument. The other end is stopped by 'culinariums' (that's 'restaurant areas' to us). Plenty more gorgeous wood forms an almost traditional chalet, topped off by a glass treehouse.

No doubt creator Matteo Thun would take exception to such vulgar descriptions. He's a classically trained artist who can apparently turn his hand to anything he chooses. Vigilius is so beautifully functional and quietly inspiring that it's hard to believe it was one of his first architectural projects.

We're greeted very personally in a wide, loungey reception. This area doubles as a place to stretch out and flick though glossies. Mrs Smith is keen to try a cowhide sofa the size of an ocean liner. 'No rush, take your time,' seems to be the Vigilius way, but I'm eager to take the tour.

Our eyes are immediately drawn up to the glass ceilings as we're led along the museum-like corridors.

We pass by a split-level library that transforms into a screening room come nightfall. We marvel at the frankly enormous lightshades (seriously, each one is the size of our Fiat) and ask what's showing tonight. 'Whatever the guests want,' we're told. A few steps away is the sunken piazza. Smart, comfortable, designer furniture surrounds a fire that looks like a special effect. As in all areas of Vigilius, the views are exceptional. The glass wall also accesses a big, private verandah. There's no bar as such, but a wooden cocktail menu has been left to entice, and staff are always around to take an order.

No time for indulging right now – we're determined to cut to the chase. Behind a big wooden door lies our generously sized 'living area', which we find superbly user-friendly and totally relaxing. Open-plan, but cleverly divided with various partitions and simple, functional furniture, it's very design-mag without being cold or uninviting. Almost everything is in birch, brushed and soaped to accentuate colour and grain. Slipping out of

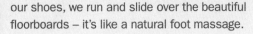

our shoes, we run and slide over the beautiful floorboards – it's like a natural foot massage.

There are no pictures in our room (or anywhere else in the hotel for that matter); the art is provided by Vigilius' stunning setting. A ruby-hued modern sofa, ripe for resting weary limbs, and a medicinally comfortable bed face another wall of glass. Our eyes are treated to the sight of a small meadow giving way to a forest of Alpine neatness, framed by bright-blue sky and the mountains, miles away, in perfect focus.

So, what's there to do at 1,500 feet? We soar and get sore. Having missed out on archery owing to our delayed arrival (note to Mrs Smith: satnav in the future, please) we are anxious to get some serious action under our belts. Stage one consists of jumping off our mountain strapped to some charming locals. Paragliding around these parts is a breeze, with plenty of ↓

locations to choose from. And it provides more of those mind-boggling views. Our flights take off a short trek from Vigilius, and turn out to be as comfortable as floating about in a favourite armchair.

After barely a panini break in a local café, we're off to stage two: riding on a couple of Norwegian/ Arabic-cross horses. What a way to see the mountains. Our posse crosses rocky rivers and steeply banked streams, picks its way through paths covered with fallen trees, and jumps the occasional boulder. Hushed fir forests give way to winding mountain paths and reach into previously inaccessible villages. Fabulous! But three hours in the saddle takes its toll. We work up some serious muscle aches with which to challenge the staff at the Vigilius spa.

If you're not fussed about treatments, Vigilius also offers infinity pools, Jacuzzi, steam and sauna rooms, all with incredible views as standard. A devoted follower of pampering, Mr Smith makes a beeline for watsu: pool-based shiatsu, involving a fair amount of floating and a few pressure points. Mrs Smith stews in a fresh-hay bath that calls for a little more mettle. Toxins are purged as the temperature rockets.

The last of our stresses and strains are serviced in the culinarium. Three amuse-bouches are followed by a delicate pig's head salad and ravioli of radicchio. Finally, sea bass with broad beans and saddle of venison with bitter chocolate and cherries work their way into our adventure. All washed down with lashings of delicious Südtirol Riesling.

On departure day, running late for our flight, Vigilius staff eyebrows are raised as we seek direction on how to travel 300 kilometres in under two-and-a-half hours. Our action-film adventure isn't over yet.

Reviewed by Mr & Mrs Smith

NEED TO KNOW
Rooms 35 room and six suites.
Rates €310–€585, including breakfast and unlimited use of the cable car.
Check-out Midday.
Room service 24 hour; restaurant menu available until 22h; picnics can also be prepared if requested the day before.
Facilities Internet. TVs on request. There are film screenings in the library at 22h every night. All rooms have balconies or terraces.
Poolside Several quartzite-lined indoor pools and outdoor sundecks.
Children Children's prices vary with age: children under two stay for €35; children under 12 stay for €90. Over-12s pay full price.
Also The hotel spa has a range of treatments, including massages. There is a steam room, sauna, fitness room and daily yoga classes. The hotel offers free archery lessons and has mountain bikes, snow-shoes and toboggans. Dogs are allowed, with a €15 charge.

IN THE KNOW
Our favourite rooms Rooms on the second floor at the front of the hotel have great views, as do the more secluded-feeling upper rooms at the back.
Hotel bar The Parlour Ida restaurant operates a bar until midnight and has an outside terrace. You can also order drinks by the log fire in the lounge.
Hotel restaurant Parlour Ida serves hearty Tyrolean cooking, including stews and strudels. The elegant 1500 restaurant serves inventive vegetarian and Mediterranean dishes. You also have the option of private dining for extra intimacy.
Top table A corner table near the window at 1500.
Dress code Active Alpine style.

LOCAL EATING AND DRINKING
The cable car to Vigilius runs regularly every 30 minutes until 19h30 in summer and until 17h in winter, thereafter by appointment only. On Monte San Vigilio, with great views across the valley, **Gasthof Sessellift** (0473 564 828) serves traditional lunches and is a ten-minute ride by chairlift from the hotel. In Merano, head for elegant **Kallmünz** within the walls of a palace on Piazza Rena (0473 212 917) for modern Italian cuisine.

 Smith members receive a free bottle of South Tyrolean sparkling wine and a free hay bath with a three-night stay.

GET A ROOM!
Use our online booking service at www.mrandmrssmith.com to check availability and make reservations. Register your Smithcard to find out about current member offers for this hotel.

Vigilius Mountain Resort
Vigiljoch Mountain, Lana
+ 39 0473 556 600
info@vigilius.it; www.vigilius.it

Tuscany

COUNTRYSIDE ANCIENT TOWNS, FERTILE SLOPES
COUNTRY LIFE PLEASURES FOR EVERY PALATE

TUSCANY

M T W T F S S M T W T F S S M T W T F S S M T W T F S S M T W T F S S M T W T
ITALIA

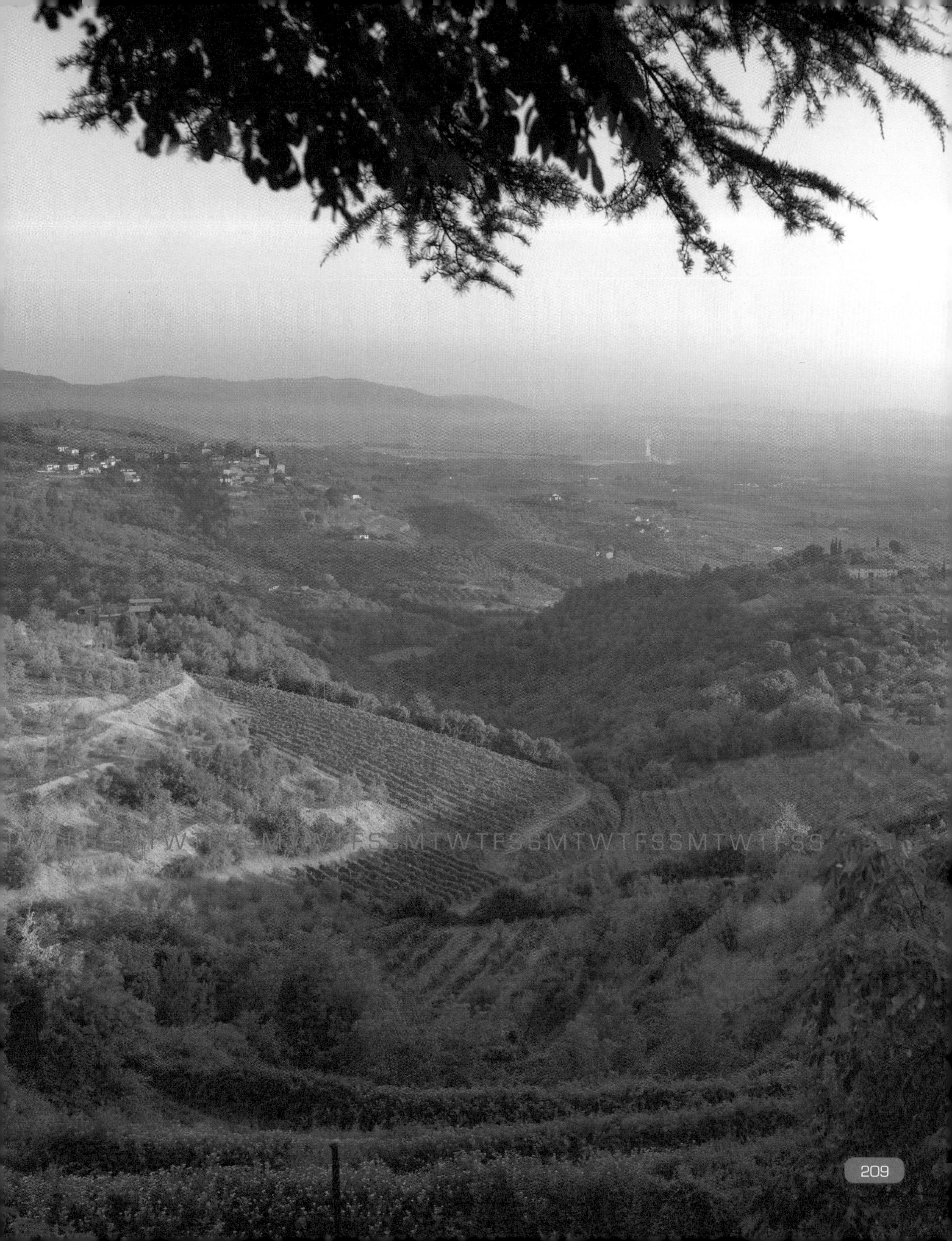

TUSCANY

When Mother Nature was handing out charm, she really slathered on the right ingredients when it came to this above-the-knee patch of Italy. If the slopes dotted with cypress trees and olive groves don't win your heart, the aromas and flavours of flourishing farmlands will do, via your stomach. Perfectly preserved Renaissance treasures in culture-packed ancient cities vie for your attention alongside discounted designer-label emporia. And don't let Tuscany's popularity fool you into thinking you can't get away from it all here. Sure, this beloved province will treat you to the gamut of holiday activities, but whether you feel like touring mediaeval hilltop villages or flopping on a lounger-for-two for a poolside sun-kissed snooze, Tuscany's allure can be enjoyed at every pace.

GETTING THERE

Planes Florence, Siena and Pisa airports are the gateways to the Tuscany region for air travellers.

Trains The main station in Florence is behind Piazza Santa Maria Novella. The overnight Palatino Express leaves Paris at 19h and arrives at Florence's Campo di Marte station at 07h15.

Automobiles The cities are best explored on foot, but there's nothing more fun than putting the top down and exploring the Tuscan countryside by car.

DO GO/DON'T GO

Tuscany can be busy with tourists throughout the summer months, although once you've escaped to your retreat you won't notice. The cities of Florence and Siena are best enjoyed outside the peak summer season.

TOTALLY TUSCANY

Wend your way through 'Chiantishire', between Siena and Florence, and comb this territory of vineyards for your own favourite bottles of Italy's legendary wine. But promise us that won't include one of the straw-covered variety.

LOCAL KNOWLEDGE

Taxis Your best bet is to ask your hotel to organise one.

Tipping culture Service charges aren't a huge deal here, so forking out five to ten per cent is the polite thing to do.

Siesta and fiesta Many shops close between 13h and 17h. Restaurants get especially busy between 20h and 21h.

Packing tips Bring headscarves and caps for open-top touring.

Recommended reads *A Room with a View* by EM Forster; *The Decameron* by Giovanni Boccaccio; *Under the Tuscan Sun* by Frances Mayes.

Cuisine Peasant fare is at its finest in Tuscany, with fagioli-filled tasty soups and stews often the headline acts. You may appreciate a hearty meal to soak up the irresistible liquid enticements of Chiantis, Brunellos and Montepulcianos. The sweet-toothed should sample the rainbow of tempting flavours on offer at *gelaterie*.

Currency Euro.

Dialling codes Country code for Italy: 39. Florence: 055; Siena: 0577.

DIARY

Late April–early July The auditory delights of Maggio Musicale Fiorentino is a must for lovers of classical music (www.maggiofiorentino.com). **July** Arezzo Wave is a popular music and culture festival which might get you throwing your hands in the air; we're waiting for it to catch on like the Mexican one (www.arezzowave.com). **July–August** The Palio in Siena sees bareback horsemen race round the main square (www.paliosiena.com). **Second week in September** Where better to get stuck into a wine fair than at one held in Greve in Chianti. **September** Head to the Joust of the Saracens in Arezzo for some mediaeval mayhem (www.portacrucifera.it).

WORTH GETTING OUT OF BED FOR

Viewpoint Fiesole is the upmarket hillside suburb northeast of Florence from where you will enjoy the most magnificent panoramic views of the terracotta-tiled town and its Duomo below.

Arts and culture 60 per cent of the world's most important works of art are housed in Italy and half of these are in Florence. To ogle Botticellis, Michelangelos and da Vincis, head to the world-famous Uffizi Gallery. Don't waste time queuing; book at www.polomuseale.firenze.it.

Activities Rent a vintage car and explore the countryside (www.clmviaggi.net). Villa Bordoni in Greve in Chianti offers cookery courses (from half-day to six-day courses). There are also courses at the Osteria di Passignano in Badia a Passignano (www.osteriadipassignano.com).

Daytripper Tourists flock to Tuscany in peak season, but head to the sites early or off-season and you should miss the hordes who hit the hotspots in the middle of the day. Siena's Gothic greatness is worth setting your eyes on, as is pretty San Gimignano, but the ancient village of Volterra beats them both if you want your architecture unsullied by spandex or bumbags.

Perfect picnic From Greve, *strade bianche* (white gravel paths) pass through the shady forests, olive groves and vineyards of the Monti del Chianti to mediaeval Panzano, situated above the Conca d'Oro (Golden Valley). You're sure to find the perfect spot.

Something for nothing Siena's famous horse race – Il Palio – is contested by the city's 17 *contrade* (town districts), each with their own symbol, such as eagle, panther and… snail. You can enjoy a wonderfully haphazard tour of the city by trying to finding the statues of all 17.

Shopping All of the major labels have their factory outlets in Florence, and fashion aficionados can pick up some satisfying bargains. Shopaholics must visit Mall 8 on Via Europa, Leccio Regello (055 865 7775), which offers discounts of up to 70 per cent off last season's lines.

CAFES

Sample the best of Florence's café culture: overlooking Michelangelo's David in Piazza della Signoria, **Caffè Rivoire** is a people-watching hub and has fabulous hot chocolate; **Caffè Pitti** in Piazza Pitti becomes a restaurant at night, specialising in truffle dishes.

BARS AND RESTAURANTS

Enoteca Fuori Piazza on Via Primo Maggio in Greve in Chianti is a charming little wine bar. **La Cantinetta di Rignana** in Località Rignan near Greve (055 852 601) is a smart choice for typical Tuscan food in a rustic farmhouse setting. Try the veal chop grilled over a wood fire, washed down with Fontodi Chianti Classico Riserva Vigna del Sorbo. If you're in Florence and fancy sophisticated Italian cooking in contemporary surroundings, visit Villa Bordoni's sister restaurants, **Beccofino** on Piazza degli Scarlatti (055 290 076) or **Baldovino** on Via San Giuseppe (055 241 773; closed Mondays). Legendary **Enoteca Pinchiorri** on Via Ghibellina (055 242 777) is a pricey thrice-Michelin-starred wine-lovers' paradise; grab a table on the jasmine-scented courtyard. Only open Tuesday, Thursday to Saturday.

NIGHTLIFE

Fiorentini keen to see and be seen (which is all of them) flock to the terrace at **The Lounge** on Piazza Santa Maria Novella. A chic cocktail bar/restaurant from neighbouring hotel JK Place, it's an extension of the hotel's neo-classical calm, with a downstairs where the city's beautiful folk cosy up on white leather banquettes.

'Built in the 16th
century, it has been
lovingly modernised
to combine original
features with
present-day luxury'

Villa Bordoni

DESTINATION TUSCANY
STYLE RUSTIC DELUXE
SETTING CLASSIC CHIANTISHIRE

MTWTFSSMTWTFSSMTWTFSSMTWTFSSMTWTFSSMTWT
ITALIA

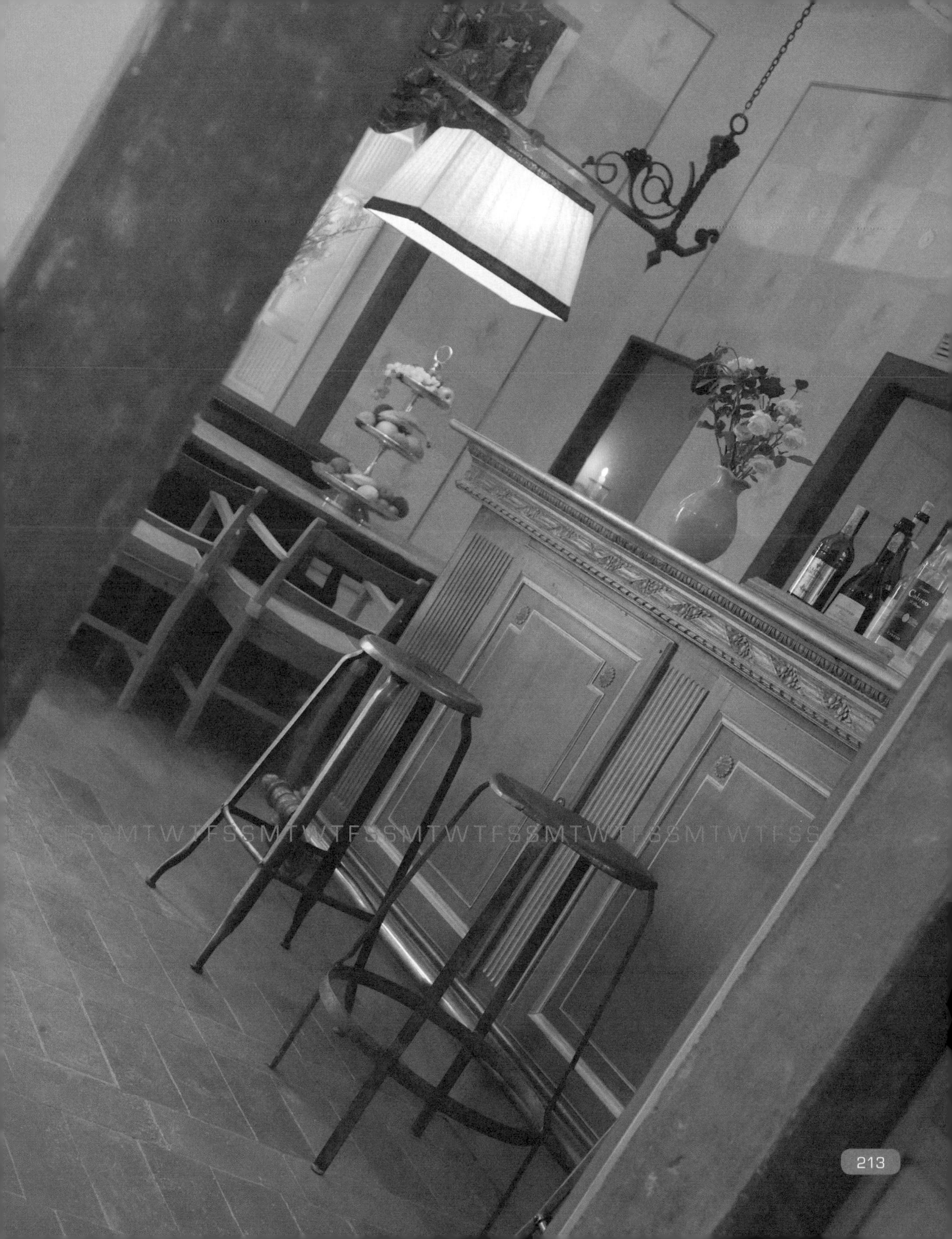

Villa Bordoni, Tuscany, Italy

A lazy escape to the Tuscan hills is not supposed to induce anxiety, but as we crunch along the tiny gravel drive that leads up to the Villa Bordoni, Mr Smith and I are a little nervy. Partly because we're dyed-in-the-wool urbanites, and Greve in Chianti is just so very rural, and partly because I have just been executive-producing the TV series based on the travels of Mr & Mrs Smith's editor and publisher. Weirdly, I've seen the Villa Bordoni on TV already and, weirder still, I feel I've 'met' the owners David and Catherine, having watched them being interviewed. Surely they'll see through me the minute I arrive, and our undercover role will instantly be blown sky-high?

I manage to keep a lid on my déjà vu and fear of exposure as a fraud. And the moment we step into the Villa Bordoni for the first time, my anxieties melt into the kind of sigh of blissed-out relaxation for which you usually have to pay top

dollar to a masseur. Just three years ago, the Villa Bordoni was a roofless ruin. Built in the 16th century by nobility, it has been lovingly modernised. The real skill has been in combining the original features of the house, from terracotta floor tiles to a spooky wine cellar, with present-day luxury.

The decor is a cunning blend of rich and poor, to emulate the grandeur-on-a-budget that the impoverished aristos might have favoured: a twig tassel on a curtain is very sumptuous-on-a-shoestring. Our room, too, combines the rustic with the elegant, housing a vast bed with a draped canopy. But for Mr Smith, the high point is the shower. A massive green-tiled wet room contains a hi-tech system capable of pumping gallons of water at you from every angle; a hydrotherapy spa would probably class it as a treatment in itself. Mr Smith is so entranced he begins to calculate whether he could knock down any walls back home to incorporate this kind of indulgence into his daily bathing habits. I can't say I'd complain.

If indoors at the Villa Bordoni is wonderful, outdoors is sublime. We're seated under a pine tree at the edge of the property's walled garden, tucking into the freshest mozzarella and tomato salad ever, and we find that, after some chilled wine, we become hypnotised by the huge butterflies that glide over the lavender bushes.

Beyond the garden wall, via paths where lizards skitter past us, we find the saltwater swimming pool, with its view of olive groves and rolling hills. Under private pergolas, we occupy double sunloungers – all the better to talk rubbish without offending some of the more sophisticated guests. Lounging by the pool with the sun on my belly and a view of a lightning storm in the valley opposite is my idea of heaven, but Mr Smith has managed to find something to fret about. How, he worries, will he fit in a four-course dinner on top of the huge boozy lunch we've just eaten? Here again, David and Catherine have thought of everything, installing a thatch-roofed outdoor gym with a view.

The great cultural magnets of Florence, Siena and Pisa are within reach, and many of the hotel's other guests are Americans keen to do the Grand Tour. But Mr Smith and I are rather more in the mood to explore the other great draw of Tuscany: its food and world-class wine. Guided by the concierge, we head out for a walk through the vineyards, hoping to get a feel for the rural heritage of the region that produces our favourite Chianti Classico. We got slightly more than we'd bargained for, and ended up having a rather too close encounter with a local dog that seemed spellbound by Mr Smith's knees.

A bit further on through the fields, we stumble across a very elderly man in an eye-wateringly tiny pair of shorts and a skintight vest tending his vines, only to turn a corner and bump into his identical twin, identically dressed. David Lynch couldn't concoct anything more out-there. Suitably spooked out by the countryside, we ↓

head towards the nearby village of Montefioralle – a cluster of stone houses clinging to a steep hill – where a few glasses of the local vintage help to restore our equilibrium.

The villa's restaurant doesn't open on Mondays, so the endlessly charming and helpful David sorted us out with a table at his favourite local, the Cantinetta di Rignana. The view of the valley, and the ravioli with ricotta and fresh truffles, had Mr Smith and me beaming with joy. And we earn our Wildlife Spotters badge by practically colliding with one of the famous local wild boars as we head back to the hotel. (I'm now convinced the You Are What You Eat adage is true; I swear the *Sus scrofa* looked us two porkers in the eye and saw kindred spirits.)

Breakfast on the terrace at the Bordoni is simple and elegant – fresh fruit, just-squeezed orange or pink-grapefruit juice, local breads and home-made jams, and traditional cheeses and cold meats.

The owners' restaurateur credentials are a huge part of Bordoni's allure. For lunch, chef Francesco's four-course tasting menu is, in Mr Smith's view (and personal experience), worth bursting a button off your new shirt for. The squid-ink risotto is rich and perfect, and a dessert modestly called cheese mousse has us chasing the last smears round the glass like greedy kids in an ice-cream parlour, and regretting like mad that a car is already revving up on the drive to take us back to the airport.

Reviewed by Helen Veale

NEED TO KNOW

Rooms 10 rooms, including five suites.
Rates €170–€395, including breakfast.
Check-out 11h.
Room service Restaurant and snack menus are available 11h–23h30.
Facilities LCD TV, DVD/CD player, wireless Internet.
Poolside Saltwater pool set in terraced olive groves with views of the Chianti hills.
Children Welcome. There is no charge for children under seven sharing with their parents.
Extra beds and cots are available for a charge of €30–€50.
Hotel closed From the second week of January until 28 February.
Also Open-air gym, hill-walking trails and mountain bikes. Horse riding can be arranged, as can
cookery lessons and winetasting. The villa and its grounds are non-smoking.

IN THE KNOW

Our favourite rooms Montefili has pale grey and crimson decor and fabulous views over the olive
groves and the valley.
Hotel bar Open until midnight. There is an 'aperitivo hour' (between 18h30 and 19h30) with
complimentary *antipastini* at the bar. There is an excellent selection of Chianti Classico from
regional winemakers. We can't recommend a long lazy lunch fuelled by Batar more
wholeheartedly. The Montrachet-alike 2001 vintage from Querciabella is liquid heaven.
Hotel restaurant The villa's original wood-burning stove is used to produce local specialities.
Lunch is from 12h30 to 14h30, dinner from 19h30 to 22h; closed Mondays.
Top table On the patio or among the umbrella pines in the summer; next to the log fire in winter.
Dress code Chiantishire chic.

LOCAL EATING AND DRINKING

La Cantinetta di Rignana in Greve-in-Chianti (055 852 601) is an informal trattoria serving
Tuscan and Chiantigiana dishes, including cold cuts, cheeses and hearty game dishes and
there are exquisite views. Better still, why not get a taste for the wines of Chianti by visiting local
vineyards; give Lawrence d'Almeida a call and he can not only arrange a table for you for lunch,
but guide you round the grapes (055 642 828; www.wineandchianti.com). For a taste of some
of the best prosciutto and salami in Tuscany, try **L'Antica Macelleria Cecchini** in the village of
Panzano (055 852 020).

A complimentary bottle of Castellare's Chianti Classico and a snack of wild boar salami.

GET A ROOM!

Use our online booking service at www.mrandmrssmith.com to check availability and make
reservations. Register your Smithcard to find out about current member offers for this hotel.

Villa Bordoni
31/32 Via San Cresci, Mezzuola, Greve-in-Chianti
+39 055 884 0004/+39 329 986 5927
info@villabordoni.com; www.villabordoni.com

Villa Fontelunga

DESTINATION   TUSCANY
STYLE   GRAND GUESTHOUSE
SETTING   GLAMOROUS GARDENS

MTWTFSSMTWTFSSMTWTF**SS**MTWTFSSMTWTFSSMTW
ITALIA

'Well-travelled fans of contemporary cool will appreciate a flavour of
the locale injected into its decor: think Starck mixed with Jacobsen'

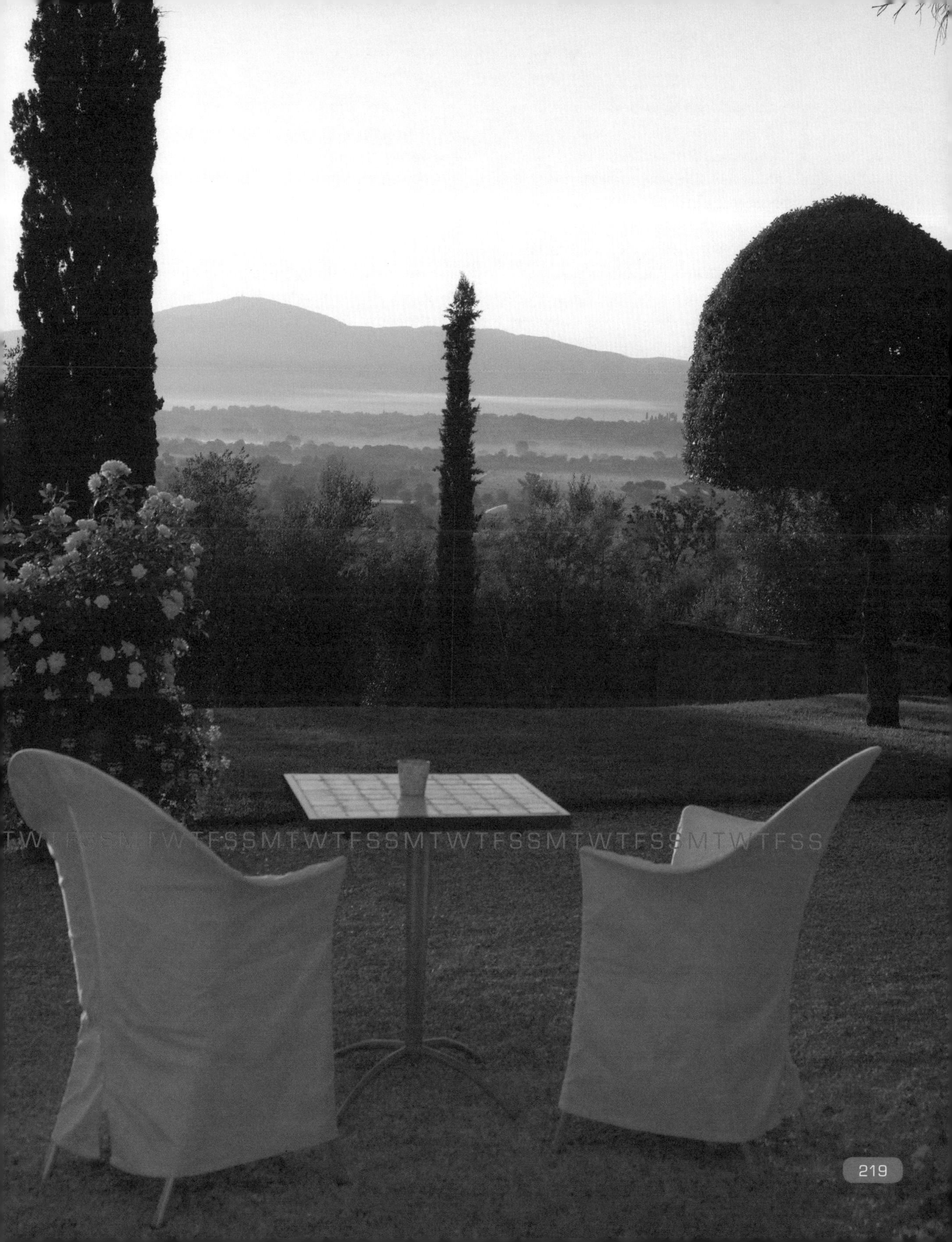
TWTFSSMTWTFSSMTWTFSSMTWTFSSMTWTFSS

Villa Fontelunga, Tuscany, Italy

Thank the Virgin Mary for Villa Fontelunga, a designer den near Cortona in Tuscany. I first visited the hotel when it opened in 2001 and I was a little worried about going back – not because it was bad, but because it was so wonderful. Like a first-time encounter with a new lover, the pleasure of a first visit to a great hotel can rarely be matched. But, with hotels as with past passions, there is comfort in knowing what to expect when you revisit them – especially when the hosts welcome you with open arms and actually remember you from all those years ago.

Crafted from a traditional *padronale*, the villa is a marriage of traditional Tuscan style and contemporary design. It is homely and stylish, and the personalities of owners Paolo and Philip (film-set designer), Simon (landscape gardener) and Paolo's Mamma (domestic goddess) combine to make guests feel like part of an extended family. The cosy atmosphere is also heavily indebted to

a troop of dogs who scamper around the terracotta house and rambling grounds, occasionally taking a dip in the swimming pool. We fell in love with Dylan, a black scottie, now almost entirely deaf and blind, who bumbles along in carefree bliss, occasionally colliding with guests and revelling in the attention of his new friends.

The guests eat together, either outside on the terrace or in the main dining room. When we arrived at the end of a meal, an intimate gang of ten were already a few sheets to the wind and had clearly bonded (Germans, Americans, French and Brits all getting on swimmingly). Sleepy and hungry, we settled into a gazebo-style nook outside to dine by candlelight. All the stress of a cancelled flight and our tiring two-hour drive from Bologna quickly floated away over lasagne and a lovely bottle of local red wine.

Well-travelled fans of contemporary cool will appreciate that Villa Fontelunga has had a flavour of the locale injected into its decor: think Starck and Jacobsen mixed

with vintage Italiana. It's always a shame to stay in a hotel and feel you could be anywhere in the world. Here, you are firmly embedded in Tuscany, but without the clutter and fuss that often weigh down more traditional Italian hotels. There are nine rooms, each individually designed. Ours had a double aspect and, as I discovered when I flung open the shutters on our first morning, the stunning views across the Val di Chiana provided a perfect start to the day.

We spent our time being gloriously decadent by the pool, occasionally knocking a ball about on the tennis court which, thankfully, is hidden from view by an olive grove. We planned jaunty outfits, attempting to capture some sort of Mr Ripley look with white deck shoes, preppy pastel Ralph Lauren polo shirts and cashmere jumpers thrown nonchalantly across the shoulders. The ball rarely went over the net, but we looked the part, at least.

The gravelled terrace was the perfect spot for an alfresco Tuscan lunch, prepared by Mamma's own fair hands. We were served the *crostini Toscana*, a mixture of minced meat, chicken liver, onion, carrot and celery cooked in olive oil on a very slow heat and served with bread. We found ourselves back on the terrace for early-evening cocktails with the pups before heading out to one of the twinkling hilltop villages for supper. The drinks situation at Villa Fontelunga is characteristically relaxed and generous; low-maintenence types will love the absence of highfalutin pomp and ceremony. I enjoyed making us G-heavy G&Ts at the self-serve bar.

Paolo and Philip are chatty and treat you like a special guest in their home (which, of course, you are), but they have also perfected the art of knowing when to back off and give you space. It's a skill I greatly admire, staying so jolly and always having something to say beyond 'Ooh, looks like it's going to turn out nice again.' I respect their ability to be intimate and personable without getting too up close and personal – there needs to be some distance between guest and host, after all. ↓

At Villa Fontelunga, there is no hint of an upstairs/downstairs boundary; rather it's a seamless guest/friend/owner dynamic.

So if it's a 'I *vant* to be alone' hideaway you're after, this may not be quite the place for you. If you're on a romantic escape, however, you might benefit from the group dynamic here. On my previous visit, it all went horribly wrong for my partner after a day in the sun without protection, causing inflammation of skin and tempers. The most soothing aftersun treatment for me was to retreat to the company of new friends downstairs while things cooled down a little in our boudoir.

If you tire of sun-worshipping, Villa Fontelunga is less than an hour by car from some of Italy's most beautiful cities: Florence, Siena, Arezzo and Cortona. You can indulge in another kind of worship too, at the shrines of Gucci, Dolce & Gabbana, Prada and Jil Sander, which all have shops nearby.

I found my way to the Mall (see Shopping, in our guide to Tuscany on page 209), which offers discounts of as much as 70 per cent off last season's lines. This region is home to the Italian textile industry, and the major labels have their factory outlets here, so you can pick up some astounding bargains.

Togged up to the nines in our newly purchased white Prada jeans (somehow this homage to Elizabeth Hurley works on Italian soil), we returned to the homely charm of Fontelunga and realised that rolling around in the gravel with the puppies while sweet smells wafted from the kitchen, where Mamma was cooking up a feast, far outshone the high-octane thrill of a retail relay. Many hotels claim to be a home away from home. This really is one.

Reviewed by Richard Bence

NEED TO KNOW

Rooms Eight rooms, and a junior suite in a separate building. Three self-catering villas in the area can be booked through the hotel.

Rates €154–€370, including breakfast.

Check-out 11h.

Room service Not available.

Facilities CD players. Each room has double-aspect views. There is a tennis court, and guests can use the villa's mountain bikes for excursions.

Poolside Outdoor pool amid the olive groves.

Children Under-14s are welcome only if the villa is booked in its entirety.

Also A minimum stay of two nights is usually required.

IN THE KNOW

Our favourite rooms The Oro room has wonderful views over the secret garden and the valley. The junior suite is in its own separate cottage with private terrace.

Hotel bar There is a 24-hour honesty bar.

Hotel restaurant Lunches of home-made Italian dishes can be provided daily for guests staying at the villa. A five-course dinner party is held twice a week, on Tuesdays and Fridays. Light snack meals are available at other times. The restaurant is closed on Wednesdays and Saturdays.

Top table Outside in the gardens.

Dress code Villa vogue.

LOCAL EATING AND DRINKING

In the pretty hilltop town of Cortona, **Pane e Vino** on Piazza Signorelli (0575 631 010; closed on Mondays) serves hearty local dishes and has an extensive wine list. In nearby Marciano, book a table upstairs under the painted ceiling at **La Vecchia Rota** (0575 845 362), which serves excellent pizzas. **L'Agania** on Via Mazzini in Arezzo (0575 295 381) serves traditional local cooking. Try the tagliatelle, and creamy polenta with the classic Tuscan sauces. A little further afield, **Pizzeria di Nonno Mede** on Via Camporegio in Siena (0577 247 966) has great pizzas and super views of the black and white Duomo.

Smith cardholders receive a free upgrade whenever possible, a bottle of prosecco and a bottle of extra-virgin olive oil from the hotel's own olive groves.

GET A ROOM!

Use our online booking service at www.mrandmrssmith.com to check availability and make reservations. Register your Smithcard to find out about current member offers for this hotel.

Villa Fontelunga
5 Via Cunicchio, Pozzo della Chiana, Arezzo
+39 0575 660 410
info@fontelunga.com; www.fontelunga.com

Villa Sassolini

DESTINATION	TUSCANY
STYLE	CONTEMPORARY COUNTRY HOUSE
SETTING	TRANQUIL CHIANTI

MTWTFSSMTWTFSSMTWTF**SS**MTWTFSSMTWTFSSMTWT
ITALIA

'As we tread the slate-coloured
wooden floors that run
throughout, it feels as though
we're the only guests here'

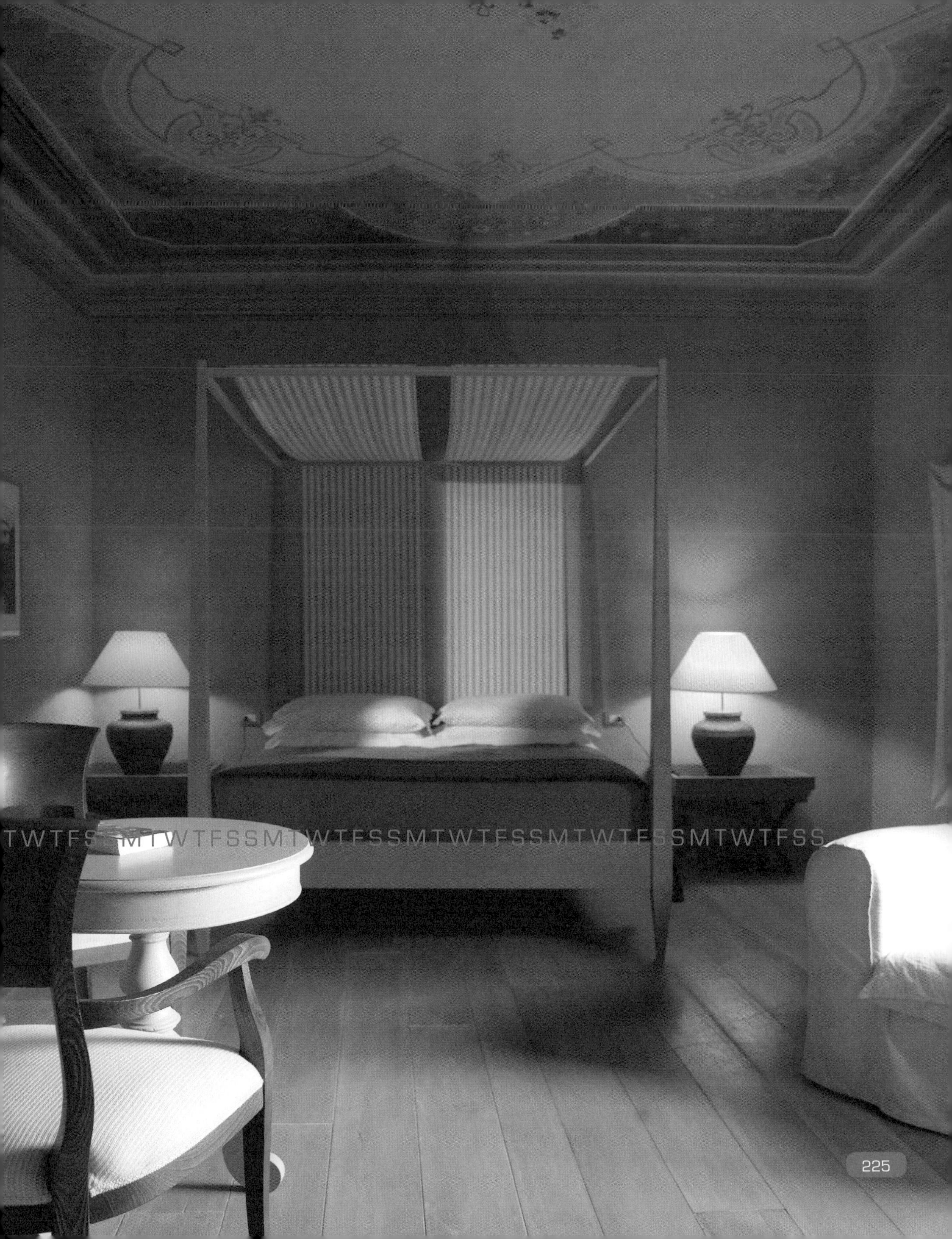
TWTFSSMTWTFSSMTWTFSSMTWTFSSMTWTFSS

For the first time in my life, when I get off the plane in Florence, I walk through customs and straight past the baggage-carousel area. For a woman who loves and lives fashion, this is a great accomplishment – I have packed my whole weekend into a carry-on (ladies, take note: gold flip-flops will save you packing endless shoes in summer, since you can dress them up or down). I feel like my old, breezy Californian self once again, travelling short-haul for a relaxed weekend away, with few wardrobe rules to worry about.

It is 15h when we arrive at the Villa Sassolini. The charming hotel manager, Andrea, comes to meet us at the gate of what appears to be a village monastery hiding behind a strong stucco façade. Mr Smith remarks that Andrea has an air of Lex Luther about him. It might be fair to say that his levels of passion are comparable to the comic-book villain but, rather than obsessing about global domination, Andrea's focus is clearly to ensure the world is a better place – especially for guests at Villa Sassolini. As we enter the lobby, it feels as though no one is home, and that we're the only guests here. We tread the slate-coloured wooden floors that run throughout, past a spacious living room with a fireplace, books and oversized lampshades. The low yellow lighting enhances a pervading sense of calm. There is a small reception, but the greeting at the gate counted as check-in.

Andrea shows us to our room on the top floor, helping with Mr Smith's bulky baggage while I saunter up the stairs with my carry-on. Mr Smith notes that, though we have a lounge and bedroom with beautiful old white-painted beams, what we don't have is a bathtub. Without so much as a whiff of irritation, Andrea lumbers himself with Mr Smith's luggage once again and takes us off to another room on yet another floor. Our new abode has a lovely four-poster bed, fresco-painted ceiling, grey walls and a bathroom large enough to house a whole family – with a beautiful, oversized bath in the middle of it.

With the heat absolutely scorching at 30 degrees, the pool beckons. I am reminded of my childhood in the Californian valley, where pools were more important than passports. Having had to adjust to leisure-centre versions in London, it is a joy to swim outdoors again. We've come straight from the airport, with no lunch pitstop, so we are starving: Andrea, who is nothing short of a miracle-worker, whips together a plate of cheeses, pears, honey and rolls, while we have a cooling splash about.

It's such a beautiful night that we decide to eat outside again at sunset. There are two options at Villa Sassolini: inside is a softly lit dining hall near the tower, with a vaulted ceiling and a wine cellar; outside there's a honeysuckle-framed garden full of overgrown rosemary and lavender bushes. We choose a garden table, where my handbag is even given its own pedestal – how nice to be in a hotel where the staff anticipate the whims of a fashionista. The food is gorgeous, but beware: don't fill your belly on the tasty traditional Tuscan fare. Make sure you save room for the homemade puddings – namely the chocolate fondant and the cheesecake.

We're back in the garden once more for breakfast and to plan our day out. Nothing is too far, but nothing is quite on the doorstep either, so a car is crucial; taxis aren't really an option out here. We begin with a stop at the local Prada outlet. There are lots of charming hilltop mediaeval villages to visit, but shopping is taken just as seriously as heritage around here. (We pull in to a petrol station on the way to check where we're going and, without prompting, a serviceman approaches us and says, 'Next light, left and left again.' Three shopping bags later, I realise my hand-luggage-only approach might not work for the return journey.

Our next foray is to Badia a Coltibuono, an old monastery and vineyard where we enjoy a light lunch with a stunning view of the hills and valleys. It is clearly marked on the tourist map, though, and in high season we feel like dots in the crowd, so we set ↓

off on a mission to seek out a rather more intimate wine-tasting experience. At our first stop, Monterotondo, the owner gives us a private tour of the cool cellar and a broken-English explanation of his wines. We're no connoisseurs and, after several tastings, we have to confess that everything tastes like a glass of Canaletto Primitivo. When Mr Smith points out that a particular vintage tastes a bit like Um Bongo, I take it as a sure sign that it is time to go back to the hotel.

As we say farewell to Sassolini, I realise that the place has caused me to reconsider exactly what accommodation means. This is a small hotel with a relaxed ethos and wonderful service, whose atmosphere serves as a valuable reminder that a holiday in Tuscany is best enjoyed unhurriedly. I see the region as a little like my home of Napa Valley, but quainter and more personal. And I have yet to find a hotel as unique in style and personality as

Villa Sassolini in the Californian wine country. Our break doesn't end with the simple pleasure it began with: at Gatwick, I stand by the carousel waiting for my luggage, smiling in the knowledge that I am returning laden with rewards both sartorial and spiritual.

Reviewed by Casey Gorman

NEED TO KNOW

Rooms Ten.

Rates €200–€400, including breakfast.

Check-out 11h.

Room service The restaurant menu is available from 07h30–22h. An early breakfast can be provided.

Facilities TV, Internet. Guests can use the villa's mountain bikes for excursions.

Poolside Outdoor pool with bar, panoramic terrace and formal garden. A light lunch is served by the pool between 12h30 and 14h30.

Children Under-12s stay free when sharing a room; an extra €40 is charged for those aged 12–16.

IN THE KNOW

Our favourite rooms The Marrakech room has fantastic views over the pool. The A Caccia suite has its own balcony and is decorated with hunting prints and has views of the wild hills of Chianti.

Hotel bar On the terrace next to the pool.

Hotel restaurant The hotel's seasonal menu presents a modern take on fresh, traditional Tuscan ingredients, such as Chianina beef and wind-cured ham.

Top table Alfresco on the terrace by the swimming pool.

Dress code Chianti chic.

LOCAL EATING AND DRINKING

Osteria Locanda Il Canto del Maggio in Terranuova (0559 705 147) is a family-run restaurant set in a wild garden, famous for its goose pappardelle and home-made desserts. **Fontebussi** on Borgo di Fontebussi in Cavriglia (055 916 811) serves traditional Tuscan dishes and has great views from the terrace. **Osteria di Starda**, in Starda Castle in Gaiole (0577 734 100) is set in the vaulted cellars and has a traditional menu.

 Smith cardholders receive a free bottle of champagne.

GET A ROOM!

Use our online booking service at www.mrandmrssmith.com to check availability and make reservations. Register your Smithcard to check current members' offers for this hotel.

Villa Sassolini
Largo Moncioni, Località Moncioni, Chianti
+39 0559 702 246
info@villasassolini.it; www.villasassolini.it

MTWTFSSMTWTFSSMTWTFSSMTWTFSSMTWTFSSMTWT

● CASCAIS

PORTUGAL

CASCAIS
Farol Design Hotel

TWTFSSMTWTFSSMTWTFSSMTWTFSSMTWTFSSMTWTFSS

PORTUGAL

CASCAIS

Cascais

COASTLINE   ATLANTIC ROLLERS, IMPOSING CLIFFS
COAST LIFE   COSMOPOLITAN FISHING VILLAGE

MTWTFSSMTWTFSSMTWTFSSMTWTFSSMTWTFSSMTWT
PORTUGAL

TWTFSSMTWTFSSMTWTFSSMTWTFSSMTWTFSSMTWTFSS

CASCAIS

Once a small fishing village, Cascais (pronounced 'kesh-kysh') grew into a genteel summer resort under the patronage of the Portuguese royal family. During World War II, this peaceful town on the edge of Europe buzzed with exiled royalty and spies trawling for news. Cascais still draws in the crowds, and it has kept its laidback and carefree atmosphere. Weekend lovebirds mingle happily here with strolling families and sunbaked surfers, while yachts bob alongside the brightly painted fishing boats in the bay. The relaxed elegance of the town and its hip restaurants and friendly bars make for perhaps the most sophisticated spot on the Portuguese Riviera.

GETTING THERE

Planes Lisbon airport is roughly 40 minutes from Cascais by car. There's a bus from the airport for about €1; taxis cost around €40.

Trains From Lisbon's Cais do Sodré station to Cascais, trains take 30 mins and cost €1.50. Sit on the left-hand side for scenic views of the Atlantic coastline.

Boats If you want to get to Cascais by boat, you'll have to sign up as crew on a yacht – or take your own.

Automobiles It's worth hiring a car for coastal exploring, but public transport connections to Lisbon are very good.

DO GO / DON'T GO

The climate is generally mild; from April to October, fine weather is virtually guaranteed. The coast is pounded by the Atlantic surf in winter but is rarely cold.

COMPLETELY CASCAIS

For a slice of street theatre, make sure you head to the harbour at dusk and watch the fishermen selling the day's catch. You may not be in the market for a whole side of salmon, but it's a great spectacle nonetheless.

LOCAL KNOWLEDGE

Taxis If you venture to Lisbon, there are plenty of cabs to hail on the street. In Cascais, ask your hotel to book one for you.

Tipping culture Discretionary; ten per cent is appreciated.

Siesta and fiesta Portugal's valiant Association of Friends of the Siesta continues its noble fight to defend the two-hour lunch break and power nap between 13h and 15h. We pledge ourselves to the cause. Many restaurants don't open until 21h.

Packing tips Surf dudes should pack their coolest threads, but leave some space in your suitcase for all those lovely bottles of vintage port you'll want to take home with you – particularly if you taste some 20-year-old tawny.

Recommended read *Distant Music* by Lee Langley.

Cuisine Must-trys include cozido à Portuguesa, a stew with beans, veg and cuts of meat. Fish-lovers will be in seventh heaven here, as fresh fish and squid land daily. Try the cataplana, a seafood platter served with rice or potatoes. The sweet-toothed will find the custard tarts hard to resist.

Currency Euro.

Dialling codes Country code for Portugal: 351. Cascais: 21.

DIARY

June or July Cascais Sailing Week is a major event, attracting an armada of international competitors (www.cncascais.com). **July** Jazz on a Summer's Day takes place in Palmela Park Auditorium, and scores of musicians supply the soundtrack to balmy evenings. **Late July** The Festival of the Sea is an annual event run by the town's fishermen. Besides music and dancing, the event sees a herd of bulls released onto the beach. Anyone brave or foolish enough to grab one by the horns is rewarded with a dubious prize of dried fish. Fireworks, folk singing and bizarre games go on into the night.

WORTH GETTING OUT OF BED FOR

Viewpoint For the best sunset views, take a drive up the coastal road past Guincho to Cabo da Roca, and sit by Europe's most westerly cliffs as the big Atlantic rollers crash beneath you.

Arts and culture The Convent of Mafra is considered the world's best example of baroque architecture, with its imposing dome and magnificent 88-metre-long library. In Lisbon, the Gulbenkian Museum and Gallery is particularly wonderful (www.museu.gulbenkian.pt).

Activities Sailing is a major draw; Cascais marina often hosts major regattas. There are several outfits in town hiring out sailing dinghies, yachts and motorboats. Guincho and Carcavelos are some of the best surfing beaches in Europe.

Daytripper Follow in Lord Byron's footsteps northwards and visit Sintra for its glorious Gothic and Renaissance palace and tropical micro-climate. In low season, it's misty and mysterious, with empty streets and a fairy-tale feel. If you drive there, stop off on the way back at Cabo da Roca and look out to the open sea from the westernmost point in Europe.

Best beach The sheltered sandy beaches of Praia da Rainha and Praia da Ribeira are popular with families. To the northwest of Cascais lies Praia do Guincho, a magnificent beach whose exposure to the full force of the Atlantic makes it popular with surfers.

Something for nothing Check out Boca do Inferno ('Mouth of Hell'), just to the west of Cascais. Legend has it that this crater-shaped rock formation is the entrance to the underworld.

Shopping There's a lively market in Cascais on Wednesdays and Saturday mornings, and a daily fleamarket. The designer-label zone in Lisbon is Rua Garrett in the Chiado area. Glove emporium Luvaria Ulisses is worth a look just for its tiny exterior and drawer upon drawer of kid-leather mitts. Stock up on port and Madeira.

CAFES

In Cascais, **Casa Velha** on Avenida Valbom is the place for a light seafood snack and a glass of port on the balcony. Heartier appetites should try the lunchtime special of superb paella.

Pastéis de Belém, on Rua de Belém in Lisbon, has been serving delicious custard tarts since 1837. The top-secret recipe was acquired from some hard-up monks.

BARS AND RESTAURANTS

Head to **Refúgio da Roca** on Estrada do Cabo da Roca in Azoia (21 929 0898) after watching the sun set behind the cliffs. This traditional seafood restaurant with its wooden decor and huge lobster tanks has an easygoing informality. In Lisbon's Santos district, **Kais** on Rua da Cintura (21 393 2930) is a theatrical experience, set in a huge waterfront warehouse. For fine dining in a thoroughly modern context, futro-chic **Bica do Sapato** on Avenida Infante D Henrique (21 881 0320) is the hippest restaurant in the capital; if you're not in the mood for a big event, try the sushi bar upstairs. Opulent **Pavilhão Chinês**, on Rua Dom Pedro V, is an opulent rendezvous in Lisbon's buzzing Bairro Alto – definitely the district of choice for night owls.

NIGHTLIFE

If it's supercool clubs you're after, head to Lisbon. In the riverside Docas area, **Lux**, next to Bica do Sapato in Lisbon, is where the glamorous go to pose with a caipirinha (www.luxfragil.com). Closer to Cascais itself, friendly **Bally Bally** pub on Rua Marquês Leal Pancada is open until 3h30 every night. Largo Luiz de Camões Square is the hub of the hotspots.

Farol Design Hotel

MTWTFSSMTWTFSSMTWTFSSMTWTFSSMTWTFSSMTW

PORTUGAL

'It's the fruit of an unusual
marriage: that of a traditional
19th-century Portuguese villa
and a Corbusieresque extension'

Farol Design Hotel, Cascais, Portugal

Our weekend on the Portuguese coast is a double quest; Mrs Smith is on the prowl for the perfect room, Mr Smith is seeking the ideal surf beach. So when we walk into Farol Design Hotel and note the view straight through to the sea, mile-wide smiles appear on our faces. For reasons too humdrum to be hinted at, we arrived worn out, irritable and craving a spot of tranquillity. Farol Design Hotel has ticked two out of three of our boxes before we've even taken our shoes off.

Perched on an outcrop of rock a few feet from the Atlantic Ocean, Farol's contemporary style is the fruit of an unusual marriage: that of a traditional 19th-century Portuguese villa and a Corbusieresque extension, built to encase a slick restaurant and additional rooms. The blend of old and new is a triumph. The exterior that greeted us is white and minimalist; the interior is sleek and wood-panelled. The result is a stylish box of tricks, in which you don't know what to expect next.

Of the hotel's 34 bedrooms, ten are the creation of esteemed Portuguese fashion designers, such as Ana Salazar and José Antonio Tenente, hence its Design Hotel mantle. We're excited to see what the USP of our room will be. We are spoilt with a big, blue view – 180 degrees of ocean – and although there's no balcony, we don't miss one, since what we do have is simply stunning: a superior mix of vintage chic and modern finish.

We've been booked into a suite, and we can't help but wonder if that's why we've struck gold in terms of our accommodation. As a life-long addict to all things interior-design, I have to find out what individual wonders the other bedrooms contain. I swiftly befriend a chambermaid, and Mr Smith and I get our noses around a few doors.

Our investigations reveal one space blessed with a great big bath that you could simply tumble into straight from bed – perfect for a karma-sutric weekend.

Next, room 204: 'a cross between *Boogie Nights* and an African safari?' I suggest to my partner in boudoir voyeurism. 'Now there's a film I'd pay to see,' says he. I peek into another dwelling, this time a blanched-out abode with floor to ceiling white curtains. Just as we're feeling that the vibe here is more sanatorium than sexy sleepover, the drapes open and the need for such minimalism becomes clear. The focus is the stupendous view. (If you are a vistaholic, make sure you ask for one of the west-facing rooms, which all have wonderful panoramas over the Atlantic.)

The design savvy at Farol extends to its grounds, which are very *Café del Mar*. Daybeds shrouded in muslin are positioned superbly for watching the surf breaking on the rocks and the ships slowly disappearing over the horizon – a perfect retreat from the Ibiza-style pool area, where girls bobbing about in teeny bikinis hold Mr Smith's interest. The thoughtfully designed set of private spaces means I'm able to drag him off for a more secluded, less distracted sunbathe. We colonise a grassy knoll, with

beanbags crying out to be settled on for sunset, and the ubiquitous soundtrack of blissed-out beats making the perfect accompaniment.

I wasn't sure what to expect from Portuguese gastronomy. Firstly there were those delicious custard tarts from my local patisserie in London, but then I'd also heard horror stories of unidentifiable green soups and oily stews. Luckily we discover that the hotel's restaurant, Rosa Maria, is doing wonders for its country's international reputation. Serving up high-quality southern European dishes, and doffing its cap to national favourites, the kitchen executes everything with modern-minded finesse.

Side-stepping any what-to-have quandaries, we jump on the adventurous *menu desgustación*. We're not quite courageous enough to try the Gorgonzola ice cream, but we do manage to indulge in a 20-year-old tawny port, and a cigar for señor, in the easy chairs in the opulent red library-style bar. ↓

There is no shortage of daytime distractions to be had around the hotel. After a pretty ten-minute stroll along the seafront, we find ourselves right in the centre of Cascais. It's a pretty, chocolate-box town that gets cooling sea breezes – no wonder Portugal's royal family liked to retreat here from the capital during the sweltering summer months. It remains just as popular today with couples and families from Lisbon, eager for a good dose of sea air. The promenade is the ideal place to spend a few hours ambling and building up an appetite for some spicy piri-piri chicken and grilled squid on the seafront.

We still had one mission left to accomplish: our search for the perfect surf. After quizzing a few locals, we seek out Bar do Guincho, the Portuguese equivalent of a lido. A few euros gets us a good parking space and a beach a lot less crowded than many others; we shell out a smidgen more, and get an umbrella and wind-blocker thrown into the bargain. The breeze is stiff and, within seconds, Mr Smith disappears. He's seen the sign for

kite-surfing. Still, I have a secret weapon. As soon as I feel that it's time to return to our chic retreat all I have to do is dangle that room key. Even the waves can't compete with a splash in the hydro-massage tub, big enough for two, awaiting us back at Farol.

Reviewed by Mr & Mrs Smith

NEED TO KNOW

Rooms 34, including one suite and 11 rooms styled by different fashion designers.
Rates €100–€400, including breakfast.
Check-out Midday, but ask for flexibility.
Room service 07h–23h: restaurant menu. At other times there's a snack menu with sandwiches, salads and puddings.
Facilities Outdoor saltwater pool, massages on request in your room.
Poolside The pool and secluded sun terrace overlook the sea.
Children Welcome, but the hotel's location on a rocky shoreline could be considered hazardous for smaller children.

IN THE KNOW

Our favourite rooms For a modern influence, choose the new wing; for high ceilings and more space, go for the old building. Ask for a balcony overlooking the sea. Room 216 is very rock 'n' roll in black and gold. Room 215, all-white, is sleek with breathtaking views.
Hotel bar Stone Bar is cosy, with doors opening onto the terrace. Open until 02h.
Hotel restaurant Rosa Maria is modern and airy, with floor-to-ceiling windows affording you a greedy view out onto the deck and rocky coast beyond. Dinner for two can be arranged on a jetty below. Sushi lounge every day except Monday.
Top table Outside on the terrace.
Dress code Gloss up for the evening.

LOCAL EATING AND DRINKING

For Italian flavours, oysters and sushi, **La Villa** on Praia do Tamariz (21 468 0033) is a chic eatery, 15 minutes away by car; for a panoramic sea view, ask for table 20 by the window. For similar fare, with humbler price tags and an Ibiza-style buzz, try **Pizzeria Lucullus** (21 484 4709). €100 will get you a seafood platter and some wine at **Mar do Guincho** on Estrada do Guincho (21 485 8280). The decor is not what you go for, but there's plenty of eye candy in the form of seafood tanks and a view of the beach. **Furnas do Guincho** (21 486 9243) is just down the road and ideal for Portuguese meat and fish specialities. A short distance from Guincho beach, and with an ocean view as perfect as the fresh seafood, **Porto de Santa Maria** (21 487 9450) is one place where you'll definitely want to reserve a window table.

Smith members receive a bottle of Portuguese wine and a fruit basket in their room on arrival.

GET A ROOM!

Use our online booking service at www.mrandmrssmith.com to check availability and make reservations. Register your Smithcard to find out about current member offers for this hotel.

Farol Design Hotel
7 Avenida Rei Humberto II de Itália, Cascais
+351 21 482 3490
farol@farol.com.pt; www.farol.com.pt

take

the

perfect

picture

How to...

HOW TO… TAKE HOLIDAY PHOTOGRAPHS

It's time for some hard truths. No one, not even your very best friends, wants to look at lame holiday snaps. Sunsets? Forget it. That cute lizard on the steps to your suite? Send it to *Reptiles Monthly*. Another washed-out series of you in a bandanna, proudly clutching a snowboard? Please, God, no more.

The digital era, great though it is in terms of instant gratification, has spawned umpteen times more bad holiday photography. Without worrying about wasting film on wait-and-see cameras, we snap away merrily, then compile endless slideshows back home on the PC. The paradox is that it doesn't have to be this way. Digital photography's great upside is that you can learn from (and delete) your mistakes, and shoot, shoot and shoot again, using various angles and different light, until you've got the perfect picture. Combine that with some of the following top tips, and the days of friends inching away from you and your laptop will be long gone.

Use the 'magic hour' This delightful phrase describes the quality of the light in the early morning, and an hour before sunset. The morning light is crisp and clear, the evening light soft, giving photographs more dramatic qualities. If you're shooting people, go for the late magic hour, since most of us look better as the day goes by… It also means you avoid subjects squinting into the bright midday sun like Mr Magoo.

Give the shot depth A sense of scale can mean the difference between 'so what' and 'wow' shots. If you're shooting a landscape, try it with something in the foreground. Include strong lines and colours in the frame; stand on a rock or your car to get a different angle. Don't be afraid to try unexpected positioning to accentuate perspective.

Be a people person Technical skills are less important than social skills when you're taking pictures of people. A smile and a joke will get your subjects to relax. Be quick and confident: the longer you take, the more stilted a subject will become. If possible, photograph people in natural light and keep the camera just above their eye level, or make sure chins are tilted down. We've all seen flared-nostril wedding snaps, as people instinctively throw back their heads and pose. If it's midday, look for a doorway or other area of shadow to create a strong image. You don't always need your friends smiling straight at the camera – catching them unawares will give a less contrived, more relaxed result.

Keep it steady You know the manual that came with the camera? Read it, so you can figure out how to use the remote release or self-timer function. Both will help eliminate camera shake. This isn't a problem during the day, but the slower shutter release can result in blurry night shots. A mini-tripod and remote release make the ideal set-up, but balancing your camera on a bag or coat and setting the self-timer will do at a pinch.

Flash tactics If you're shooting at night or at a party, try your camera's fill-in flash mode, which lets you capture some of the atmosphere, as well as your subjects.

Go low-slung Yes, sometimes it pays to literally shoot from the hip. Digital lets you shoot more than you need, so don't stop, even if you think you're done. Try a few different angles to mix it up a bit: set your camera on self-timer and spin it by the strap; or walk along firing off shots without checking the composition. You could end up with one or two fantastic images – or a bunch of blurred shots of feet. And on that note…

Find a theme A surprisingly successful Internet site we've heard about is simply a collection of shots of celebrities' feet. This may be a little down-at-heel for your holiday pics, but it's worth considering a theme. Your thing, for example, might be lovehearts – from graffiti in a souk to giant ad hoardings.

Practicalities Hot climates can affect equipment: if you are moving from air-con to the humid outdoors, give your camera a few minutes to acclimatise before you start shooting. Finally, don't forget to carry all the spare batteries, mains chargers and adaptors you need: it is frustrating to spot the perfect photo opportunity and realise you're short of power.

MTWTFSSMTWTFSSMTWTFSSMTWTFSSMTWTFSSMTW

● SOUTHERN EXTREMADURA

● MALLORCA

● SEVILLE PROVINCE   ● IBIZA
● RONDA
● COSTA DE LA LUZ

SPAIN

TWTFSSMTWTFSSMTWTFSSMTWTFSSMTWTFSSMTWTFSS

ESPAÑA

SOUTHERN EXTREMADURA

Southern Extremadura

COUNTRYSIDE   WILD, WILD WEST
COUNTRY LIFE   MUCHAS SIESTAS

M T W T F S S M T W T F S S M T W T F S S M T W T F S S M T W T F S S M T W T
ESPAÑA

SOUTHERN EXTREMADURA

The sunshine state in a land that gets plenty, this uncrowded rural region gets fantastic weather when much of Europe is still shivering. The lack of coastline has kept mass tourism at bay: this is a part of Spain where donkeys plod through quiet olive groves, and life passes slowly with the changing of the seasons. Sleepy fortified towns overlooking the Portuguese borderlands bear traces of Roman, Moorish and mediaeval glory and are graced by Conquistador mansions paid for with plundered Aztec and Inca gold. Today, the treasure troves of Pizarro and Cortés are matched by an El Dorado of regional delicacies to tempt a new breed of explorer.

GETTING THERE

Planes The region has very few international airports. The nearest are Seville, Madrid and Lisbon.

Trains Badajoz is on the Madrid-Lisbon train line. Infrequent express trains stop at Cáceres, Mérida and Badajoz.

Automobiles Roads are of a high quality, and driving is the only practical way to see the region in a short space of time. When you hire a car, make sure you ask for a map, or fork out the extra for GPS.

GO OR DON'T GO

You get really good weather from April to October – July and August are not crowded (because everyone has headed for the sea) but might be too hot for some people. Winters are generally mild with some snow in the hills.

ESSENTIALLY EXTREMADURA

Extremadura's tracts of pastureland are criss-crossed by ancient drove roads called *cañadas reales* (royal roads) and *vías pecuarias* (drove roads), which were once used to transport vast flocks of sheep to market. They now make excellent hiking trails.

LOCAL KNOWLEDGE

Taxis Best to ask your hotel to order one.

Tipping culture Ten per cent is normal. Be aware: in 'local' places the waiters often do the sums in their head and you won't get a written bill.

Siesta and fiesta You'll need to embrace siesta in the summer heat. Some larger shops stay open but many close between 13h and 17h.

Packing tips The strong sunshine means it's wise to bring a hat.

Recommended reads *The Broken Spears: The Aztec Account of the Conquest of Mexico* by Miguel León-Portilla; *Don Quixote* by Cervantes.

Cuisine Extremadura's cooking is almost mediaeval: roast suckling pig, game (especially in autumn), and wild frog all feature on menus in the region. There's also a good range of local gazpacho recipes, sheep's-milk cheese and cured ham, including jamón de bellota, made from acorn- and herb-fed pigs. Yemas (candied egg yolks) and licor de cereza (cherry liqueur) are delicious if you have a sweet tooth. Ribera del Guadiana whites are the region's most famous wines.

Currency Euro.

Dialling codes Country code for Spain: 34. Badajoz: 924.

DIARY

Semana Santa aka Easter Week is one of the year's biggest and most colourful festivals. In Cáceres you can see penitents walking through the streets dragging logs. **24 June** The week-long Feria de San Juan is the biggest festival in Badajoz, with fireworks, fairs and celebrations. **July–August** Mérida hosts a classical theatre festival, with plays staged nightly in the Roman amphitheatre (www.festivaldemerida.es). **August** Albuquerque's Mediaeval Folk Festival features costumes, music and drama. **First week of September** Mérida hosts its own lively festival with funfairs and cultural events.

WORTH GETTING OUT OF BED FOR

Viewpoint The towering Castillo de la Luna in Albuquerque, north of Badajoz, was once the centrepiece of a network of border defences and has wonderful views over the Portuguese frontier.

Arts and culture Over the centuries, Extremadura's harsh and impoverished environment has produced some of Spain's toughest and most famous adventurers, such as Pizarro and Cortés. The new MEIAC Museum of Contemporary Art in Badajoz explores the region's relationship with the Americas. Many local towns and villages have familiar namesakes on the other side of the Atlantic.

Activities The network of ancient drove roads makes for excellent hiking. Your hotel can also arrange 4x4 and donkey treks, as well as horse riding, wine-tasting and paragliding.

Daytripper Mérida was once the largest Roman city in Iberia and it's definitely worth exploring the remains of the temples, amphitheatres, aqueducts and hippodromes. There's also a wealth of local finds in the National Museum of Roman Art.

Perfect picnic The Cornalvo Nature Reserve, just outside Mérida, is a hilly spot ideal for both a picnic and an amble.

Something for nothing The town of Zafra, southeast of Badajoz, is nicknamed Little Seville; its beautiful whitewashed Old Town has a distinctly Andalucian feel. It is an agreeable place for an idle wander.

Shopping You won't be browsing designer-label boutiques here, but Extremadura is an excellent place to pick up cheeses, smoked ham and good-value wine. Keep an eye out for traditional leather, pottery and linen items, too.

CAFES

Gran Café Victoria on Calle San Juan de Ribera in Badajoz is a great place for a late-morning coffee and pastry. **LaCasaBar** next to Puerta de Jerez in Zafra (closed Sunday evening and Mondays) is set in a beautiful old house, and the roof terrace is perfect for drinks and tapas. Part of the town's defensive wall is inside the bar.

BARS AND RESTAURANTS

In Zafra, **La Tertulia** on Plaza Chica has a terrace out in the square and serves excellent tapas. **Casa Crespo** just off Calle Sevilla near Plaza de España (924 551 000) serves typical Extremaduran dishes, and its internal patio is a fine place for a lunchtime drink. In Mérida, **Altair** on Avenida José Fernández López (924 304 512) does traditional cuisine with a modern twist, and has a wonderful view of the fantastic new Calatrava-designed bridge across the Guadiana. On the other side of Lusitania Bridge, **Cachicho** (924 372 847) serves classic dishes on a sunny terrace. Over the border in the Portuguese town of Elvas, **El Cristo** (+351 268 623 512) is very popular for its fresh seafood.

NIGHTLIFE

You don't really come here for nightlife, but the bars will stay open if there are enough people in them, making it very easy to stay up until the wee small hours by mistake. There are several late-night bars near the cathedral in Badajoz – exotic **Samarkanda** on Calle de la Virgen de la Soledad is one of the best, sometimes featuring live music.

Hospedería Convento de la Parra

DESTINATION SOUTHERN EXTREMADURA
STYLE DIVINE RETREAT
SETTING SUNNY BADAJOZ

MTWTFSSMTWTFSSMTWTFS **S S** MTWTFSSMTWTFSSMTWT

ESPAÑA

'The main activities are lolling
and reading; the whole space
is incredibly relaxing, with
a special serenity to it at night'

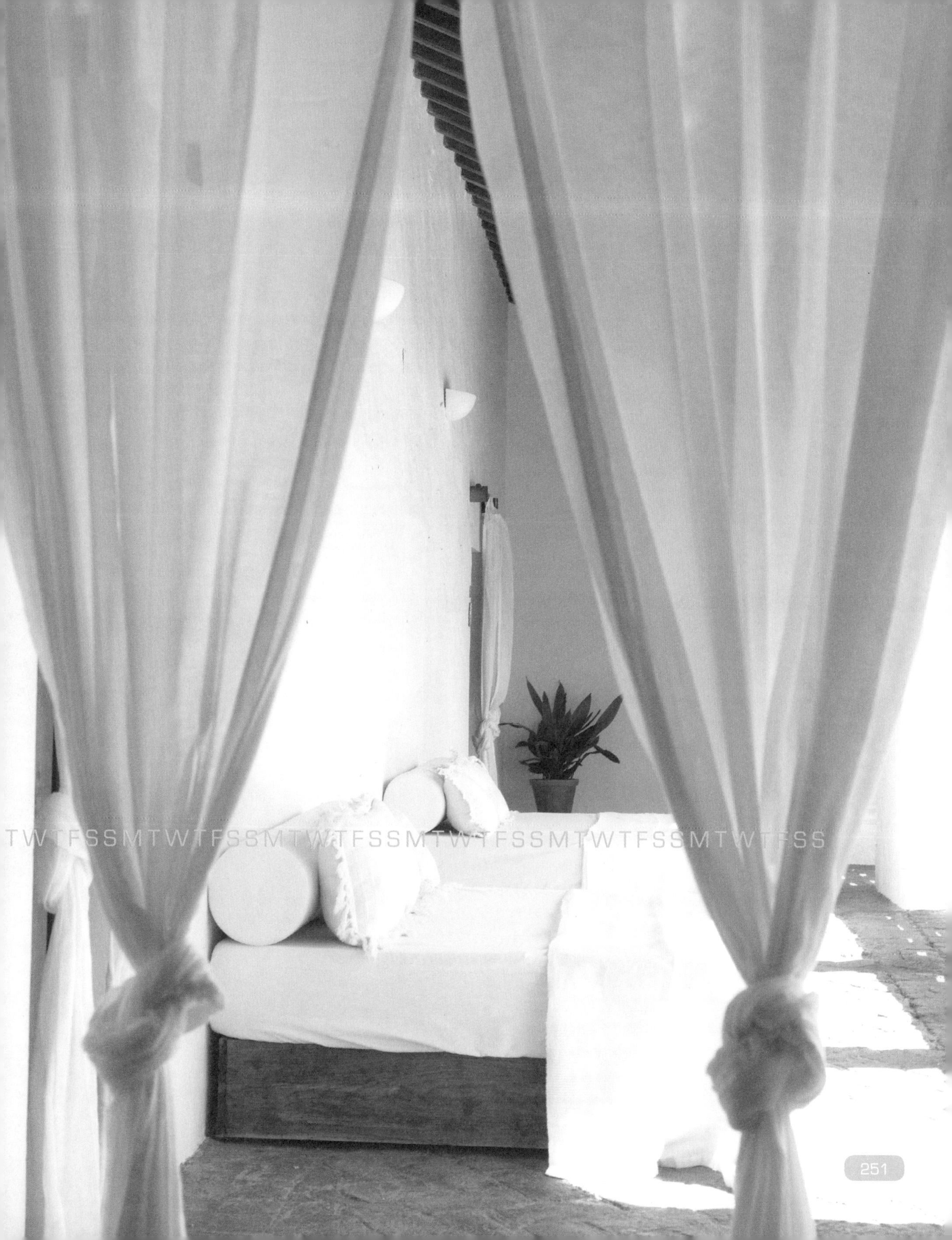
TWTFSSMTWTFSSMTWTFSSMTWTFSSMTWTFSS

Hospedería Convento de la Parra,
Southern Extremadura, Spain

and lit space for a quiet evening moment. We left only to explore our new home, and found plenty of other peaceful corners. There's a courtyard, a solarium leading from the library, and definitely no gym. The main activities here are lolling and reading. (You'll need to bring your own books unless you fancy grappling with *Oliver Twist* in Spanish.)

A stylish little bar area does exist, but we never saw it in use; it just stood there waiting to serve as the backdrop for a magazine shoot, since guests seem to choose their own spots to hang out. The whole space is incredibly relaxing, with a very special serenity about it at night, perhaps something to do with its former occupants; it was built in 1673 for nuns, who only gave it up in the late Seventies. We were particularly fond of the health-and-safety-busting amount of naked flame around the place, and found the lighting level to be romantic enough for both cooing and reading – just right after a long journey.

Whitney Houston once sang, 'I believe that children are our future.' That's all very well, but you don't necessarily want them messing up the clean lines of your boutique hotel. At Hospedería Convento de la Parra, you need to be at least 12 to get in, which is a good thing: the multitude of white surfaces would surely provide an irresistible challenge for crayon-wielding nippers. The designer of the hotel's small but very beautiful salt pool did not make provision for slides, inflatables, jumping or bombing when he drew up his plans. Indeed, poolside at La Parra has been designed as a quiet, reflection-friendly space; mobile phones are discreetly discouraged in the hotel's welcome note.

We arrived late at night and were warmly welcomed by the demure but friendly staff. It was the hour when poolside becomes what might once have been called a chill-out area: a perfectly designed

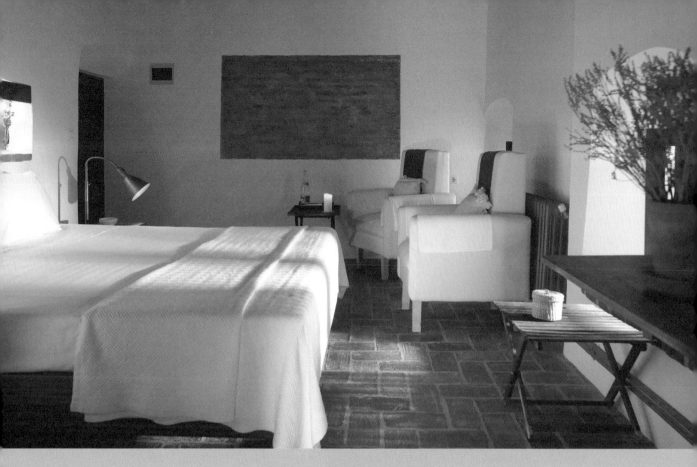

We took our Spanish-measure G&Ts up to our room, which overlooked the courtyard. Appropriately for a former convent, the vibe is reflective rather than showy, but we found it design-conscious, with rusty lampshades and retro fans, and wood and candles lending an upmarket rustic feel. It was built for comfort, too, with lots of cushions, a super-comfy bed... Sleep came easy. As there are so many original fixtures and fittings, and the building is too old to seriously tinker with, there is no air-con at La Parra. This is nice and eco, and the thick walls and shutters do their best to keep the heat out in the way they have done for centuries.

Breakfast is served until a leisurely noon. The freshly squeezed orange juice could not have been more locally sourced, and the chocolatey muesli, and bread and cheese did the business. The hotel dazzles in the Extremadura daytime, night-time nooks and crannies turning into places where you can take the sun in style. No beach (and the fact that the international airport is a couple of hours away) means hardly any tourists around here. The kind of Englishman who might be wearing a football shirt has headed for the overcrowded coast. This is great news for us and our fellow guests. They struck us as early adopters, who might have headed to Tuscany a few years ago. The visitors' book suggests a wide Euro mix: as well as plenty of Brits, there were lots of in-the-know folk from across the border in Portugal as well as other parts of Spain.

We picked up a map from reception and went for a wander. The unspoilt countryside is perfect for walking (outside of peak heat) and we ambled between olive groves, hills and farms, spotting donkeys. Stopping off for tapas in a local (telly on very loud, but friendly) bar, we explored the village, which took no more than ten minutes. Time for a drive, then. This meant cranking up the air-con in our hire car and taking advantage of excellent roads by embarking on a whistle-stop tour of the Moorish, Roman and mediaeval towns within ↓

striking distance. There isn't much traffic in this part of Spain, and easy parking, pretty views and tolerant road users meant that our jaunt was a real pleasure. And I only drove on the left once.

Good job La Parra is defiantly non-spa in its atmosphere. I'm told spas don't particularly encourage guests to round off a day's lazy driving with a pork kebab. The hotel's restaurant serves up the best in traditional Spanish regional cooking (plenty of pork, black-pudding croquettes, fish, game pie in cooler months), with a modern sensibility, and slightly erratic service. Eating and drinking are popular activities in this part of the world: traditional, regional and seasonal menus in nearby restaurants might offer wild frog and roast suckling pig. Be warned that the local smoked ham is not much less addictive than crack.

This boutique hideaway is certainly a destination hotel – and the staff made us feel very special for making the effort, by being perfectly charming, and even saying complimentary things about my rather sub-par Spanish. La Parra is one for the grown-ups: off the beaten track, so not for urbanites who get twitchy when removed from a major metropolis, but a perfect place to avoid noise and effort for a few days. My favourite memory will certainly be moonbathing with Mrs Smith in the solarium on our final evening. I had slowed down physical activity to panda levels by this point, and I wasn't thinking of anything much apart from what fantastical lie I could tell my co-workers in order to snatch an extra few days here.

Reviewed by Nick Raistrick

NEED TO KNOW

Rooms 21, including two suites.
Rates €111–€170, including breakfast.
Check-out 11h, but midday is possible if the room is not booked out.
Room service 21h–23h for restaurant menu.
Facilities Solarium. No TVs or air-con, but there is an extensive library and lots of board games.
Poolside Outdoor saltwater pool, in pristine-white surroundings.
Children Over-12s are welcome.
Hotel closed First three weeks of January.
Also The hotel can arrange a host of activities, including 4x4 excursions, wine-tasting, cooking courses, paragliding and donkey treks.

IN THE KNOW

Our favourite rooms Room 22 is a spacious double with lots of light. Room 24 is slightly darker but cool, with an open-plan bathroom. Room 18 is a lovely regular double. Ask for a room facing the courtyard.
Hotel bar You can order drinks anywhere you like, all hours within reason.
Hotel restaurant Set in the vaulted refectory, or the cloisters in balmy weather, serving a fresh take on Extremadura's traditional cuisine, and local Ribera del Guadiana wines. Lunch served 14h–15h30; dinner 21h–23h30.
Top table In a candlelit corner of the cloisters.
Dress code Natural fabrics, to harmonise with the hotel's organic feel.

LOCAL EATING AND DRINKING

In Zafra, **La Rebotica** on Calle Botica (924 554 289) is in the prettiest part of town and serves excellent traditional cuisine, like chicken breast with mulberry sauce. The elegant **La Barbacana** on Calle López Asme (924 554 100) also serves delicious regional food, including sautéed green asparagus and roast suckling pig. If you find yourself in Badajoz, the dignified **Gran Café Victoria** on Calle San Juan de Ribera (924 263 223) is a great place for a late-morning coffee and pastry.

 Smith members receive a complimentary bottle of Spanish cava.

GET A ROOM!

Use our online booking service at www.mrandmrssmith.com to check availability and make reservations. Register your Smithcard to find out about current member offers for this hotel.

Hospedería Convento de la Parra
16 Calle Santa María, La Parra, Badajoz
+34 924 682 692
convento@laparra.net; www.laparra.net

COSTA DE LA LUZ

Costa de la Luz

COASTLINE   WINDSWEPT WAVES
COAST LIFE   DOLPHINS AND SURFERS

MTWTFSSMTWTFSSMTWTFSSMTWTFSSMTWTFSSMTWT
ESPAÑA

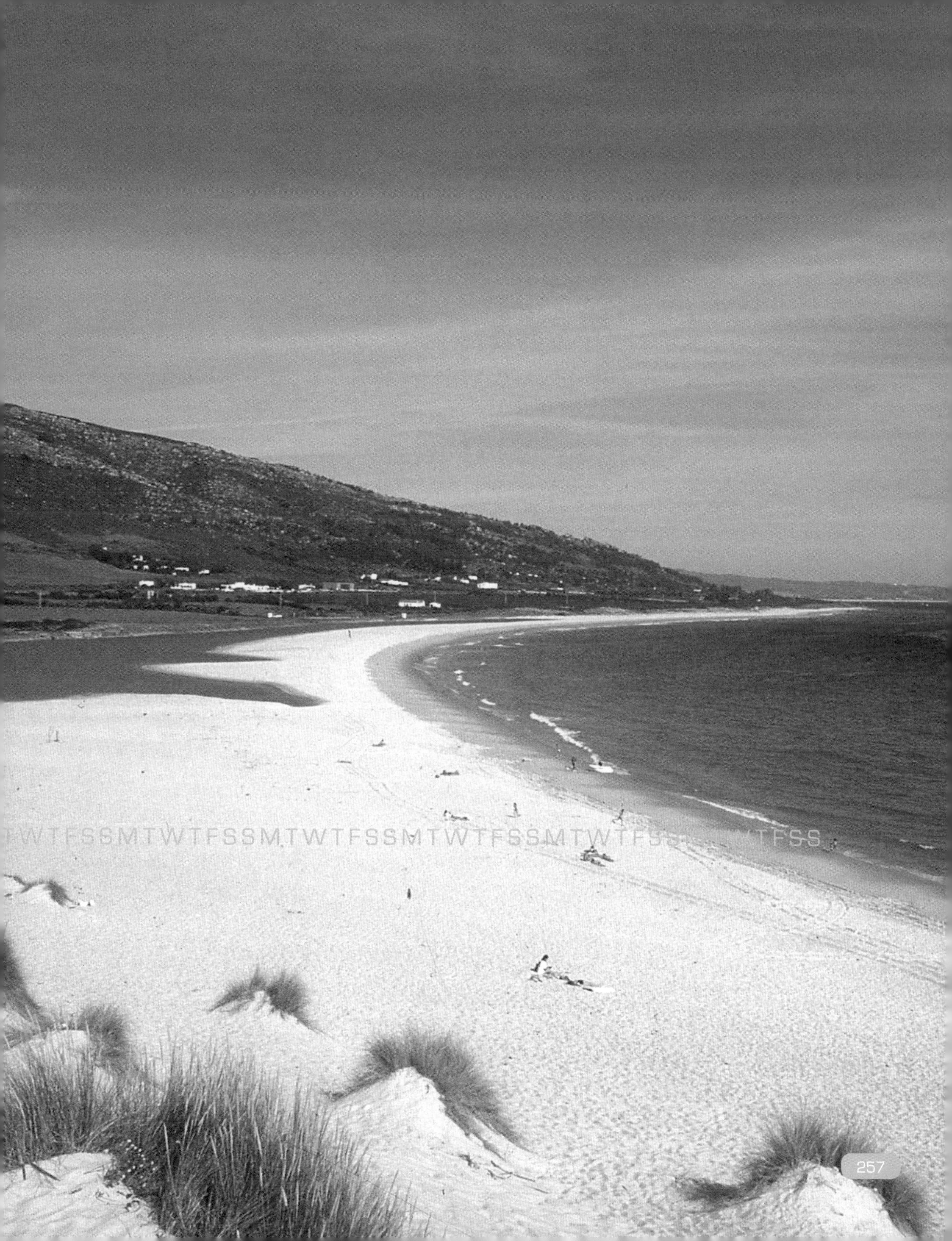

COSTA DE LA LUZ

On the Costa de la Luz the blue skies and pristine beaches seem to stretch on endlessly, and Atlantic breakers crash against a wild and windswept shore. Surfers have long been flocking to this coast at the southern tip of Europe, where sun, sand and big waves combine to perfection. Beyond the sublime solitude of the Costa lies a quintessentially Spanish land: the home of fiery flamenco; the breeding farms of fighting bulls destined for the sand of the arena; unspoilt sugar-white villages in which to while away the day with tapas and sweet sherry. The Costa de la Luz is slowly giving up its secrets, but even in high summer, you may still have just the seagulls to share the beach with.

GETTING THERE

Planes Jerez and Gibraltar airports are less than an hour away. There are regular flights year-round. You might come across slow traffic at the border with Gibraltar.
Trains The coast is not very accessible by train, but there is a scenic mountain line between Algeciras and Ronda.
Boats Fast ferries run from Tarifa to the Moroccan port city of Tangiers (35 minutes; €25).
Automobiles It's worth renting a car to explore the great beaches along the Atlantic coastline, as well as for daytrips to the cities of Seville, Jerez or Cádiz.

DO GO/DON'T GO

The coast is busiest during Easter and throughout July and August, but the warm climate makes the region perfect for a quiet holiday whatever the time of year.

VERY VEJER

The Costa is considered the best destination in Europe for kiting, windsurfing and kitesurfing, with dependable wind and surf throughout the year. Contact Club Mistral on Carretera N340 (956 689 098).

LOCAL KNOWLEDGE

Taxis You will find taxi ranks in most small towns and villages. In Vejer, call 956 451 744, or ask your hotel to order a cab for you.
Tipping culture Ten per cent in restaurants is appreciated; with drinks or tapas, a few euros is sufficient.
Siesta and fiesta Banks and shops close between 14h and 17h during the week, and at 14h on Saturdays. Restaurants don't get busy until after 21h.
Packing tips A kite, windbreaker or umbrella for the blustery beach. Pack a pashmina for the cool evenings.
Recommended reads *As I Walked Out One Midsummer Morning* by Laurie Lee; *Moorish Spain* by Richard Fletcher.
Cuisine Fresh fish and seafood figure heavily, including delicious barbecued sardines. The region is the home of tapas, so you can enjoy wonderful plates of Serrano ham, olives, roast peppers and anchovies. Try the beef, too; this is the breeding area for Spain's fighting bulls. Seasonal game is also excellent here.
Currency Euro.
Dialling codes Country code for Spain: 34. Cadíz province: 956.

DIARY

Late February/early March The International Flamenco Festival in Jerez is a riot of energetic dancing (www.flamenco-world.com). **Early April** Seville's Semana Santa, aka Easter Week, is one of Spain's greatest fiestas, with flamenco, bullfights and equestrian parades. **Early May** Jerez Horse Fair showcases Spanish horsemanship. **September** Jerez's month-long Autumn Festival covers everything from grape-treading to fireworks.

WORTH GETTING OUT OF BED FOR

Viewpoint Bar El Poniente, on the ridge above Vejer, has sweeping views down the coast to El Palmar and Conil. The ramparts of Castillo de Guzmán el Bueno in Tarifa have fine views across the Straits to north Africa.

Arts and culture NMAC is an excellent contemporary sculpture park near Vejer, featuring works by international artists (www.fundacionnmac.com).

Activities The coast has superb conditions for windsurfing and kitesurfing. You can ride through the surf on deserted beaches; ask your hotel for information on local stables. The Straits of Gibraltar are excellent for dolphin-spotting and whale-watching; FIRMM on Calle Pedro Cortés in Tarifa runs excursions (www.firmm.org). Light aircraft offer scenic flights along the coast, and daytrips to Morocco from Jerez (www.fly-in-spain.com).

Daytripper Jerez de la Frontera is famous for its dancing horses, flamenco and sherry. Follow the Thursday show at the Royal Riding School (www.realescuela.org) with a visit to one of the sherry bodegas to sample treacly oloroso and nutty amontillado.

Best beach The beautiful sandy coves at Los Caños de Meca, southwest of Vejer, were once a hippie hang-out and maintain a laidback air. Nearby El Palmar is one of the best surfing beaches around. For adrenalin sports, head for El Porro beach, northwest of Tarifa.

Something for nothing The white-sand beach at Atlanterra is the perfect place for a picnic. Even at the height of summer it's rarely crowded and, because it's relatively sheltered you won't get sand in your cucumber sandwiches. Ask at the hotel for directions.

Shopping In Tarifa, shop for Moroccan leather goods at the Bazar Hispano Arabe on Avenida de Andalucía. You can buy extremely tasty sherry from bodegas in Jerez; try Pedro Domecq (www.alvarodomecq.com) or González Byass (www.gonzalezbyass.com). Don't forget to take home some sherry vinegar as a variant on balsamic.

CAFES

On Plaza España in Vejer, **Bar Papaya** has great fruit juices and sandwiches. **La Taverna** is a good tapas option, especially for vegetarians. **La Chozita** is a creperie but has a varied menu.

BARS AND RESTAURANTS

La Chanca on El Palmar beach (956 232 214) is a restored tuna factory and a relaxing place for a lunch of fresh grilled fish. **Costigo el Cartero** is a busy *chiringuito* near Conil, popular with surfers on summer evening. **La Castillería** in the pretty village of Santa Lucia, just outside Vejer (956 451 497; summer only), is renowned for melt-in-the-mouth steaks. **Bar Juanito** on Pescadería Vieja (956 334 838) is one of the best tapas bars in Jerez. In a traditional long, low white building, **El Faro** at Calle San Felix in Cádiz (956 211 068) serves tasty seafood, including parga (red snapper) and cazón (dogfish). Beachside **Miramar** at the Hotel Arte Vida, on Carretera N340 near Tarifa (956 685 246), has tuna steaks as perfect as the sea views.

NIGHTLIFE

Flamenco is traditionally a private and spontaneous event but **La Peña Flamenca**, on Calle Rosario in Vejer, is where night-owls go every Saturday night in summer. The garden of **El Claustro** on Calle Castillo, near the church, is also a popular option in the warmer months. **La Bodeguita** on Arco de la Segur is a popular meeting place throughout the year.

Escondrijo

DESTINATION   COSTA DE LA LUZ
STYLE   MODERN MOORISH
SETTING   COBBLED VEJER

M T W T F S S M T W T F S S M T W T F **S S** M T W T F S S M T W T F S S M T W T
ESPAÑA

'We walked up steep, cobbled streets, under alabaster archways, past vast wooden doors, until we found the right one'

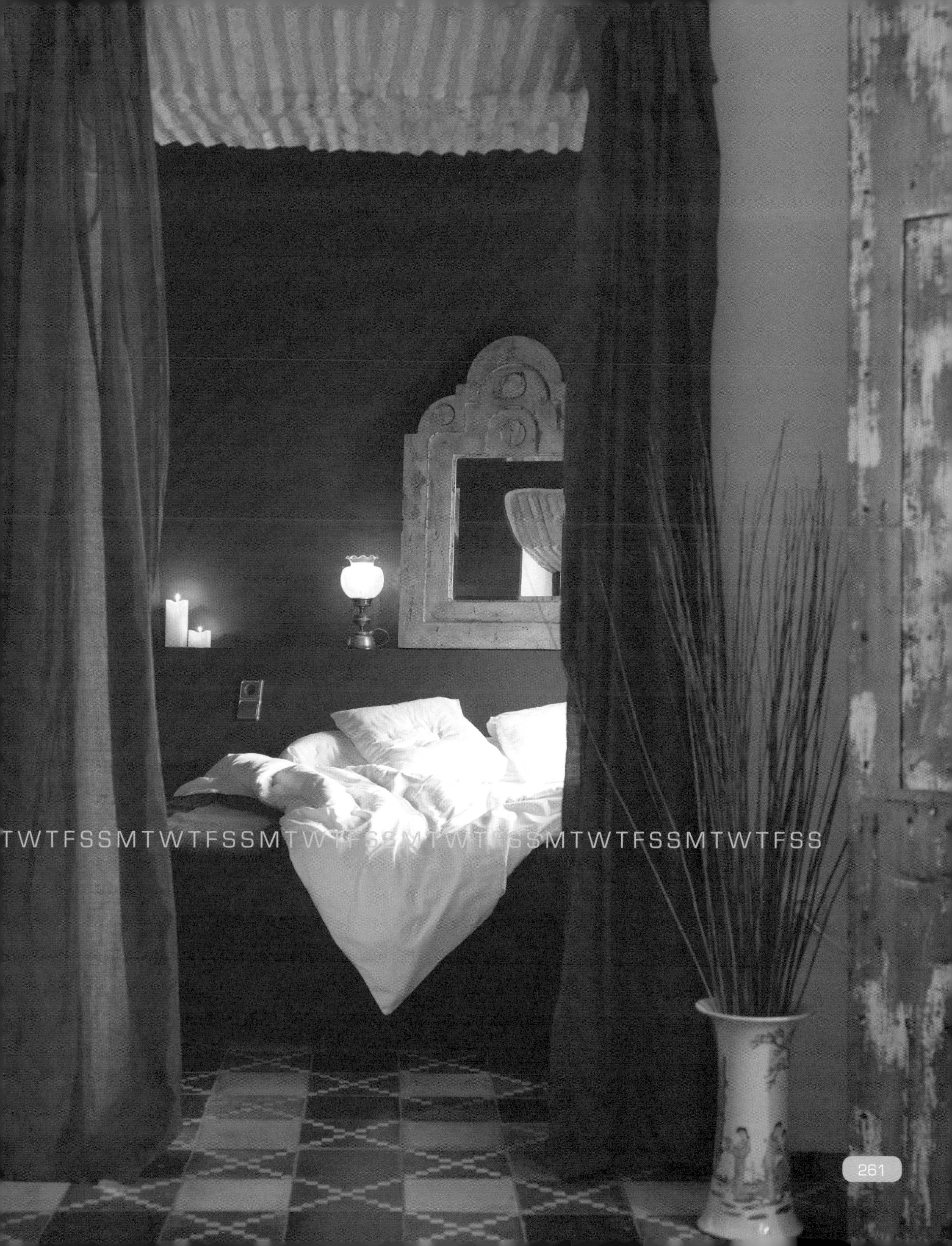
TWTFSSMTWTFSSMTWTFSSMTWTFSSMTWTFSSMTWTFSS

Arriving in any whitewashed Andalucian village, and especially one with deep, dark Moorish roots like Vejer de la Frontera's, I am always reminded of Laurie Lee, the great writer and traveller who passed this way in the Thirties. For him, it was all about being a pathfinder, a naïf with his life in a handkerchief hanging from a stick. He was invited by crinkly old women in black veils into mazy white alleyways, up marble staircases lined with Andalucian tiles, into houses barred with slender ironwork, roofs open to the sky. He paints a picture of central courtyards full of palms and potted grasses, the food simple, the beer cold, the mediaeval stone walls keeping the interior cool in the hot afternoons.

And that is exactly what you get at Escondrijo, except that it's not a crinkly old woman who leads you down the mazy alley to her home, but Tenette Ludlow, who is not crinkly at all. Or possibly her partner, Nigel Anderson, who is only a bit crinkly. They are two British refugees from urban servitude who brought what was once a chapel back from the dead in 2005, and have made it something that, depending on how you look at it, is either a tiny, stunning boutique hotel, or a private home with four rooms set aside for paying guests.

And that is the great thing about it: for as long as you are in Vejer – whether it's a month or just a night – this is your home. And it's not some shonky self-catering duplex with a view of the petrol station: it is a dream of the Spanish Golden Age. Travelling can so often be about simply observing a foreign lifestyle and environment, about witnessing historical continuity and low-key exoticism, rather than living it, that you wonder if it is worth doing at all. And then you come somewhere like Escondrijo (which means, I believe, 'hidden place'), and you know that it is.

We arrived at the village after midnight and parked in a small square where children were running round the

tiled fountain and people sat out drinking and eating. We walked up steep, cobbled streets, under alabaster archways, following our written directions past vast wooden doors, until we found the right one and pounded on it.

'Aha – we thought the plane might be late,' said Tenette, peering through the slidey spyhole in the door, before opening up. 'Can I get you a drink? Beer? Or maybe a glass of wine? I've no bread but there's ham and cheese and stuff if you're hungry.' Not only prescient and generous, but low-carb, too…

Then we followed her in through the entrance to what would soon become our own little bolthole at the end of our own white alleyway, and up the cool marble steps lined with tiles (our marble steps, our tiles) and through another, more highly polished wooden door, and we were on a four-sided balcony, iron-railed, that looked down to a stone-floored bar and dining area and up to another balcony and then to the sky.

The drama of black wrought iron against white walls looks as attractive inside as it does out in the village streets. But here there are many-coloured tiles, too, restored and relocated, and rich fabrics, and gently pulsing music. Down in the internal courtyard we had our beers and smelt the cool air and the teak oil on the furniture. It was like going to stay with one's very posh Andalucian friends – except that if it belonged to one's posh Andalucian friends it would probably still be falling down.

We spent our first two nights in a vast and dazzling room with a hammock on its mezzanine floor, and its own roof terrace with wide views over the dusty plains. We lolled on the many-cushioned chaise longue, and leafed through the home-dec magazines full of nothing as beautiful as the home we were in (such a nice feeling), and enjoyed a minibar full of icy Cruzcampo and cava. Stacked on sills were lots of good books – I sampled Don DeLillo, Banana Yoshimoto and Julio Cortázar. We snuggled down in thick, silky ↓

cotton sheets and woke to breakfast on fruit and homemade granola and yoghurt (in less lovely circumstances I have gone for weeks in Spain without seeing fruit or roughage) and then all the jam and sheep's cheese you can roll onto bread. And great coffee. And proper tea.

When we refused to leave, they hived us away in another bedroom – smaller, nookier, more Moorish still, with a similarly dramatic and exciting bathroom and an elephantine, steaming, rushing shower. We liked the roof beams in the high ceilings, and the ferns that were riffled by breezes through the windows. The suite was horizontally arranged this time, not vertically, and the little bedroom was deep red, with a central bed and wide wooden running boards.

Not that you want to stay in quite all the time. Nigel is a master of maps, and his hastily sketched diagrams directed us not only to lovely local bars and restaurants but to wide, white, windy beaches and sheltered coves not ten minutes away. To Tarifa where hundreds of lunatic kite-surfers fill the sky with their blazing sails. And to ancient Cádiz, a dazzling city climbing back now after years of decline. And to Cape Trafalgar, where Nelson whupped the French in 1805.

There is history, too, in Vejer. First a Phoenician then a Carthaginian then a Roman settlement, it became a Moorish hub, where women of the village (though Christianised these last 500 years) wore the head-to-toe black chador until as recently as the Forties. It wasn't far from here that Christopher Columbus sailed out down the river Guadalquivir to the sea. He set out to find China and, unfortunately, found a malarial swamp in the Caribbean. Some might say he shouldn't have bothered. If only he had had somewhere nice to stay, like the Escondrijo, he would probably never have left.

Reviewed by Giles Coren

NEED TO KNOW

Rooms Four; two have private terraces.
Rates €75–€130, including breakfast.
Check-out Midday, but can be flexible. There is a shower room and luggage store for use by guests after check-out.
Room service None, but rooms have drinks and snacks.
Facilities CD players; a selection of music and books.
Poolside No swimming pool.
Children No under-12s.
Hotel closed Early December to end February.
Also You will need to park in Plaza España or the main carpark, because you can't drive to the door of the hotel. Call from Plaza España when you arrive and someone will come to meet you.

IN THE KNOW

Our favourite rooms Room 1 is a spacious duplex with large verandah on the upper level.
Hotel bar There's an honesty bar.
Hotel restaurant There isn't a restaurant, but Tenette and Nigel offer a wonderful breakfast of ham and eggs, fresh fruit, coffee and home-made muesli.
Top table On the terrace, with a sea view.
Dress code As you like.

LOCAL EATING AND DRINKING

In Vejer, **Café Bar Arriate**, on Corredera, is a perfect tapas pitstop if you arrive on the late flight. For a more refined meal, walk just around the corner from Escondrijo to French restaurant **La Vera Cruz** on Calle Eduardo Shelly (956 451 683). **El Jardín del Califa** on Plaza de España (956 451 706) is part of La Califa hotel, and is a wonderfully romantic spot in which to enjoy Moroccan cuisine. For after-hours drinks, head to **Janis Joplin** and **La Bodeguita,** which are side by side on Marqués de Tamarón. **La Brasa de Sancho** on Calle Sancho IV (615 591 919) is a great brasserie, and **La Castillería** (956 451 497; only open in summer), in the neighbouring village of Santa Lucia, is renowned for its succulent steaks.

 Smith members receive a 20 per cent discount at the Hammam Andalusi, Arabic baths in Jerez.

GET A ROOM!

Use our online booking service at www.mrandmrssmith.com to check availability and make reservations. Register your Smithcard to find out about current member offers for this hotel.

Escondrijo

3 Callejón Oscuro, Vejer de la Frontera, Cádiz
+34 956 447 438
info@escondrijo.com; www.escondrijo.com

Ibiza

COASTLINE   SOCIAL-SCENE BEACHES
COAST LIFE   BOHO BARS AND SUPERSTARS

MTWTFSSMTWTFSSMTWTFSSMTWTFSSMTWTFSSMTW
ESPAÑA

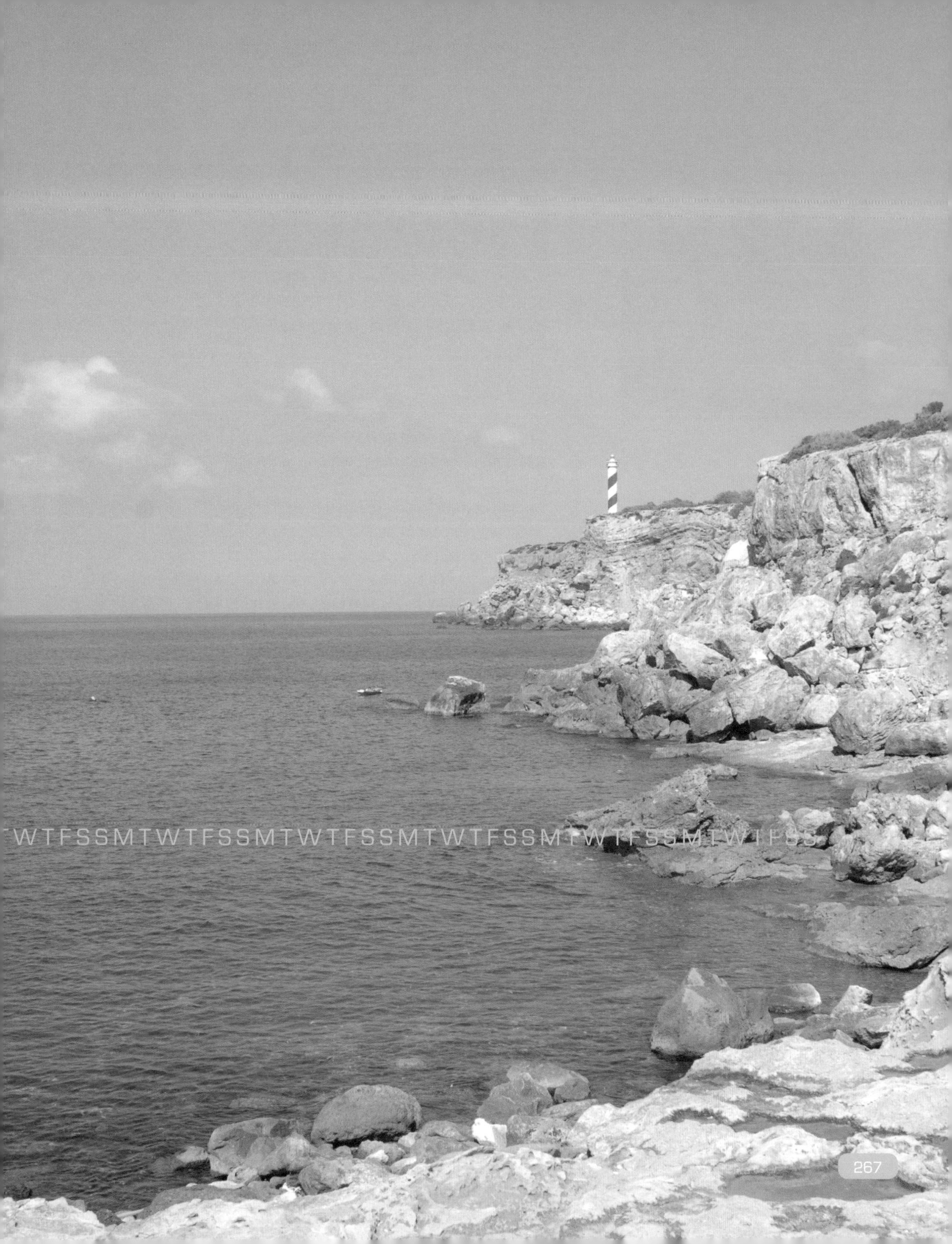
WTFSSMTWTFSSMTWTFSSMTWTFSSMTWTFSS

IBIZA

Crystal-clear waters, quiet beaches, pine forests and great seafood may not be the first things that spring to mind about Ibiza, but the legendary nightlife is only one aspect of this lovely Mediterranean island. It has long been luring a cool, cosmopolitan crew, following in the footsteps of Phoenicians, Romans, Moors and Catalans, all drawn to the tranquillity of the rural interior and the natural beauty of its lesser-known coastlines. Of course there are always the world's best clubs, and the charming narrow streets of Ibiza Town's old quarter on hand if you feel you're getting a little *too* relaxed.

GETTING THERE

Planes Lots of flights in the summer; far fewer in winter.
Boat Ferries to Barcelona (4hrs), Valencia (3hrs), Denia (2hrs) and Palma (2hrs) run regularly; see www.trasmediterranea.com for more details. The ferry to Formentera takes 25 minutes.
Automobiles Driving on the coast roads is a thrill. Go off-road in the northern pine forests with a 4x4.

DO GO/DON'T GO

May, September or October are perfect, although in summer you can find uncrowded beaches on Formentera and the north coast. The opening and closing parties in June and September are highlights of the clubbing calendar.

IRRESISTIBLY IBIZA

Ibiza sunsets have graced a thousand compilation CD covers. We love Benirràs beach with its impromptu sunset drumming on Sundays, and the secluded cliffs near Portinatx lighthouse.

LOCAL KNOWLEDGE

Taxis Try to use licensed taxis. You can flag one down if its green light is lit; prices are metered and reasonable. It costs around €10 from the airport to Ibiza Town.
Tipping culture If you experience good service, it's nice to leave up to about ten per cent, though it's not always expected.
Siesta and fiesta Some shops close for siesta between 13h30 and 17h. Restaurants don't get busy until after 21h. Head for the clubs after midnight. Of course it's also possible to party 24 hours a day throughout the summer if the urge takes you.
Packing tips Hippie chic forever; style here is always about boho luxe. Pack something glam for those indulgent evenings out.
Recommended reads *Ibiza Surprise* by Dorothy Dunnett; *The Life and Death of a Spanish Town* by Elliot Paul; *The White Island: The Extraordinary History of the Mediterranean's Capital of Hedonism* by Stephen Armstrong.
Cuisine Seafood is unsurprisingly popular. Local specialities include ray with almonds, Fideuá seafood stew with pasta, and anglerfish casserole. Fish stews can be exceptionally good, and fresh lobster and squid are delicious.
Currency Euro.
Dialling codes Country code for Spain: 34. Ibiza: 971.

DIARY

See in the **New Year** at Space, DC10 or Pacha. **February** Carnaval street parties in Ibiza Town lend a flavour of Brazil with samba parades and music. **June** The clubs come out of hibernation with a bang and set up for another long summer of excess. **24 June** The Festival of Fuegos de San Juan sees a fantastic fireworks display over Ibiza Town. **Last week of July** The five-day Ibiza Jazz Festival is held on the Santa Lucia bulwark in Ibiza Town and attracts international artists. **September** Clubbing season comes to a fitting climax with closing parties. **December** During the two weeks before Christmas there's a festive daily market at Las Dalias near San Carlos.

WORTH GETTING OUT OF BED FOR

Viewpoint Clamber up the lookout towers of Las Salinas for a lovely view of Es Vedra island.
Arts and culture The Carthaginians built the amazing salt flats, Las Salinas – especially beautiful when dotted with flamingos. Hippie culture thrives at Las Dalias Saturday market near San Carlos (summer only). Go in the morning or evening to avoid the heat and crowds.
Activities Hire a 4x4 and take to the dirt tracks that criss-cross the pine forests in the north of the island. There's limitless opportunity for sailing, water-skiing and windsurfing, too.
Daytripper Charter a speedboat or yacht and cruise to Formentera, Ibiza's quieter neighbour, where there are natural mud baths at Espalmador. Contact Danyboats (www.danyboats.com).
Best beach North-coast Cala d'en Serra near Portinatx is a well-kept secret. Aguas Blancas on the northeast coast has a great *chiringuito* serving caipirinhas and steak sandwiches.
Something for nothing The clubs put on parades in Ibiza Town on summer evenings to draw in the crowds. The strategy is simple: the more outrageously eye-catching the better.
Shopping For boho threads, pop into Ganesha on Montgri in Ibiza Town. For designer labels, try Atelier at 12 Vara de Rey. Deseo on Benirràs Beach is great for sarongs and sexy bikinis.

CAFES

El Chiringuito on Es Cavallet beach caters to a clientele accustomed to being waited on hand and foot; snacks are brought to the sunloungers. Watch the sun set at **Café Benirràs** on the celebrated beach on the north coast. **Montesol**, in the grand colonial-style hotel on Paseo Vara de Rey in the heart of Ibiza Town, is the perfect spot to sit and people-watch. For no-nonsense tapas, try **Bar Destino** in San José, opposite the church, and **Bon Lloc** on the roadside in Jesus.

BARS AND RESTAURANTS

For lunch, try the humble **Es Bigote** on Mastella beach, serving only fish stew; you'll eat like royalty – provided you can get a table. There's no phone so book in person a few days in advance. **Es Torrent** (971 802 160) is in a beautiful bay near Porroig and does excellent seafood. Book a week in advance in summer and order your fish the day before. Have lunch at the **Jockey Club** on Salinas beach (971 395 788). Bring a yacht – everyone else seems to. For dinner, **La Brasa** on Calle Pere Sala in Ibiza Town (971 301 202) serves local dishes in a courtyard garden; ask for a table on the right. **El Ayoun** in San Rafel (971 198 335) is a cool Arabian Nights-style Moroccan restaurant. San Rafel's **L'Elephant** (971 198 056) attracts a crowd every bit as stylish as its French menu. For sundowners try its rooftop bar, **Las Dos Lunes** (971 198 102), a favourite with the air-kissy set. On the road between Ibiza Town and San Jose, **KM5** (971 396 349) is decked out with Bedouin tents and loungers. Get the lowdown on the best parties over cocktails at **Base Bar** on Placa sa Riba in Ibiza Town. At the far end of the bay, **Macao Café** is another stylish hang-out.

NIGHTLIFE

The creation of **Pacha** in 1973 marked the dawn of a new era of decadence (www.pacha.com). Friday night is best. Gay night on Wednesdays at **Amnesia** is one of the best parties on the island. **Privilege** hosts the wild ways of Manumission on Mondays (www.manumission.com), when folk fork out €5,000–€10,000 for a table in the VIP area. The party continues through the day at **Space** (ww.space-ibiza.es), or at hardcore **DC10** on Mondays between 09h and 21h.

Atzaró

	IBIZA
	AFRO/ASIAN FINCA
	BACKCOUNTRY OASIS

S S
ESPAÑA

'The converted century-old farmhouse is a *típica* Ibiza finca
– all-white walls, windows and throw cushions'

TWTFSSMTWTFSSMTWTFSSMTWTFSSMTWTFSS

'Agroturismo?' Mr Smith asked, sounding slightly terrified, as we approached the hotel. 'Does this mean we'll be mucking out stables and milking the cows?' 'Don't be ridiculous', I answered, quietly eyeing the man pushing a wheelbarrow in the distance. I sure hoped we wouldn't be singing for our supper. Thankfully, at Atzaró, one of Spain's new agrotourism hotels, where a holistic approach to holidaying is the focus, you don't have to harvest your own meals.

The converted century-old farmhouse is a *típica* Ibiza finca – all-white walls, windows and throw cushions. This hotel oozes what many folk would label 'Zen' and, seriously, from the moment we arrived, we felt relaxed. Usually this takes days, if not weeks, to achieve.

We came in on the early flight, so our room wasn't ready, but Bea, the enthusiastic front-of-house (with great Ibiza-made gladiator sandals) greeted us with a smile and proceeded to show us around the grounds, which we were welcome to enjoy until our room was ready (and you knew when she used the word 'welcome', she meant it). And what grounds they are… Off the breakfast room (which serves a delectable feast until a very civilised 13h) is a large pool, surrounded by plush loungers, massage tables, and the requisite reclining daybeds. A highlight is definitely the cool-water Jacuzzi. Why hadn't we thought of this back home?

We could have stayed there, basking in the sun, listening to the Balearic beats that were playing unobtrusively in the background, but Bea urged us to explore some more. Down a few stairs, we were led to Atzaró's luxury spa, consisting of a lap pool (very chic, very skinny), several treatment rooms, a swish marble-laden changing room and, again, daybeds – one of which I instantly marked as my own (using a towel – not in the tomcat sense). Staff glided around in breezy billowing whites, and subtle signs reading 'silence, please' swayed from orange trees. I highly recommend a deep facial (they use a brush on special cases; clearly my urban pores were highly polluted). A quick look around made me realise why Kate Moss is said to have spent £30k here in one week on a spa holiday. This was pure luxury.

Ibiza is funny that way. Hedonists and hippies live harmoniously. And Atzaró seems to reflect that effortlessly. There's nothing bootcamp about this set-up: champagne and mojitos are as much a part of the schedule as yoga and massages. Yet respect for nature and the body is at the root of everything. So is balance – something most of us city-dwellers are sorely missing.

After our tour, we decided to hop in the car and do a bit of exploring. After what we thought would be a brief chat, but was in fact a 45-minute animated 'conversation' in Spanglish, Catalan, Ibicenco, with the man holding the fort at the roadside grocery shop, we made a jaunt to some local beaches he recommended. Anyone who

thinks that Ibiza's beaches are made up only of strips of burnt tourists hasn't seen the island properly. In two hours we drove through what felt like deserts, bushland and the tropics. We pondered how such a great variety of vegetation thrives here (and all so green!) in between trips to vacant beaches.

On one stop – Cala Boix – Mr S leaned over and said: 'I feel like painting – this scenery is truly inspiring.' Painting? It had been years since he'd felt so artistic. After begging El Bigote ('The Mustache') to let us into his eponymous waterfront restaurant (he said no – the same response the King of Spain received when he turned up unannounced, so we felt in good company), we returned to the hotel to be taken to our room by the lovely Bea. After passing under our own personal grapevine, we were led into a corner cove, which, complete with outdoor sofas and carved driftwood recliners, and the scent of lavender filling the air, was home for the next two days. ↓

We had a sitting room with fireplace, so cosy for winter; a large cavernous bedchamber, with a raised Japanese platform-style bed; and a well-stocked minibar, with contents including Veuve – nice touch. The ensuite, however, was the main attraction. After stepping through what felt like a secret door, we emerged in a terracotta-tiled oasis. The Asiatic/Arabic/African artwork and artefacts in here were as attractive as the ones in the lobby. The room had all the mod cons, but with scenery as good as this, they were duly ignored.

We spent a blissful day by the pool, splashing and falling in and out of consciousness, only to rally ourselves for a quick trip to Benirràs (the legendary bongo-beating sunset hang-out), and then back to the hotel for dinner. When we arrived at the outdoor restaurant, we again rejoiced at how well they do it in España. You can spend all the money in the world at some of London's top haunts, but there's nothing quite like dining alfresco for hours, amid palms and candles, fountains and statues, under the stars. The modern Catalan cuisine was delicious, the service was refreshingly unhurried (no 90-minute tables here), and the entertainment impressive. There was live opera, full orchestra during dinner, then a DJ into the wee hours.

After dinner, we took a stroll around the hotel, trying to decide how we could recreate the lily-pad pond look in our inner-city garden. More importantly, could we keep the fish alive? Sipping cocktails from the moonlit outdoor bar, we decided this was as good as it gets. I'd never have thought I'd be going to Ibiza to recharge, but that's exactly what we did. Two days here felt like two weeks – it was like a giant power nap. And I definitely plan on doing it again. Actually, forgive me the clichéd Smith sign-off but, seriously, we've already booked.

Reviewed by Taryn Ross

Rooms Ten rooms, including two suites.
Rates €240–€500, including breakfast.
Check-out Midday, but flexible depending on availability.
Room service Hot and cold snacks provided 12h–20h.
Facilities Spa, gym and sauna. Massage on request, from €60 for an hour.
Poolside Outdoor swimming pool with sun terrace in a landscaped garden.
Children Welcome. Baby cots are free; extra beds are €40 each.
Hotel closed From November until March.

Our favourite rooms Each room has a private terrace and great view, and the majority of rooms have fireplaces. The suites in the new villa enclave are bigger and away from the main building, providing extra privacy. We love room Llevant.
Hotel bar There is live music three times a week (jazz, bossa nova, world music); DJs provide the soundtrack on other evenings.
Hotel restaurant A nouvelle take on tapas and Mediterranean meat and fish sees dishes presented with finesse and elegance, at no cost to the full flavours.
Top table Anywhere in the garden is good, but a table for two by the fountain is especially lovely.
Dress code Laidback luxe.

For all your favourite Spanish lunchtime fare, head to **Restaurante Cala Xarraca** (971 33 35 18) in the cove of the same name; the fish stew is especially tasty. It's very popular, but you can sit on the beach while waiting for a table to become available. **La Paloma** in San Lorenzo (971 32 55 43) offers delicious Italian cooking at dinnertime. The ambience is so relaxed that it almost feels as though you're in someone's home. For a respite from Mediterranean flavours, the **Cardamom Club** on Camino Puig de Missa in Santa Eulalia (971 33 00 17) is a stylish Indian restaurant. Far from the madding crowd, **S'Illot** is just off the road to Portinatx (971 32 05 85), and is a great plastic-tables-and-chairs beach restaurant that specialises in paella and fish; you can build up an appetite splashing in the lovely clear waters there.

Smith members receive a bottle of cava on arrival.

Use our online booking service at www.mrandmrssmith.com to check availability and make reservations. Register your Smithcard to find out about current member offers for this hotel.

Atzaró
Carretera San Juan Km15, Santa Eulalia, Ibiza
+34 971 338 838
agroturismo@atzaro.com; www.atzaro.com

Les Terrasses

DESTINATION   IBIZA
STYLE   DISTINCTLY FRENCH
SETTING   LEAFY SANTA EULALIA

MTWTFSSMTWTFSSMTWTF **SS** MTWTFSSMTWTFSSMTWT

ESPAÑA

'The ambience here is
strictly chilled – even
the resident dog is too
blissed out to bark'

TWTFSSMTWTFSSMTWTFSSMTWTFSSMTWTFSSMTWTFSS

Les Terrasses, Ibiza, Spain

Ibiza, closing weekend parties, a clear blue sky and keys to a Renault Mégane from Hertz – life in the fast lane indeed. Pedal to the metal, 8km outside Ibiza Town on the road to Santa Eulalia and you see an Yves Klein blue stone. No, you are not hallucinating: this is the surreal marker informing you have reached the boho-riche hangout that is Les Terrasses.

Off the main road, up the dirt track and there you are. It is a haven of eight guest casitas, each built on its own individual level, and designed with its own eclectic mix of antiques, linens, fabrics and finishes. So far, so French, in an Ibicencan kind of way.

We pull up to the main house, purchased some 15 years ago by owner Françoise Pialoux. The restored finca has been rebuilt, remodelled and redesigned by the French hotelier. Terracotta flooring, whitewashed walls and eye-catching

photo art – it's all effortlessly reminiscent of a wealthy artist's home. One central space serves as reception area, lounge and dining area, with a large adjoining terrace, enabling its cosmopolitan clientele to either socialise around the family-sized tables, or pair off for more intimate conversation.

The ambience here is strictly chilled – even the resident dog is too blissed out to bark. If Ibiza's infamous nightlife is your poison, then this is the perfect antidote. As we walk out onto the terrace, beautiful French models waft past and we are welcomed by Julian, a photographer who's been using Les Terrasses as a location for a glamorous shoot, and now appears to be moonlighting as concierge, to foot his bill.

He informs us our room is still being made up, but invites us to relax around the pool with a refreshing drink. We take him up on his offer, unpack our swimwear, and enter the garden of Eden. Well, that is after Mrs Smith insists on a snoop around the boutique. Just as she's clutching enough crockery and cutlery to host a dinner party, I remind her we're missing out on sunrays. A semi-precious-stoned necklace later, I manage to prise her away. The pool is sumptuous, housed in a sunken walled botanical world of palms and tumbling bougainvillea. As we lie on the luxurious sunloungers, our hometown in Blighty suddenly feels a long way away…

Just as I'm dropping off into la-la land, Julian rocks up and informs us our room is ready. We follow him as he struggles with our suitcase, and fills us in on the highly flexible mealtimes and lack of house rules. Our casita, admittedly the most expensive of the eight, is breathtakingly beautiful. If rustic sophisticated romance is your bag, unpack it here.

We enter via our own private curtained terrace, through the mosaic-tiled bathroom, into a huge square room. The bed is massive; I'm six foot four, and even

my legs won't be dangling here. There are sofas covered in linen to recline on, and huge French doors leading to our own secluded back garden. Satellite TV, fridge, hi-fi and Internet connection take care of any need for gadgetry, but we run a bath and light some candles to create our own more laidback groove.

The bath is plenty big enough for the two of us to recline and enjoy a drop of champagne in, before liberally applying the house moisturisers to our weary limbs. Then it's time to hit the beach. Although inland, Les Terrasses is ideally located for such endeavours. Ibiza Town and the beaches to the south are a mere 15-minute drive, but we head north, to a more rural part of the island, in search of Benirràs, the legendary home to Sixties hippies and the full-moon parties. Benirràs is a beachy cove steeped in mythology. Some say it is the strongest convergence of ley lines anywhere on the planet. I say 'hippie schmippie' to that and take the plunge for a refreshing swim. before striding out to dry ↓

off with a refreshing vodka. Never mind the ley lines: this is also a land with a strong convergence of techno DJs – and the music starts as soon as the sun goes down.

Our next hankering is for some food, something we think Ibiza does better than anywhere else in Europe. We retrace our steps, back past Les Terrasses and its close proximity to the renowned eateries of Casa Colonial and Bambuddha Grove, heading for La Brassa in the heart of Ibiza Town. Excellent service and exquisitely prepared and presented food framed in a gorgeous, exotic-flower-ensconced courtyard make this my new favourite restaurant in the world.

Some slugging back of the complimentary liqueurs signals witching hour for late-night shenanigans, a facet the island has been famed for since Roman times – but for which it charges handsomely in the modern era. (If you're smart you'll get yourselves guestlisted. Throughout the summer, Friday night is Roger Sanchez at Pacha, and even if you are past your pills-and-thrills period, this or the Sunday session at Space cannot fail to impress. In Ibiza you are never too old!)

However, I am old enough to know when it's time to leave. On returning to Les Terrasses, we head straight for the most important aspect of a romantic hotel – bed. It is probably the most comfortable night's sleep I've had this year. A big bed, with a firm mattress, a generous supply of pillows, a light southerly breeze and nothing but my partner's deep sleep noises to fill the air. The sound of romance, indeed.

Reviewed by Charles Martin

NEED TO KNOW

Rooms Ten.
Rates €115–€310.
Check-out Midday, but flexible in low season.
Room service 08h30–midnight. Hard-partying guests can have breakfast at any time of the day.
Facilities Satellite TV; some rooms have DVD. The hotel has a grass tennis court.
Poolside Two outdoor pools with pergolas, sun awnings and loungers.
Children Welcome in limited numbers. Extra bed: €30.
Hotel closed From mid-November to March.

IN THE KNOW

Our favourite rooms Number 1 has a light and airy style and sunny patio. 10 has a shaded terrace and rich textured walls. Number 7 is a lovely cool shade of blue, with a warming fire for cooler months. The entrance to roomy Number 3 is through some magnificent glass doors.
Hotel bar There is no bar but guests can enjoy drinks throughout the hotel and gardens.
Hotel restaurant The menu changes daily. Cuisine is international, with a French influence; couscous is usually served on Tuesdays.
Top table Outside in the garden by the pools in the summer; we particularly liked the corner table.
Dress code Balearic boho.

LOCAL EATING AND DRINKING

Pop next door for Thai-tinged mod Med at **Casa Colonial** (971 338001), accompanied by great views. **Amalur** on Carretera San Miguel (971 314554) is one of the best restaurants on the island, serving richly flavoured Basque cooking in a charming garden. Stylish **El Ayoun** in San Rafel (971 198335) has a fantastic bar scene on Wednesdays among its bedouin tents. **Bambuddha Grove** on Santa Eulalia del Rio near San Juan (971 197510) is set in a striking Balinese *banjak* (meeting hall) filled with the aroma of its Asian-fusion cuisine. You'll need to book in advance for the ever-popular **El Olivo** on Plaza de Vila in Ibiza Town (971 300680) where fine French cuisine is served by attentive waiters. The outdoor restaurant at **Atzaró** (see page 270) is somewhere really special, only 15 minutes away. If you fancy some Italian cuisine, try **Cicale** on Carretera San Juan (971 325151) or, for a super-romantic setting and home cooking, there's **La Paloma** (971 325543), 20 minutes away in San Lorenç.

 Smith members receive a surprise gift from the hotel's shop.

GET A ROOM!

Use our online booking service at www.mrandmrssmith.com to check availability and make reservations. Register your Smithcard to find out about current member offers for this hotel.

Les Terrasses
Carretera de Santa Eulalia Km1, Ibiza
+34 971 33 26 43
info@lesterrasses.net; www.lesterrasses.net

MALLORCA

Mallorca

MTWTFSSMTWTFSSMTWTFSSMTWTFSSMTWTFSSMTWT
ESPAÑA

TWTFSSMTWTFSSMTWTFSSMTWTFSSMTWTFSS

MALLORCA

The biggest of the Baleares, Mallorca is a varied surprise: a rural patchwork of wheat fields, olive groves and tranquil villages; a cosmopolitan destination with well-edited boutiques and white-cube galleries; a series of beautiful beaches for party people and peace-seekers alike. Palma is the island's self-assured capital, where yachts and cocktails cohabit happily with ancient winding streets beneath the towering pink-hued Gothic cathedral. Drive for an hour, and you can escape the 21st century on the dramatic north coast or among the Serra de Tramuntana mountains. The hilltop village of Deià, with its literary credentials and an insouciant elegance, epitomizes Mallorquin glamour – the original boho chic.

GETTING THERE

Planes Palma airport is 10km from the capital, with numerous flights year-round.
Trains Take the vintage electric train from Palma to Sóller, then enjoy the scenic route from there to Port de Sóller by tram.
Boats There are several ferry services to the mainland: Barcelona (4hrs); Valencia (6hrs). See www.trasmediterranea.es for details.
Automobiles Driving is a breeze on this island, and roads are well signposted. The mountain roads through the jagged Serra de Tramuntana are spectacular.

DO GO/DON'T GO

The temperature rarely dips below 30ºC in summer, when the island gets very busy. Autumn is less hectic and the water is at its warmest. In winter and spring, Mallorca is mild, sunny and peaceful.

MARVELLOUSLY MALLORCA

The 10th-century Arab baths in Palma are a rare reminder of the Moorish period of Mallorca's history. There's no bathing these days, but you can see the underground chambers and relax in the flower-filled courtyard.

LOCAL KNOWLEDGE

Taxis Cabs are cheap and easy to find in Palma itself, but you're better off hiring a car if you plan to do any longer journeys around the island.
Tipping culture Mallorcans don't usually tip. A few euros is sufficient.
Siesta and fiesta Banks close at 14h. Most bars and cafés open at lunchtime and stay open until midnight or later. It generally doesn't get busy at restaurants before 21h, or before 23h at bars and clubs.
Packing tips Take a Mallorquin phrasebook with you and try out a few words of the island's mother tongue along with your Spanish.
Recommended reads *A Winter in Majorca* by George Sand; *Snowball Oranges* by Peter Kerr.
Cuisine Snack on pa amb oli, the Mallorquin take on bruschetta. Other specialities include lubina a la sal (salt-baked sea bass), slow-roast lamb, and frito Mallorquin – deep-fried offal and vegetables. If you want to get hands-on, Jay Ciccarelli offers excellent cookery courses (971 619320) at C'an Torna near Es Porles.
Currency Euro.
Dialling codes Country code for Spain: 34. Balearics: 971.

DIARY

16 January The festival of San Sebastián brings Palma onto the streets with barbecues and live bands. **March–April** During Santa Semana, aka Easter Week, ghostly, hooded penitents, representing the island's 50 brotherhoods, parade through the streets of Palma. **Late July–early August** The Copa del Rey is arguably the most important and glamorous yachting regatta in the Med. **2 August** Good-natured street battles in Pollença recreate historic wars between Moors and Christians. **Late September** Festa d'es Vermar is Binissalem's foremost wine festival – go with the flow.

Viewpoint There are unparalleled views over Palma from the fortress of Castell de Bellver. Alternatively, drift sedately above the landscape in a balloon (www.mallorcaballoons.com).
Arts and culture The imposing Gothic cathedral, Sa Seu, dominates Palma's skyline. For modern-day eye candy, the Es Baluard museum, on Plaça Porta de Santa Catalina, has exhibitions showcasing works by Picasso and Dalí (www.esbaluard.org). There's also a great gallery and sculpture trail on an estate in Malpas, near Alcudia (www.fundacionjakober.org).
Activities Drive the twisting mountain roads of the Serra de Tramuntana between Lluc and Pollença. There are beautiful walks around the glamorous village of Deià. You can go canyoning and mountain biking in the interior, or sailing and diving on the coast. Adrenalin junkies can contact Sloane Helicopters (www.sloanemallorca.com), for tours of the island.
Daytripper To find the best beaches and remoter coastal stretches, hire a motorboat or a yacht. Contact Marítimo Yachts (971 707669; www.maritimoyachts.com).
Best beach Pine-fringed Platja de Formentor near the island's northern tip, and white-sand Es Trenc, on the east coast, are idyllic. Puro beach in Palma is best for hip Riviera-style lounging.
Something for nothing Take in the dizzying views from the clifftops near Cap de Formentor.
Shopping In Palma, a browse of the chic Chocolat Factory on Plaça d'es Mercat (www.chocolatfactory.com) is worth it just for the samples. Don't miss Corner on Paseo del Borne, and Custo on Calle San Miguel, which stock a wide range of designer brands. Fleamarket lovers should visit Rastrillo on Avenida Gabriel Alomar I Villalonga, where a market is held on Saturday mornings, 08h–14h. Perlas Majorica, in Avenida Jaume III in Palma, has a fine selection of Mallorcan cultured pearls.

Palma's museum café at **Es Baluard** on Plaça Porta de Santa Catalina is a great spot for a salad at lunchtime, under the shade of a parasol, overlooking the marina. **Ca'n Joan de s'Aigo** on Calle de Ca'n Sanc has served fluffy pastries since the 17th century.

In Palma's Paseo Mallorca, Claudia Schiffer's favourite, **La Cuchara** (971 710000), is great for organic tapas. **La Bóveda** on Carrer Boteria (971 714863), is also tapas heaven. Elegant **Caballito de Mar** on Passeig Sagrera (971 721074) is great for seafood on the terrace. In Soller, ask for a cliffside table at **Bens d'Avall** on Carretera Soller-Deià (971 632381), which is renowned for its rich Mediterranean cuisine. **Es Faro** (971 633752) has decent local dishes and amazing views over Port de Sóller. **El Olivo** at La Residencia in Deià (971 639392) offers fine dining in a romantic setting under the olive trees. Dress up – shorts are not allowed. **Es Cellar** in Petra (971 561056) is a rustic bodega serving traditional game dishes. **Casa Manolo** in Salinas (971 649130) serves the best lobster stew on the island.

Palma is the heart of Mallorca's nightlife. Cliffside **Abraxas** at 42 Paseo Marítimo has great views of the glitzy gin palaces in the marina. Top-name DJs play throughout the summer. It also opens in winter, Thursday to Saturday. **113**, on Ca'n Barbara, is a chilled-out, intimate club, popular with Palma's most stylish set.

Can Simoneta

DESTINATION   MALLORCA
STYLE   21ST-CENTURY FARMHOUSE
SETTING   VERDANT CLIFFTOP

MTWTFSSMTWTFSSMTWTF S S MTWTFSSMTWTFSSMTWT

ESPAÑA

'The hardest decision we have to face is whether to clamber
into the Jacuzzi or walk down to the monk's pool'

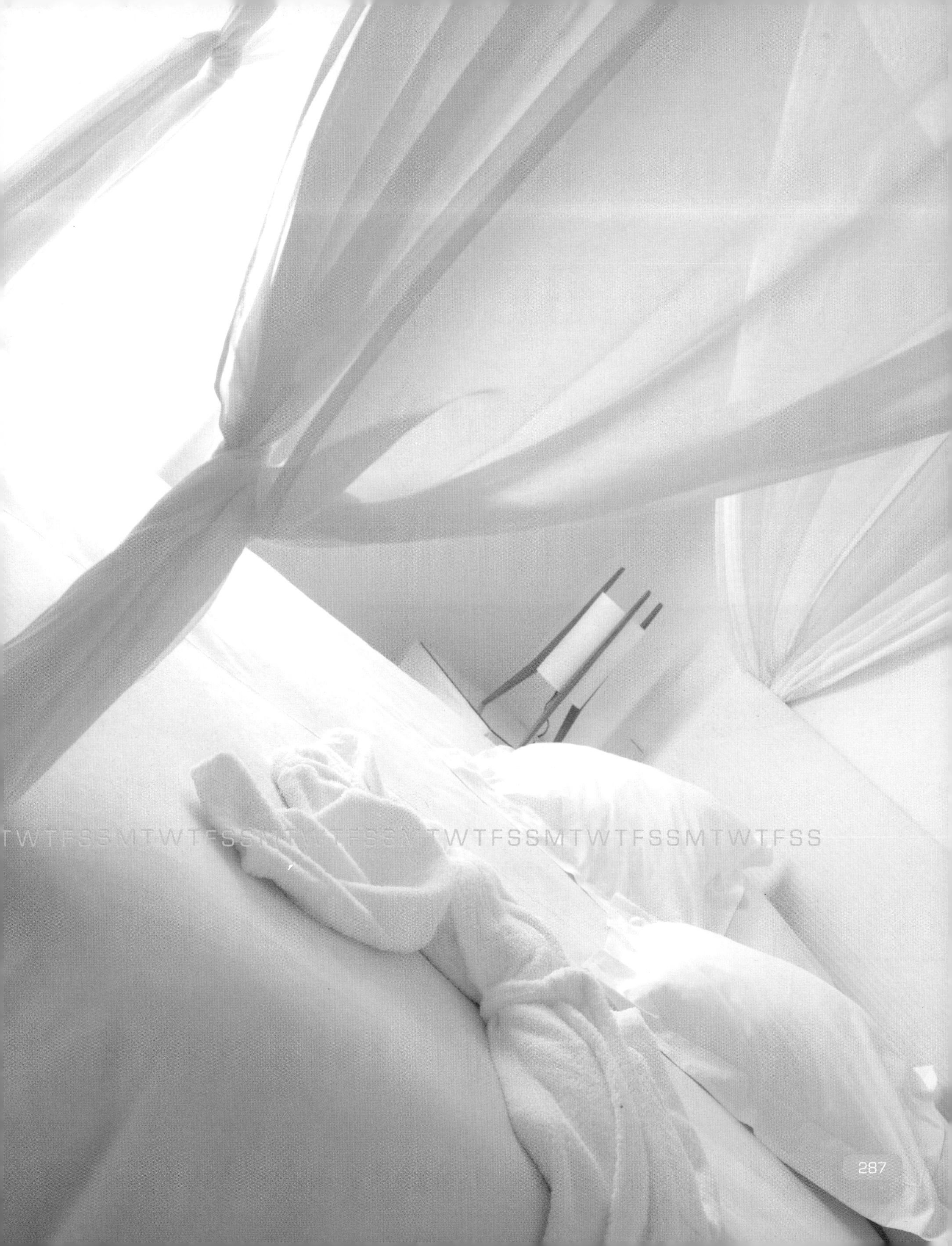
TWTFSSMTWTFSSMTWTFSSMTWTFSSMTWTFSSMTWTFSS

We found out before we set off for Spain that our clifftop hotel, Can Simoneta, was originally built well over a century ago, as a house for a monk whose doctor had prescribed a course of seawater treatments for some unspecified medical condition. We realised a couple of things immediately: 19th-century monks would not be impressed by the NHS, and our weekend in Mallorca was going to be a profoundly peaceful affair. After all, a poorly monk is likely to live in a nice tranquil spot, rather than heading for the noisy, bustling charms of somewhere like Magaluf.

We were right, about the second thing anyway. This was one brother who knew how to choose his location. Just an hour's drive from Palma airport, we find ourselves standing on the edge of a cliff, gazing and sighing at the spectacular views over the Mediterranean towards the island's smaller sister, Menorca. It is the perfect place, if you're so inclined, to contemplate the wonders of God's creation – or, in my case, to get up to some thoroughly un-monkish frolics with my own Mr Smith.

That monk must have had a pretty good time here, too. The house is way up on the cliff, and a staircase was cut out of the rock so that he could saunter down and take the waters in an amazing, secluded bath – like a natural Jacuzzi – carved straight out of the rocks on the beach at the foot of the stairs.

The hotel itself consists of two imposing stone houses that were lovingly restored and refurbished in 2004. One of the houses is much closer to the clifftop than the other, and this is the one to ask for. Its suites are exceptional, with muslin-draped four-poster beds, large windows to let in the summer breeze and, of course, those views over the sea. There is great variety of rooms in the second building, including one which is smaller and darker, with a very small window

(presumably as a defence against the heat). Ask for either a terrace or a high room with big windows if you're in this house.

All the rooms have satellite TV and an Internet connection, although we wouldn't have minded if they didn't. Of course there are those who want to check emails or watch the news, but in a place as calm and secluded as Can Simoneta, modern communications can feel like an unnecessary addition. That said, our bathroom, always a good indicator of the quality of a hotel, is thoroughly modern and immaculate. And if we needed any help getting to sleep, the sound of running water from the fountain outside our window would prove more effective than Temazepam.

Not that we spend much time inside, anyway. In the morning, we prescribe some seawater therapy for ourselves, on a very nice beach a short walk away. Unusually for the Mediterranean in high season, and

Mallorca in particular, the pale sands are blissfully uncrowded. Back at the hotel, we spend the afternoon beside the pool, lounging on the rattan chairs all decked with the whitest of white linen cushions, seeking refuge from the sun and drinking in the view (as well as a few cocktails).

The hardest decisions we have to face during our stay are whether to have a massage in the hotel or under the pine trees overlooking the sea, whether to clamber into the Jacuzzi at the top of the cliff or walk down the stairs to the 'monk's pool' at the bottom, and whether to take advantage of the yoga classes or simply lounge about in one of the hammocks hanging in the hotel's extensive and beautiful gardens. There are plenty of other activities to do in the surrounding area, should we wish to venture away from our clifftop haven: farms and caves to explore, the mediaeval tower at Canyamel that looks so beautiful in the distance, churches and prehistoric settlements. After less than 24 hours in ↓

the hotel, though, we are so relaxed that just imagining doing these things seems far too strenuous. Of course, we end up doing nothing, and it's absolutely lovely.

We do devote a little bit of mental energy to wondering why more of the hotel facilities are not closer to the edge of the cliff, rather than 50 metres inland. It seems odd. Are they worried about erosion? Did the sickly monk also suffer from vertigo? No – the answer lies in the hotel's location on the margins of a nature reserve. Can Simoneta has a very special position on the coastline, and apparently it's a miracle they even got planning permission for the pool.

Though it is the location that sets it apart from similar boutique hideaways, the interior of the hotel is superb, too: elegant and simple. The staff are all extremely professional and discreet, and the peaceful restaurant serves delicious, refined Mediterranean food (it has to be excellent, we decide, to match the view from the terrace). For anyone looking to escape the natter and nonsense of the everyday and unwind in a spectacular, peaceful and soul-soothing environment, Can Simoneta is a very fine retreat indeed. In fact, you could say it's just what the monk's doctor ordered.

Reviewed by Alison Chow

NEED TO KNOW

Rooms 18, including five suites.
Rates €245–€410, including breakfast.
Check-out Midday, but flexible.
Room service 24 hours, but limited after hours.
Facilities Restaurant, massage area, Internet access. Direct access to the sea by a curved stairway carved into the cliff.
Poolside There's a large pool and clifftop Jacuzzi.
Children There is a 50 per cent discount on rates for one child and 75 per cent for a second. Because the hotel is close to a cliff edge, parents may consider it unsafe for very young children.
Also The hotel has private access to a secluded cove with bathing pool cut out of the rock. Hotel guests get a ten per cent discount at three local golf courses.

IN THE KNOW

Our favourite rooms Most importantly, ask for a sea view. Two of the suites and two of the doubles have terraces. Otherwise, recommended rooms are 4, 7, 21 and 22.
Hotel bar Snuggle up with drinks on the sofas under the awning, or struggle down the steps to the monk's pool with your drinks.
Hotel restaurant The restaurant has views over the bay of Canyamel, and specialises in Mediterranean dishes. If the weather is good, get a table on the terrace.
Top table Both indoors and outside, the corner tables are best. The hotel can arrange a secluded dinner for two perched on the cliff.
Dress code Relaxed, but dress for dinner.

LOCAL EATING AND DRINKING

Ses Rotges on Cala Ratjada (971 563 108) is Michelin-starred, with a dining area out in the garden during summer. **Renaissance** in Capdepera (971 563 713) is a romantic restaurant serving great French cuisine. Enjoy fresh fish at **Can Maya** in Cala Ratjada (971 564 035); see if you can get a table on the terrace looking over the small harbour. The best beach restaurant, or *chiringuito*, for lunch is at nearby Cala Torta, but the one in Canyamel is also great. Set in a beautifully restored old mill, **Es Moli Den Bou** on Calle Sol in Sant Llorenç (971 569 663) is a great Michelin-starred option for Mallorquin cuisine.

Smith members receive a bottle of Mallorquin wine and a basket of fruit, as well as traditional Mallorquin jam and liqueurs on departure.

GET A ROOM!

Use our online booking service at www.mrandmrssmith.com to check availability and make reservations. Register your Smithcard to find out about current member offers for this hotel.

Can Simoneta
Carretera Arta a Canyamel, Capdepera, Mallorca
+34 971 816 110
info@cansimoneta.com; www.cansimoneta.com

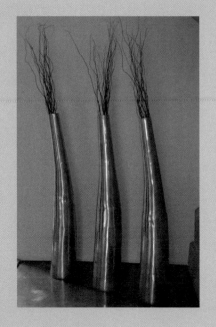

'Vast olive-oil presses
on which the monks
once toiled line the
walls of a candlelit bar'

Son Brull Hotel and Spa

DESTINATION   MALLORCA
STYLE   BALEARIC SPA RESORT
SETTING   UPSCALE POLLENÇA

MTWTFSSMTWTFSSMTWTF**SS**MTWTFSSMTWTFSSMTW
ESPAÑA

293

Foolishly, our hearts sank as we approached the austere-looking walls of Son Brull – it just seemed so far from our mental picture of design-hotel comfort. Little did we realise: the monks who once inhabited this converted 12th-century monastery/farm would be amazed at the heights of relaxation achieved by the sybarites occupying their old home.

The vast wooden olive-oil presses on which the monks once toiled line the walls of a candlelit bar scattered with low-lying Scandinavian chairs. Beyond the courtyard where horses were once kept, an infinity pool gently overflows. Further inside, down stone-cut steps, nestles the quiet haven of the spa and the greenish waters of a connected indoor and outdoor pool. A religious experience, perhaps, but not the kind that the brotherhood had in mind. After the hour-long trip from Palma airport on the twisty Mallorcan roads, Son Brull proved itself to be exactly the oasis we'd dreamed of.

The beaming receptionist, whose black outfit matched the carpeted stairs, took us to our room. A vision of discerning good taste, with little wooden shutters on the tiny windows, and views over the gardens, the room had tons of space for unpacking and general lounging on the Scandinavian oak chairs, as well as a Bang & Olufsen TV. A vast bed with silky cotton sheets, linen throws and white sofas kept the room feeling cool (teamed with top-notch air-conditioning). And in the bathroom with brushed-concrete floor, double sinks, shower room and 'therapy' bath with water jets, there were enough bottles of potions for us to have our own in-room spa experience (although there are massages and facials on offer in the sauna rooms here, too).

Just as folk back home would be contemplating crumpets and tea, we were assured that we'd arrived in time for lunch, which is served until 18h30 (don't you love the Spanish timetable?). Some Spanish guests obviously needed all the time

over lunch they could get, we thought, as we watched them neck-deep in glasses of Armagnac with their coffee. Beneath a reed screen that blocked out the overhead sun, we ate *pa amb oli* (local bread with Serrano ham and Mahón cheese) washed down with cold beers, enjoying the breeze and views of ancient olive trees. Shady areas beckoned for a siesta, scattered with sculptures and scented flower beds planted with giant blue agapanthus, roses and jasmine; it was time to let out a deep breath and ponder if there was any need to leave the hotel at all over the weekend.

There are several secluded spaces at Son Brull that allow you to get away from people, so you never feel crowded, and the walls of the rooms are of a solid mediaeval thickness that leaves you wondering if there's anyone else staying in the hotel at all. With an all-important breeze and view of the landscape, the cerulean-blue mosaic tiled indoor/outdoor pool is the centre point of the hotel, right next door to

the restaurant. In order that you never feel too scrutinised by other guests, there is a raised area with enough double beds covered in vast towels for everyone. White curtains can be drawn around your bed, to blow in the breeze in a tantalising *Far Pavilions* style, though they are, of course, intended in more of a Balearic, chill-out way. At night, candles are lit around the pool, and more cushions scattered around the decking.

Clearly, some of the guests summon the energy to make the trip to clubs like Abraxas, Virtual Club or Tito's, and emerge the following afternoon for a bed by the pool. But the majority of residents are plugged into their iPods or novels, sipping cordials in a daze. We had a toddler (a bit of a challenge, with the infinity pool acting like a magnet), although, amazingly, no one batted an eyelid when she shouted at birds and laughed loudly into the quiet. The hotel is really an ideal place for romantic couples – of which there were many – and we ↓

grabbed the chance to join their ranks by hiring a babysitter for an entire afternoon.

Apart from seeing and being seen on one of Palma's hippest of dancefloors, the other temptation to lure you away from the hotel are the beaches. Cala de Sant Vicenç is a short drive from the hotel and is one of the best beaches on the island. We swam in the bay and dozed on the sunloungers, but in such midsummer heat we only lasted a few hours before deciding that the hotel's cool showers and on-tap waiters were much more appealing than feeling sticky, hot and in need of somewhere to eat.

The hotel's restaurant is outdoors in good weather (which is most of the time), otherwise meals are served indoors among the huge old olive presses. The evening menu is modern, with plenty of fashionable froth flourishes and adventurous combinations, all very well presented. It is one of the most sought-after restaurants in Mallorca and attracts lots of Spaniards, guaranteeing, in turn, an effervescent atmosphere.

As I tucked into excellent marinated mackerel, chilled almond soup and cottage cheese mousse from the *menu degustación*, I had to raise a toast to all those abstemious monks who once toiled within these walls. Son Brull is a beautifully converted building, with every comfort refined far beyond the point of necessity: this was a discipline we could happily prescribe ourselves.

Reviewed by Jo Craven

NEED TO KNOW

Rooms 23.
Rates €248–€743.
Check-out Midday.
Room service 24 hours: extensive menu available until 23h.
Facilities Spa with sauna and massage room (book treatments in advance), tennis court, B&O audiovisuals, CD and DVD library, gastronomic events in low season, including wine/olive oil tastings. The hotel can arrange boat, yacht and bicycle rental.
Poolside Connected indoor and outdoor pools with massage hydrojets, an indoor relaxation area and outdoor sun terrace.
Children Babysitting and baby-listening services; cots and extra beds provided at an extra charge.
Hotel closed December and January.

IN THE KNOW

Our favourite rooms Any with a view on the pool side of the house, as high up as possible.
Hotel bar Drinks available until midnight in the former oil-pressing room, where old beams and a well make an attractive centrepiece. In summertime, Thursday is jazz night, Saturday is more relaxed.
Hotel restaurant 365 is the chic, formal-ish fine-dining restaurant, with black banquettes, white-clothed tables and a gold-leaf ceiling. It's modern Mallorquin, nouvelle-ish food: don't expect large portions. The menu has an emphasis on local ingredients, particularly seafood. There's also a snack menu and tables by the pool.
Top table Outside is best in summer.
Dress code Spanish chic, especially for dinner.

LOCAL EATING AND DRINKING

Clivia on Avenida Pollença (971 533 635) in Pollença old town is great for dinner. It is very traditional and brightly lit, serving fresh produce and succulent fish. **Cavall Bernat** in Hotel Cala Sant Vicenç (971 530 250), also owned by Son Brull, is a fine-dining room. **Puro Beach** in Palma (971 744 744) is great for lunch or cocktails. Book early if you'd like a table or lounger during the day. To idle away an afternoon, sit outside one of the many cafés on the central square in Pollença old town and watch the world go by.

 Smith members receive the classical CD *Insula Poetica* by Joan Valent upon arrival.

GET A ROOM!

Use our online booking service at www.mrandmrssmith.com to check availability and make reservations. Register your Smithcard to find out about current member offers for this hotel.

Son Brull Hotel and Spa
Carretera Palma, Pollença, Mallorca
+34 971 535 353
info@sonbrull.com; www.sonbrull.com

● RONDA

Ronda

COUNTRYSIDE   TIMELESS GORGE
COUNTRY LIFE   SLEEPY VILLAGE PACE

MTWTFSSMTWTFSSMTWTFSS **SS** MTWTFSSMTWTFSSMTWT
ESPAÑA

RONDA

Set high on a bluff and protected by the dizzying El Tajo gorge, the mountain fastness of Ronda was one of the last strongholds of Moorish Spain. The spectacular Puente Nuevo now spans the ravine, but the almost impregnable town retains a sense of seclusion, far removed from the razzmatazz of the nearby Mediterranean coast. The dramatic sierras still guard a traditional way of life: slumbering pueblos blancos or 'white villages'; valleys of fruit orchards, olive groves and vineyards; ancient forests of cork oak trees. Ronda, with its whitewashed houses and winding streets, epitomises a land little changed since the Moors ruled these mountains.

GETTING THERE

Planes The nearest airports are Málaga (1hr), Seville (2hrs) and Gibraltar (2hrs). Expect delays at the border with Gibraltar.
Trains There is a daily morning train to Málaga (1.5hrs; no Sunday service), returning in the evening.
Automobiles It's worth hiring a car to explore the mountains and pueblos blancos, or to make the run down to the beaches and nightlife of Marbella.

DO GO/DON'T GO

Ronda attracts daytrippers from the Costa, especially in the height of summer, but after 14h the town returns to its more peaceful self. Spring and autumn are warm and tranquil. Winter weather can be changeable in the mountains.

REMARKABLE RONDA

The beautiful Palacio Mondragón was once the residence of Ronda's Islamic rulers. Extensively added to over the centuries, it has exquisite water gardens teetering precariously on the edge of the precipice. Walk there along the ridge and Calle Tenorio, by way of the Plaza de Maria Auxiliadora, to enjoy the best views.

LOCAL KNOWLEDGE

Taxis Cabs are cheap, but not always metered. Those that aren't should carry an official book of rates, so check with your driver before you set off. Taxis display a green 'libre' notice or green light at night.
Tipping culture Ten per cent in restaurants is appreciated; otherwise a few euros with drinks or tapas is sufficient.
Siesta and fiesta Banks and shops close between 14h and 17h during the week and at 14h on Saturdays. Restaurants don't even begin to get busy until well after 21h.
Packing tips Take warm layers for the winter months, when the weather is changeable. Bring good walking boots for the mountains.
Recommended reads *For Whom the Bell Tolls* by Ernest Hemingway; *Driving Over Lemons* by Chris Stewart.
Cuisine The cooking in the interior of Andalucía is dominated by Serrano mountain ingredients, with some subtle Moorish influences. Oxtail is a particularly tasty local speciality, along with smoked ham, beef with artichokes and kidneys in Jerez sherry. The mountains also produce excellent game dishes.
Currency Euro.
Dialling codes Country code for Spain: 34. Malaga province: 952.

DIARY

Semana Santa aka Easter Week sees colourful processions by the town's religious fraternities. **20–23 May** Feria de la Reconquista celebrates the defeat of the Moors with a series of noisy parades, as well as a cattle market.
First week of September The Pedro Romero Fair is the largest in Ronda, with flamenco and folklore festivals, as well as parades and bullfights featuring 18th-century period costume. Tickets are scarce and tend to sell out quickly, so book early, from July onwards (+34 954 503 794).

Viewpoint The best views of the plunging 100-metre-deep El Tajo gorge are from the Puente Nuevo and the Paseo de Blas Infante next to the bullring.

Arts and culture The neoclassical bullring, where the Romero family defined modern bullfighting in the 18th century, is one of the oldest and prettiest in Spain. Visit the museum during late afternoon when there are fewer tourists in town.

Activities The best mountain walks and off-road-vehicle routes are around the picturesque village of Grazalema. There are great views from the 1,350-metre Puerto de las Palomas (Pass of the Doves). La Fuente de la Higuera's sister hotel, Rise, offers a range of courses, from yoga to cookery (www.rise-resort.com). Pangea offers outdoor activities, including kayaking and mountain climbing. You can cycle downhill to the coast through the Sierra de las Nieves and they will drive you back up (www.pangea-ronda.com).

Daytripper Marbella is an hour (and a world) away from the villages in the mountains. The most stylish spot on the Costa del Sol, it has been reborn as a players' destination, with old-school glam, exclusive boutiques and unashamedly glitzy nightlife. Don't miss the winding streets of the Old Town, where you can still feel the faint echo of the mountain hideaways.

Perfect picnic The old Henderson railway from Ronda is also a beautiful walking trail with many beautiful picnic spots – and you can catch the train back.

Something for nothing There are several spectacular drives through mountain scenery in the area. The roads to Grazalema, El Bosque and Setenil are some of the best.

Shopping Options in Ronda are limited. For chic shopping, Puerto Banus on the coast is a honeypot of boutiques and super-yachts.

And... Orson Welles' ashes were scattered here, some say inside the bullring.

CAFÉS

There are some fine cafés in Plaza de Carmen Abela. Tiny **Bar Maestros** on Carrera del Espinel is excellent. Start the day with churros (fried doughnut pastry) and hot chocolate.

BARS AND RESTAURANTS

The Michelin-starred **Tragabuches** on Calle José Apartado (952 190 291) is Ronda's most stylish restaurant, decked out in soothing pastels and offering a wonderful, indulgent 16-course tasting menu. **Pedro Romero** on Vírgen de la Paz (952 871 110) is the place for local favourites such as rabo de toro (oxtail), cooked with onions and tomatoes. Try **Almocábar** on Calle Ruedo Alameda (952 875 977) for tasty traditional dishes. Diagonally opposite, **Casa Maria** (952 876 212) has no fixed menu, but its tables under the laurel trees are always busy with Rondeños. **Casa Mateos** on Calle Jerez is a traditional tapas bar serving delicious plates of Serrano ham and Spanish cheeses.

NIGHTLIFE

For glitz and glamour you'll need to head to Marbella down on the coast, where you'll find international-style lounge bars such as the **Buddha Bar** on Avenida del Mar. In Ronda, **El Choque** on Calle Espíritu Santo is a lively venue that often hosts live music and film screenings on its panoramic terrace. There are several popular bars clustered around Plaza del Socorro and Calle Los Remedios. **Que Me Dices** on Calle Jerez has a great vibe.

La Fuente de la Higuera

DESTINATION	RONDA
STYLE	TRAD ANDALUCIAN
SETTING	CLOSE BUT NO COSTA

M T W T F S S M T W T F S S M T W T F **S S** M T W T F S S M T W T F S S M T W T

ESPAÑA

'It is a rather stately converted
18th-century olive mill, set into
a hillside with views over to
Ronda and the rugged sierras'

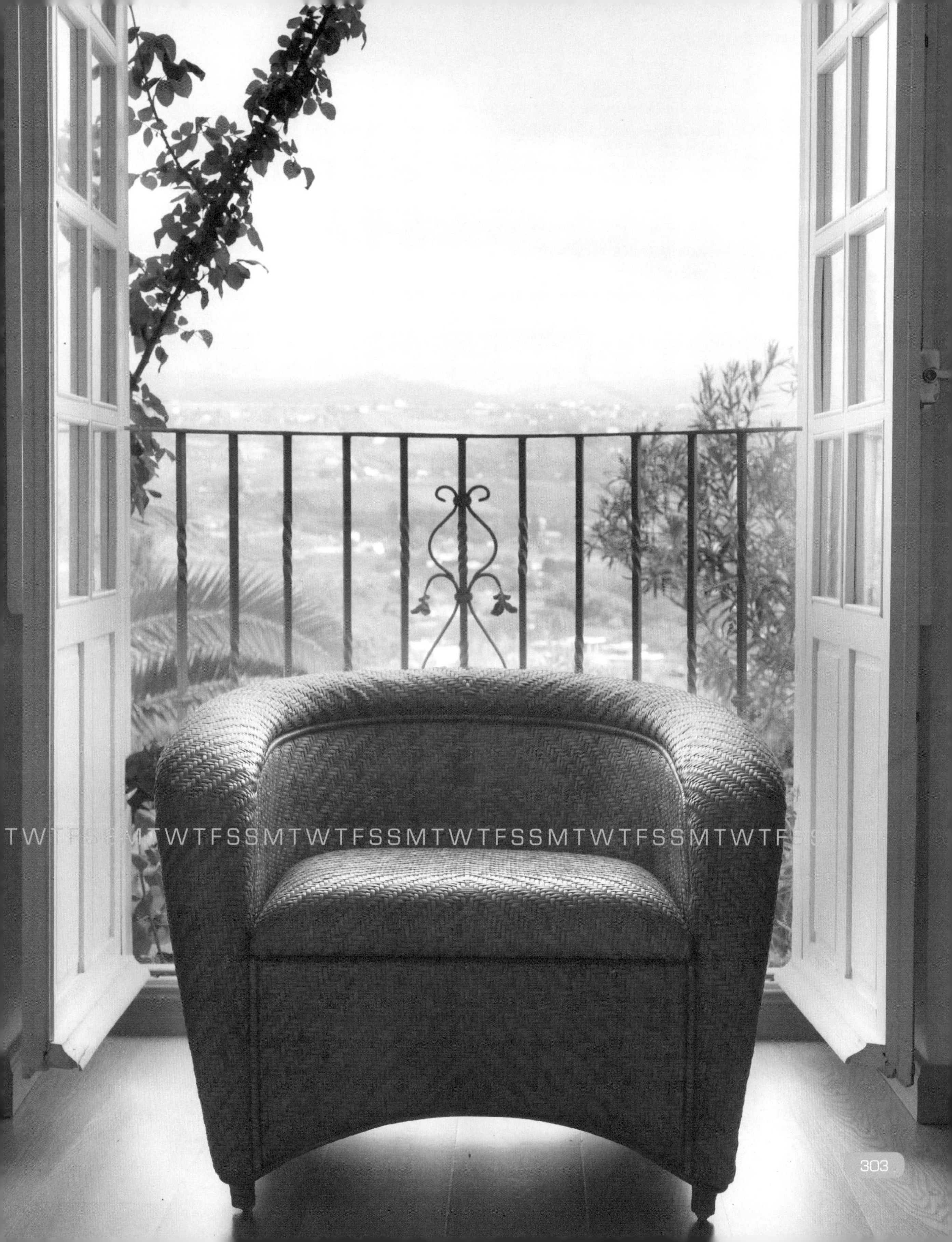
TWTFSSMTWTFSSMTWTFSSMTWTFSSMTWTFS

La Fuente de la Higuera, Ronda, Spain

While it doesn't seem quite right to start my tale of our stay in a charming and romantic old mill, nestling on an Andalucian hillside, with anything but a celebration of what made it such a wonderful weekend away, allow me a few words on Malaga, just so I can get it out of the way. Not the ideal gateway to Spain for the discerning traveller, it is a concrete theme park, with drink-all-you-can bars and eat-all-you-can restaurants fronting a burn-all-you-can beach. But there is good news, too. You soon realise that though this high-rise hell may be many miles long, it's only about four blocks deep. Head inland and the tourist trap soon vanishes. It never ceases to amaze me how close the beauty and character of real Spain is to the most overdeveloped, soulless resorts. Most of our drive from Malaga airport to Ronda was through the rugged, glorious – and almost entirely deserted – landscape of southern Andalucía.

I should also take this opportunity to mention Mrs Smith's new toy: a satnav system. This Mr Smith had long decried these devices, saying that they were for those too stupid to read maps. Reader, I was wrong. We used to fight like cat and dog over directions. No longer: now we cruise about in harmony, navigated and reassured by that strange RP voice emanating from the speakers.

Modern technology got us to Hotel la Fuente de la Higuera in under an hour, and we were instantly smitten. It is a rather stately converted 18th-century olive mill, set into a hillside with views over to Ronda and the surrounding rugged sierras. The gardens are just as impressive: a soft, lush contrast to the craggy mountains around them, forming a well-watered oasis around a swimming pool. The glorious setting meant our hopes were high for a fabulous room, too, and we were not disappointed. We walked into a beautifully cool, calm living room with an eclectic mix of furniture, including comfy wicker chairs and antique leather loungers. Curiously, there is also a fireplace – curious because it's difficult to imagine a toasty fire when it's

40°C outside. We were assured that t does snow here in the winter. Further into our suite we found a generous bedroom, with canopied beds and doors opening onto a lavender-filled garden, and a huge bathroom, whose cool stone floor is exactly what you want under your feet on a baking summer's day. The bathroom's other key feature, which we noticed perhaps a little too late, is a picture window by the bath. I didn't register the window, or the curtains hanging limply by its sides, until I'd just got out of the bath. I do hope I didn't give any of the other guests a fright.

As soon as we'd finished admiring our new temporary home, we wanted to go and explore some of the dramatic landscape around us. We got a taxi into the centre of Ronda, a beautiful and historic town that straddles the El Tajo gorge. In the cool of the early evening, we wandered around the old town and through a beautiful park before stopping for a drink at the Restaurante del Escudero, on a terrace overlooking the gorge. Sipping glasses of chilled *rosado* we watched a coppery sun set over the dusty Andalucian hills. Apologies if I've come over a little Hallmark on you, but it really was a perfect moment.

After our sundowners, we moved on to Tragabuches, Escudero's sister eaterie. Now, Mrs Smith is a veggie and, in our experience, the Spanish are not preoccupied by vegetarian needs. Worse, Ronda's culinary speciality centres around oxtail, perhaps a nod to the local bullring, one of the oldest in Spain. Luckily, Tragabuches is no run-of-the-mill tapas bar: it has a Michelin star and the food is fabulous. As well as delighting us with some gorgeous meat-free items from the tasting menu, its chefs also very graciously prepared a perfect, melt-in-the-mouth mushroom risotto especially for Mrs Smith.

Having dined at the most expensive restaurant in town (though reasonable by our London standards), it ↓

seemed only right to have a nightcap in a rough-and-ready local bar. The place was great (unfortunately the details of its whereabouts are lost in a boozy haze). On leaving, though, we ran into problems. Ronda isn't really that touristy. In many ways, this is wonderful, but it's not so wonderful when you need a cab home at 01h and the streets are more or less deserted. It's even worse when you've had a few too many sherries, and you only have your room key as an indicator of where you need to get to. Luckily, our problem became a nice little adventure when we managed to befriend some local builders, using my very patchy Spanish and a few forlorn facial expressions. By an amazing stroke of luck, one of these builders had helped renovate our hotel, and was happy to give us a lift home. I like to think this was thanks to my charming language skills, but it was more likely due to his admiration of the beautiful Mrs Smith.

The next day, a little weary from our sherry-fuelled shenanigans, we felt La Fuente de la Higuera came into its own. The garden is the ideal place to laze around reading, taking an occasional swim when the heat gets too much. Indeed, we did little except relax, enjoy our surroundings, eat the hotel's excellent home cooking, and chat to our friendly Dutch hosts, Pom and Tina.

We atoned for our laziness the following day, by visiting Grazalema and Zahara de la Sierra, two of the famous 'white villages' of Andalucía. These are in the Parque Natural de la Sierra de Grazalema, and offer rugged rural Spain at its finest. We lunched on some very fine tapas and then went hiking in the mountains. Like true Brits, we did this in the midday sun, when the temperature was up in the forties. We managed to avoid heatstroke, though, and the views were stunning. The pleasure was all the greater because we knew that, by squeezing some culture and physical activity into one day, we'd be able to do nothing by the pool of La Fuente for the rest of our stay – with a clear conscience.

Reviewed by Rhymer Rigby

NEED TO KNOW

Rooms 11.
Rates €135–€260, including breakfast.
Check-out Midday, but flexible.
Room service The restaurant menu is available until 22h. Drinks available until midnight.
Facilities All the rooms have a private garden or terrace. Most have open fireplaces. Massage on request.
Poolside Outdoor pool set in a walled garden.
Children Welcome. The junior suite has a standard room next door. An extra bed or cot is €25.
Also Yoga and flamenco classes can be arranged. The hotel can arrange English-speaking guides for visits to Seville, Granada and Jerez. A range of spa treatments is available at the hotel's sister resort, Rise (www.rise-resort.com).

IN THE KNOW

Our favourite rooms Room 10 has the best private terrace. Room 5 is a junior suite with beautiful views over the valley. Spacious Room 2 is the honeymoon suite.
Hotel bar There is a 24-hour honesty bar.
Hotel restaurant Dinner is served indoors or outdoors, depending on the weather; order during the day. The €35 three-course menu changes daily, and features Spanish fish, meat and vegetarian dishes. Last orders for lunch: 14h30. Last orders for dinner: 22h.
Top table A candlelit table by the pool.
Dress code Sierra-style insouciance.

LOCAL EATING AND DRINKING

The panoramic terrace of **El Choque**, on Calle Espíritu Santo, is a great place for coffee during the day. Ronda's finest restaurant, the Michelin-starred **Tragabuches** on Calle José Apartado (952 190 291), is famed for its creative menu. **Casa Santa Pola**, on Santo Domingo (952 879 208), does excellent Andalucian game and meat dishes and has wonderful views of the gorge from its terrace.

Smith members receive a selected bottle of wine; room upgrade subject to availability. Free massage when you stay five nights or more.

GET A ROOM!

Use our online booking service at www.mrandmrssmith.com to check availability and make reservations. Register your Smithcard to find out about current member offers for this hotel.

La Fuente de la Higuera

Partido de los Frontones, Ronda
+34 952 114 355
info@hotellafuente.com; www.hotellafuente.com

● SEVILLE PROVINCE

Seville Province

COUNTRYSIDE   WHITE COTTAGES, ORANGE BLOSSOM
COUNTRY LIFE   FIESTA AND FLAMENCO

MTWTFSSMTWTFSSMTWTFSSMTWTFSSMTWTFSSMTWT
ESPAÑA

TWTFSSMTWTFSSMTWTFSSMTWTFSSMTWTFSSMTWTFSS

SEVILLE PROVINCE

The sultry Andalucian province of Seville is the very soul of southern Spain: whitewashed villages decked with orange blossom; long hot afternoons in peaceful plazas; tapas and sherry after an evening stroll; passionate nights of flamenco and fiesta. The city of full-blooded Sevillanos is rich with Moorish influence and Catholic ceremony, and filled with cathedrals, ornate palaces and foot-stamping flamenco clubs. Equally wild and untamed, the pristine beaches of the Costa de la Luz stretch for miles along the coast. Yet only an hour's drive away, you can calm your heartbeat in the chestnut woods and sleepy *pueblos blancos* of the sierras.

GETTING THERE

Planes The nearest airports, with regular flights year-round, are Jerez (30 minutes) and Seville (45 minutes).

Trains Super-fast AVE trains run from Madrid to Seville (two and a half hours; €65). The region's local train network is limited and services can often be slow and infrequent.

Automobiles It's worth hiring a car to visit Seville, the mountains and the beautiful beaches of the Costa de la Luz.

DO GO/DON'T GO

The Seville region can be very hot in summer. Spring has fine weather and several of the year's most important festivals, while autumn is warm and peaceful. The region enjoys plenty of sunshine, even in winter.

SUITABLY SEVILLE

Seville is the home of passionate flamenco. Casa de la Memoria de al-Andalus on Calle Ximénez de Enciso has nightly performances. Alternatively, just wander through la Macarena district to find more spontaneous performances at small backstreet *peñas* (bar/clubs).

LOCAL KNOWLEDGE

Taxis Cabs are cheap and can be hailed in the street. They display a green 'libre' notice or green light at night.

Tipping culture Ten per cent in restaurants is appreciated; otherwise, a couple of euros with drinks or tapas is sufficient.

Siesta and fiesta Banks and shops close between 14h and 17h during the week, and at 14h on Saturdays. Restaurants don't get busy until after 21h.

Packing tips Jodhpurs and riding boots. Your hotel can organise horse riding with the local stables (€85 for two and a half hours). It's possible to trek along the beaches or through the Sierras de Gacalemo.

Recommended reads *The Sun Also Rises* or *Death in the Afternoon* by Ernest Hemingway; *Don Juan* by Molière.

Cuisine Freshly grilled fish and squid from the Costa de la Luz is delicious. The region is famous for its tapas, including smoked serrano ham, roasted peppers, peppery cheeses and fat, juicy olives. Sanlúcar's wonderful manzanilla sherry is the perfect accompaniment.

Currency Euro.

Dialling codes Country code for Spain: 34. Seville: 95.

DIARY

Late February/early March The International Flamenco Festival in Jerez is a riot of energetic dancing (www.flamenco-world.com). **Late April** Seville's April Fair is one of the greatest ferias in Spain, with flamenco, bullfights and equestrian parades. **Early May** The Jerez Horse Fair showcases the finest Spanish horsemanship (www.turismojerez.com). **August** Horse races take place on the beach at Sanlúcar on the second and fourth weekends.

September Jerez's month-long Autumn Festival covers everything from grape-treading to fireworks. **Second week of October** Sanlúcar has a tapas festival along Calzada del Ejército. Visit www.andalucia.org for more details.

°C
J 15
F 17
M 20
A 23
M 26
J 32
J 34
A 34
S 32
O 25
N 20
D 16

WORTH GETTING OUT OF BED FOR

Viewpoint Seville cathedral's 90-metre tower – the Giralda – was once the minaret of the city mosque, and has super views from the top. The Torre Tavira in Cádiz has a great view out to sea.

Arts and culture Jerez is famous for its beautiful dancing horses. If you miss the main Thursday show at the Royal Riding School (www.realescuela.org), the morning practice sessions are open to the public.

Activities There are bullfights every Sunday evening (usually 18h30) in Seville's Plaza de Toros, from Easter Sunday to early October (www.realmaestranza.com). The mountains of the Parque Natural Sierra de Grazalema are popular for canyoning, climbing and hiking; contact Horizon for details (www.horizonaventura.com). The hotel can also organise sailing, private yoga classes and visits to the region's bull-breeding ranches.

Daytripper The Costa de la Luz offers miles of unspoilt beaches. Conil de la Frontera is one of the coast's finest beaches. There are some beautiful sandy coves at Los Caños de Meca, southwest of Vejer, and the beach at Atlanterra, between Vejer and Tarifa, is pristine perfection.

Perfect picnic Head up through the *pueblos blancos* and the mountain scenery of the Serranía de Ronda to the village of Zahara de la Sierra for an idyllic picnic in the chestnut woods.

Something for nothing Over 100 operas are set in and around Seville. You can visit the sites associated with the most famous – Bizet's *Carmen* – including Plaza de España, the tobacco factory (now the university), and the bullring.

Shopping Calle Sierpes, north of the Giralda in Seville, is great for leather goods. Try Nicole Miller or Loewe near Plaza Nueva. You can buy manzanilla sherry from the bodegas in Sanlúcar. Your hotel can arrange a private visit to the 200-year-old Hidalgo bodega.

CAFÉS

Horno de San Buenaventura on Avenida de la Constitución in Seville has been serving excellent pastries for over 600 years. The city also has excellent tapas bars: **Bar El Rinconillo** on Calle Gerona has been popular with locals since 1670; **La Bodega Extremeña** off Calle San Esteban is perfect for Sunday snacks.

BARS AND RESTAURANTS

In Seville, **Taberna del Alabardero** on Calle Zaragoza (954 50 27 21) has a bistro with a tasty three-course menu, popular with lunchtime diners. The main restaurant is best in the evening, serving excellent game and fish dishes. **Casa Robles** on Calle Alvarez Quintero (954 56 32 72) is a great family-run restaurant specialising in Andalucian seafood dishes. In Cádiz, you'll find tasty seafood, including red snapper (*parga*) and dogfish (*cazón*) at **El Faro** on Calle San Felix (902 21 10 68). **Restaurante Gaitan**, on Calle Gaitan in Jerez (956 34 58 59), has a traditional and regional menu. Try the Jerez-style oxtail.

NIGHTLIFE

Seville is the place to head for a night out, but many venues don't get busy until late. **Bestuario** on Calle Zaragoza, just off Plaza Nueva, is nice for a relaxed drink from 21h onwards. The Alameda de Hércules attracts a cool crowd of Sevillanos to the **Habanilla Café** and **Café Central**. At the top of Calle Arenal, **Café Bohem** gets going from midnight. **Boss** on Calle Betis is a stylish upscale nightclub that livens up from 02h and keeps going until dawn.

Hacienda de San Rafael

DESTINATION	SEVILLE PROVINCE
STYLE	SPANISH STATELY HOME
SETTING	WILD SOUTHERN RANCHLAND

S S
ESPAÑA

'A stylish makeover blends the languorous sensuality
of Spanish bullfighting country with Europhile sophistication'

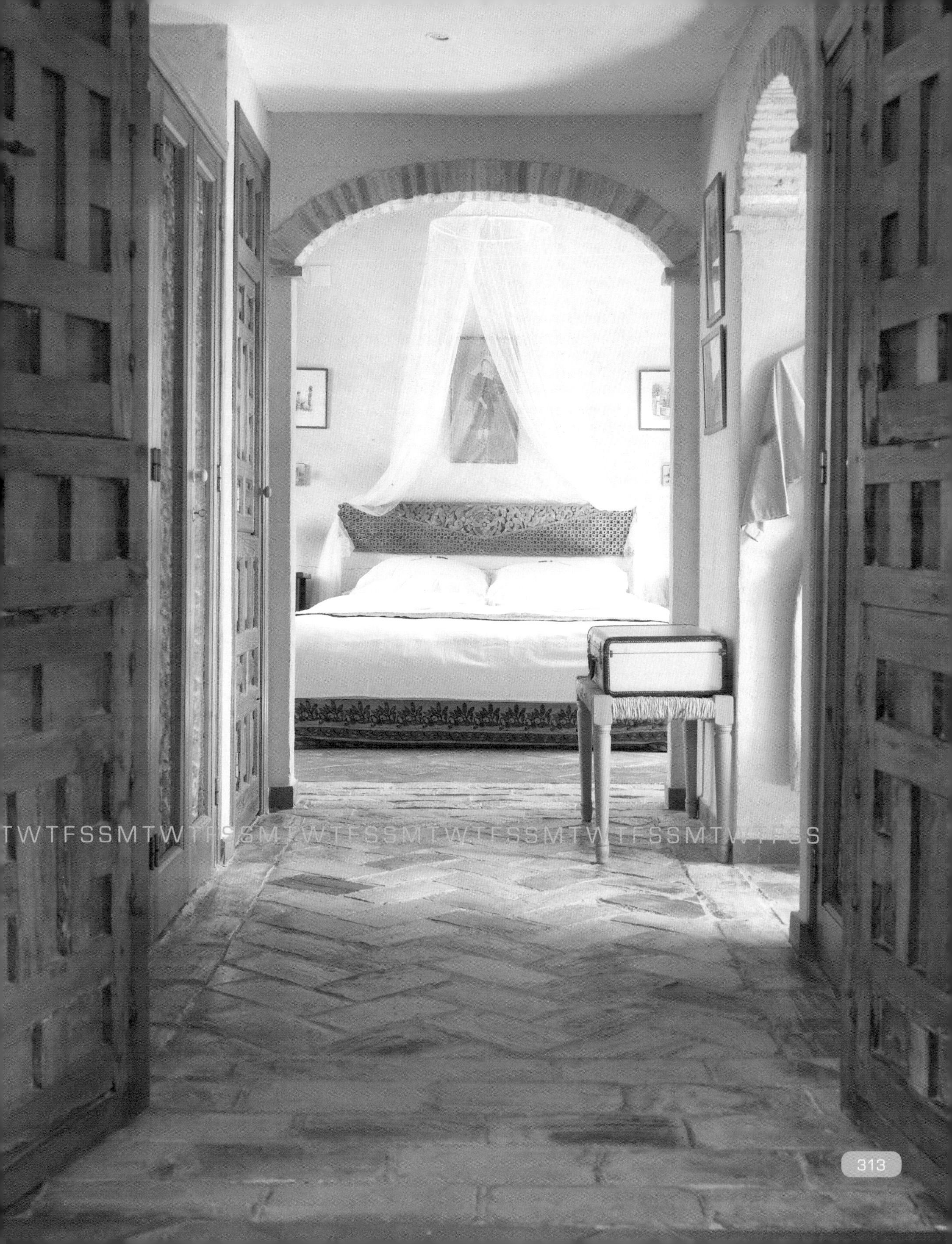

Mrs Smith and I are cruising in eerie silence along the flatlands between Seville and Jerez. She's brought her TomTom (the satnav system that cabbies swear by) and, thanks to Darth Vader telling us where to go, we haven't argued once. It's bliss, even if Vader does lend a rather surreal air to proceedings. We hang a left, down a long, dusty path that appears to be going nowhere. The setting is idyllic – you know the scene: rolling fields of sunflowers, cotton, olive trees, waving wheat… And in the warm evening light (the honey-drenched time that film-makers call the magic hour), it's like cruising into a Van Gogh. We swoosh past hedges of pink and white oleander, and the Haçienda de San Rafael smacks into view.

A gleaming-white, *cortijo*-style country house, with foot-thick walls and huge shuttered windows, the Haçienda offers grandeur without a whiff of ostentation. Two sweet-mannered Englishwomen meet us at the doorway, whisk away our bags and offer lemon iced tea. We follow them through the doorway – and past a tangle of cerise and orange bougainvillea – to a terracotta-paved courtyard. Butterflies dance around the flowers and evening birdsong fills the air. The owners are milling around and pop over for a chat. It doesn't feel much like a hotel: it's more like visiting a well-to-do friend's private residence.

The Haçienda has been in the Reid family for a century and a half and, up until the Sixties, it was a working olive farm. The youngest generation, twentysomething Anthony and Patrick, run the place. They are responsible for its recent stylish makeover: blending the languorous sensuality of Spanish bullfighting country with Europhile sophistication. Mum Kuky is from nearby Jerez, and it was her dream to turn the family farm into a small guesthouse in keeping with the surrounding white villages. Her husband, Tim, worked as a hotelier with Mandarin Oriental before setting up the superbly luxurious

Datai hotel in Langkawi, Malaysia. Patrick used to be a project manager at the Groucho Club in London, and Anthony organised swish safaris in Botswana. Between them, this family have all the skills to challenge any top resort – no wonder they got it so right here.

We are escorted into the communal living room, which contains a wild mix of upper-crust European and Far Eastern antiques that hints at the family's travels. Mrs Smith, a keen reader of interior-design magazines, loves it, and throws herself down on a huge red Thai elephant sofa, before hopping up again to inspect the antique iron bull statues on the mantelpiece, and Mrs Reid's father's 80-year-old stirrups, which hang in a line above the fireplace. Hacienda San Rafael is a trove of fascinating treasures, and most of them have a story behind them – just get Anthony talking about his grandfather, a 'horseman and

a gentleman' who won Jerez's annual Horseman of Gold award too many times to keep count of.

We are staying in a *casita*, a meticulously converted farm building with a thatched roof, away from the main house. It's expensive, but we do get a private terrace and infinity pool in a lovingly tended cottage garden. The main pool is spectacular, with manicured lawn, huge day beds and palm-trees for shade – it's just that Mrs Smith and I have developed a taste for privacy.

The family's attention to detail is what distinguishes the Haçienda de San Rafael from so many other retreats. Not only is it stunning, but there are three pools, and a full complement of staff to cater to your every whim, too. The dining experience illustrates this well. Mrs Smith is a vegetarian who likes neither eggs nor mushrooms, so eating out in Spain has previously been a pain in the posterior. There is no problem here, though, thanks to head chef Mark Dillon who whips ↓

up pumpkin and sage risotto, barbecued tofu kebabs and a delicious baked-aubergine concoction.

The food in the communal dining area is a highlight, and with the nearest café a 20-minute cab ride away, lunchtime tapas and lazy alfresco dinners at the hotel work fabulously. In fact, we spent days experiencing no urge to leave the Haçienda and its grounds, until suddenly we decided we really ought to venture out. So we trekked to Seville's mighty 15th-century cathedral, second only in size to St Paul's in Rome, and to the nearby Alcázar Palace and gardens – and the tapas bars in between – all well worth leaving our luxury cocoon for. Mrs Smith was so taken by the Mudéjar architecture, stuccoed patios and intricate mosaic that she had to buy an extra memory card for her camera.

For the more energetic holidaymakers, the hotel can arrange pretty much any activity. As keen riders, we were delighted to meet Cuko, Mrs Reid's cousin and a family member with yet more hospitality credentials, who owns a private estate with 12 horses a short drive away. His morning rides through the Andalucian mountains, and picnics in the dappled light of local chestnut forests, are hard to beat. For those times when you are feeling intrepid, there's much to do in and around the hotel: bustling Seville is a hop away; nearby Jerez has beautiful beaches and is the sherry capital of the world; and Andalucía has a long equestrian and bullfighting history. Having found this slice of paradise, though, you'd be forgiven for just flopping by the pool and ordering a martini and a massage. Just ask Mrs Smith – she became quite the expert at this by the end of our three-day sojourn. And I can't say I was too bad at following her lead.

Reviewed by Alex Proud

NEED TO KNOW

Rooms 14, including three casitas.
Rates €240–€514, including breakfast.
Check-out Midday, but ask for flexibility. There is a shower room for use by guests after check-out.
Room service 08h30–midnight. There are phones for room service in the casitas.
Facilitles Wireless Internet access, CD player. Massage and yoga on request.
Poolside There are three outdoor pools. Lunch is usually served by the garden pool.
Children The hotel welcomes children only if the property is booked in its entirety.
Hotel closed From mid-November until 15 March.
Also A picnic can be arranged for €25. The hotel has a paddle-tennis court and boules set.

IN THE KNOW

Our favourite rooms Rooms 7, 9 and 10 have bedrooms in the eaves and bathrooms. The three separate casitas have living rooms and shaded daybeds, and share their own garden and pool.
Hotel bar Luna Bar is outdoors, with music and white comfy cushions to lounge on. The Sunset Bar is next to the pool.
Hotel restaurant The indoor dining room is used in cooler weather; otherwise, dinner is served outside. Mediterranean set menu for dinner is €55 a person, including wine. The fish kebabs and the creamy blue cheese and spinach soufflé are delicious.
Top table Outside in the gardens.
Dress code Relaxed and informal.

LOCAL EATING AND DRINKING

Up in the mountains, **Mesón el Tabanco** in the village of El Bosque (956 716 081) does excellent game dishes in a rustic setting. **Egaña Oriza** on Calle San Fernando in Seville (954 227 211) is one of the city's finest restaurants, serving Andalucian and Basque cuisine. **Bar Juanito** on Pescadería Vieja in Jerez (956 334 838) is one of the city's best tapas bars, with more than 50 dishes. Also in Jerez, **La Tasca** on Calle Paraíso (956 31 03 40) has delicious fish and shellfish. The stew is particularly good.

Smith members receive a free picnic, a private bodega visit, half a bottle of manzanilla in a deluxe room, and a bottle of house champagne when staying in a casita.

GET A ROOM!

Use our online booking service at www.mrandmrssmith.com to check availability and make reservations. Register your Smithcard to find out about current member offers for this hotel.

Hacienda de San Rafael
Carretera N-IV Km 594, Las Cabezas de San Juan
+34 955 872 193
info@haciendadesanrafael.com; www.haciendadesanrafael.com

How to… be fluent behind the wheel

	FRENCH	GREEK	ICELANDIC
Excuse me	Excusez-moi	Με συγχωρείτε	Afsakid and fyrirgefdu
Could you direct me to…?	Est-ce vous pouvez me diriger vers…?	Μπορείτε να μου πείτε πώς να πάω στο…?	Geturdu sýnt mér hvar…?
Where is the nearest beach/ petrol station/carpark?	Où est la plage/ la station-service/le parking plus près d'ici?	Που είναι η πλησιέστερη παραλία/ βενζινάδικο/ πάρκιν?	Hvar er naesta stroend/ bensinstod/bilastaedi?
Can you recommend somewhere nice for lunch?	Connaissez-vous un resto sympa pour le repas de midi?	Μπορείτε να μου προτείνεται κάπου καλά για φαγητό?	Geturdu maelt med godum adegisverdarstad?
Where can I buy a map?	Où peut-on acheter une carte?	Που μπορώ να αγοράσω έναν χάρτη?	Hvar get eg keypt kort?
Fill her up, please	Le plein, s'il vous plaît	Γέμισέ τη, παρακαλώ	Fylla, takk
Baby, you can drive my hire car	Bébé, tu peux conduire ma voiture de location	Μωρό μου μπορείς να οδηγήσεις το αμάξι που έχω νοικιάσει	Elskan, thu matt keyra bilinn minn
Driving along in my automobile, my baby beside me at the wheel	Roulant dans ma bagnole/ma cherie à mon côté au volant	Οδηγούσα το αυτοκίνητό μου, με το μωρό μου να κάθεται δίπλα μου στο τιμόνι	Ek i bilnum minum, kaerastan vid styrid vid hlidina a met
Where did that ditch come from?	Ce fossé est apparu comme par miracle!	Αυτή η λακκούβα εμφανίστηκε από το πουθενά	Thessi skurdur var ekki her
That's not an official hand signal	Ca n'est pas un geste de conduire official	Αυτός δεν είναι ο κανονικός τρόπος να κάνεις σήμα με τα χέρια	Thetta er ekki venjulegt handar merki
Goodness, officer, was I really driving that fast?	Monsieur le gendarme, est-ce que je conduisais vraiment si vite que ça?	Στα αλήθεια πήγαινα τόσο γρήγορα, αστυνόμε?	Var eg virkilega a svona miklum hrada, loegreglumadur?

ITALIAN	PORTUGUESE	SPANISH
Mi scusi	Dame licença	Disculpa
Come si arriva a…?	Podia me dizer onde fica esta diração…?	¿Me podría dirigir a…?
Dov'é la spiaggi/ il benzinaio/il parcheggio più vicino?	Onde è a praia/a bomba de gazelina/o parque de carro mas perto?	¿Donde está la playa/la gasolinera/el parking/ mas cercano/a?
Può suggerire un bel posto per pranzo?	Podia recomendar algum lugar bom para almoçar?	¿Puede recomendar algún lugar bueno para comer?
Dove potrei comprare una piantina?	Onde è que eu posse comprare um mapa?	¿Donde puedo comprar un mapa?
Faccia il pieno, per favore	Encho o tanque, por favor	Lleno, por favor
Carissima, tu puoi guidare la mia macchina a noleggio	Querida, tu podes conduzir o meu carro alogado	Guapa, puedes conducir mi coche de alquiler
Guidando la mia macchinetta con la mia bella accanto a me	Tou conduzir o meu carro, com a minha querida oa meu lado	De camino en mi coche, mi chica a mi lado
Quella fossato è apparso all'improvviso!	Essa vala veio do nada!	¿De donde apareció esa zanja?
Questo non è un segnale di mano usato	Este não é um sinal de mão padrão	Eso no es una señal con la mano uniforme
Ma ufficiale, andavo davvero a quella velocita?	Eu estava a conduzir muitode presa, senhor guarda?	¿De verdad, iba tan rápido, agente?

You might want wheels to explore some of the remoter coastal and countryside destinations, and Smith members can benefit from reduced rates on car hire with Hertz. Save ten per cent off standard cars by quoting CDP 635230 when booking on www.hertz.co.uk or, if you want a really smooth ride, upgrade to a Prestige car and you'll be entitled to a 15 per cent reduction.

Every second counts when you're escaping for that all-important break, so save time collecting your hire car by registering as a Hertz #1 Club Gold member. You can have a vehicle ready and waiting at your destination with as little as two hours' advance notice. Membership of Hertz #1 Club Gold is free to Smithcard holders. Just click on www.hertz.co.uk/goldenrol to enter your details.

For the latest information on Smith offers from Hertz, check www.mrandmrssmith.com/members.

(useful numbers)

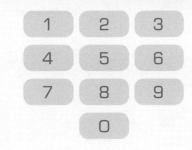

AIRLINES

Aegean Airlines (+30 210 62 61 000; www.aegeanair.com). Flights from Athens to Santorini.

Aer Lingus (08708 765000; www.aerlingus.com). Flights from Dublin to the Côte d'Azur, Tarn, Piedmont and Cascais.

Air Berlin (08707 388880; www.airberlin.com). Flights from London to southern Spain, the Balearic Islands and the Côte d'Azur.

Air France (08701 424343; www.airfrance.com). Flights from London Gatwick and Heathrow, Birmingham, Edinburgh, Manchester, Aberdeen, Southampton and Newcastle to French destinations.

Alitalia (08705 448259; www.alitalia.com) Heathrow and other UK airports to Italian destinations.

BMI (08706 070555; www.flybmi.com). Flights to Tarn, Beaujolais, Sorrento and South Tyrol destinations.

BMI Baby (08712 240224; www.bmibaby.com). Flights from airports throughout the UK and Ireland to Sorrento, Ronda, Mallorca and all French destinations.

British Airways (08708 509850; www.ba.com). UK airports to all European destinations.

EasyJet (09058 210905; www.easyjet.com). Flights from 12 airports in the UK and four in Ireland to Spanish, French, Italian and Greek destinations.

Iberia (08706 090500; www.iberia.com). Flights from London, Birmingham, Manchester and Glasgow to all our Spanish destinations.

Icelandair (08707 874020; www.icelandair.co.uk). Flights from London, Glasgow and Manchester to Reykjavík.

Meridiana (www.meridiana.it). Flights from London Gatwick to all our Italian destinations.

Monarch (08700 406300; www.flymonarch.com).
Flights from London, Birmingham and Manchester to southern Spain and the Balearic Islands.

Ryanair (08712 460000; www.ryanair.com). Flights from 20 airports in the UK and six in Ireland to our Spanish, French and Italian destinations.

TAP Air Portugal (www.flytap.com). London Gatwick and Heathrow to Lisbon.

Skyscanner Enter your flight requirements into www.skyscanner.net and it searches multiple budget airlines to give a range of prices.

HELICOPTERS AND LIGHT AIRCRAFT

Air Panarea (+39 340 366 7214; www.airpanarea.com). Helicopter transfers to the Aeolian Islands. Smith members receive a five per cent discount when staying at Hotel Raya (see page 138).

Dedalus (+39 090 983 333; www.elieolie.it). Helicopter transfers to the Aeolian Islands.

Fly-In (+34 699 77 55 01; www.fly-in-spain.com). Jerez-based light-aircraft charters for tours and destinations in southern Spain and Morocco.

Sloane Helicopters (+34 971 794 132; www.sloanemallorca.com). Recommended Mallorca helicopter charter.

CARS, BOATS AND TRAINS

Hertz (www.hertz.co.uk; 08708 448844). Smith members receive a ten to 15 per cent discount.

Holiday Taxis (www.holidaytaxis.com). Airport transfers in destinations worldwide.

Aqua Cruise (01425 673374; www.aquacruise.com). Yacht and motorboat hire on the Côte d'Azur.

Danyboats (+34 (0) 600 413 069;

www.danyboats.com). Speedboat hire in Ibiza.
Hellenic Seaways (www.hellenicseaways.gr).
High-speed catamarans from Piraeus to Santorini.
Maritimo Yachts (+34 971 707 669;
www.maritimoyachts.com). Yacht charter in Mallorca.
Moby (+49 (0)611 14020; www.mobylines.it).
Ferries from mainland Italy to Sardinia.
Nautica Sic Sic (+39 081 807 2283; www.
nauticasicsic.com). Speedboat charters between
Sorrento and Capri and along the Amalfi coast.
Onda Eoliana (+39 090 984 4200; www.ondaeoliana.
com). Boat hire in Salina. Smith members receive
a ten per cent discount when staying at Hotel Signum
(see page 144).
SNAV (www.snav.it). High-speed catamarans from
mainland Italy to Sardinia and the Aeolian Islands.
Trasmediterranea (www.trasmediterranea.com).
High-speed catamarans from Valencia, Barcelona
and Denia to the Balearic Islands.

European Rail (www.europeanrail.com). Gives
information on train travel in continental Europe.
Eurostar (www.eurostar.com; 08705 186186).
French Railways (www.voyages-sncf.com). Routes,
fares and timetables for the French rail network.
Rail Europe (08708 306050; www.raileurope.co.uk).
UK supplier of European rail tickets.
Seat 61 (www.seat61.com/europe.htm). Gives
information on travelling to Europe by train.
Spanish Railways (www.renfe.es). Details, fares and
timetables for the Spanish rail network.

MAPS
Mappy (www.mappy.com) will help you plan a route
across Europe, including times, distance and tolls.

Map Quest (www.mapquest.co.uk) has basic but
clear maps of all western European destinations.
Map Vista (www.map-vista.com) provides online
street maps for every European city.
ViaMichelin (www.viamichelin.com) provides driving
directions, route planning, and traffic and weather
reports throughout Europe.

BOOKS AND MUSIC
Amazon (www.amazon.co.uk)
Seamless Recordings (www.seamlessrecordings.co.uk)
TuneTribe (www.tunetribe.com) for downloads.

ECO-TRAVEL AND HELPFUL WEBSITES
Carbon emissions (www.futureforests.com)
Currency converter (www.xe.com/ucc)
World weather forecasts (www.weather.com)

TOURIST BOARDS
Avignon Tourist Board (www.avignon-tourisme.com)
Bergerac Tourist Board (www.pays-de-bergerac.com)
Florence Tourist Board (www.firenzetourismo.it)
French Tourist Board (www.francetourism.com)
Greek Tourist Board (www.gnto.co.uk)
Lyon Tourist Board (www.lyon-france.com)
Nice Tourist Board (www.nicetourisme.com)
Piedmont Tourist Board (www.piemontefeel.org)
Puglia Tourist Board (www.pugliaturismo.com)
Reykjavík Tourist Board (www.tourist.reykjavik.is)
Sorrento Tourist Board (www.sorrentotourism.com)
South Tyrol Tourist Board (www.suedtirol.info)
Spanish Tourist Board (www.spain.info)
Tarn Tourist Board (www.tourisme-tarn.com)

All phone numbers are given as dialled from the UK.

So, who are Mr & Mrs Smith?

Our reviewers are a panel of people who know all there is to know about style, fun and originality. They all visited their hotels anonymously, so they received no special treatment, and are able to give you an honest account of a stay there – which means you get the same kind of inside scoop as you'd get from your best friend

REVIEWERS WHO'S WHO

THE ACTOR
Born in London, actor **Nick Moran** is best known for his film roles (most notably in *Lock Stock and Two Smoking Barrels*). His career has resulted in something of a world tour. 'I've got 14 visas from nine countries, and more air miles than Alan Whicker,' he says. As a result, he's no stranger to hotel accommodation. He has written for *The Guardian*, *The Times* and the *Evening Standard*; is the author of the award-winning West End play *Telstar*; and is narrator of *The Smiths: Hotels for 2*.

THE BOUTIQUIER
Alison Chow, co-founder of Coco Ribbon, has lived in Sydney, Hong Kong and New York, so she travels frequently between them to visit family and friends. Buying trips take her to Paris, Brazil and Shanghai, and her favourite holiday spots include Marrakech and Verbier, where she indulges her passon for skiiing.

THE BON VIVEUR
Howard Marks's experience of overnight accommodation is fairly singular, stemming from several years spent in five-star hotels throughout southeast Asia as an international fugitive; then nine years in European and United States prisons. Over the past decade, he has written travel articles for *The Observer*, *Time Out* and *The Daily Telegraph*.

THE BUYER
Hus Mozaffar whetted his cultural appetite studying fine art at Brighton University, after which he made a move into buying and product development. For the past four years, he has been honing his skills at the Conran Shop. He considers himself to have the perfect job: he gets to travel the world, and find and design new stuff. His ideal getaway would be a trip to see the aurora borealis.

THE JOURNALISTS AND EDITORS
Richard Bence contributes to *Elle* and *High Life*, and is lifestyle editor of *Attitude*. Recent exploits include a spring break in Palm Springs, and a weekend on the Costa Smeralda, where he coincided with the visiting Argentinian polo team for the second time in a year. Come summer, Richard will decamp to Ibiza for his annual dose of sunshine and hedonism.

Jeroen Bergmans graduated from Bristol University a decade ago, and immediately put his six languages to good use, working as a guide to American high-school kids on 'Europe in a week' educational tours. After a stint in the arid world of business travel, he joined the launch team of the Hempel, London's first minimal, East-meets-West hotel. There he discovered a passion for design, inspiring his move to *Wallpaper** magazine where, four years ago, he became travel editor.

Giles Coren After spells as an elf in Harrods' Santa's Grotto, a barman, a hospital porter and a shirt salesman in Paris, Giles got a job as a secretary at *The Daily Telegraph* in 1994. He has been restaurant critic of *Tatler* and *The Independent on Sunday*, and diary editor and parliamentary sketch-writer of *The Times*. His debut novel, *Winkler*, was published in 2005. He regularly pops up as a pundit and presenter on TV.

In her role as features editor of *Vogue*, **Jo Craven** frequently agonises over the stylishness and suitability of hotels and travel destinations for the magazine. As a young mother of two, she also obsesses about two illusive ideals: travelling light, and locating on-tap butler and nanny services.

William Drew has been the editor of *Arena* for the past year, having served almost four years' apprenticeship as deputy. He got his first job on a fashion mag because they urgently needed 'a straight man in the office', and has built his career on similarly dubious principles, working across a variety of travel, style and health titles. He lives in suburban bliss in Wimbledon with his wife and three sons, and is passionate about magazines, motivation and Man City.

Neil McLennan is lifestyle director of *Grazia*, the UK's first weekly glossy. When not supervising food shoots, flicking through pictures of inspiring houses and dining at fine tables, he can be found travelling to boutique hotels in far-flung places. Born and bred Down Under, Neil has spent the past 20-odd years genning up on thread counts, premium brand vodkas and accruing a fine collection of travel-sized grooming products. Previously, he has managed to pass off having a good time as hard work at *Time Out*, *ES* magazine and *Elle*.

Danielle Proud (aka Mrs Alex Proud) is an interior design columnist for *Sunday Times Style* magazine. Her first book, *House Proud*, hit the shelves in November 2006. She spent years cutting her teeth as clubs editor and assistant to the TV editor at *The Guardian Guide*. This gave her a good grounding in identifying comfy furniture and making mean martinis. These skills, coupled with her designer's eye and marriage to fastidious hotel snob Alex Proud, whose review she ghostwrote, make her an ideal commentator on a place's suitability for R&R, as well as its easiness on the eye.

In the mid-Nineties, **Nick Raistrick** was based in Prague but it got too cold, so he ended up living in Barcelona and Madrid, where he picked up Spanish and rediscovered his Middlesbrough accent. He currently works for the BBC World Service Trust, training journalists in developing countries like Somalia. His favourite destinations are Nepal, Guatemala and Borneo; he'd like to get paid to visit the Antarctic next, please.

Rhymer Rigby's work has led him to investigate corporate espionage and the male beauty industry, and seen him eating deep-fried tarantulas in Cambodia. His tales have appeared in the *Financial Times*, *The Daily Telegraph* and *The Observer*, as well as magazines such as *GQ* and *Condé Nast Traveller*. He lives in London with his wife and Monty the cat.

Taryn Ross has been sniffing out what's hot and not professionally for over a decade now. With travel in her blood, and three passports under her belt, Taryn lived in New York, Chicago, Vancouver and Barcelona, before moving to London to pursue a career in fashion. After a spell in fashion PR, four years ago Taryn founded UrbanJunkies.com, London's daily e-mag. In addition to her role as MD and editor of the website, Taryn edits *MIDAS* magazine, and is on the steering committee of On|Off, a unique art/fashion/design initiative during London Fashion Week.

THE HANDBAG HEAD HONCHO
Casey Gorman moved from California to London in 2000 and worked for Escada UK before joining British accessories designer Lulu Guinness as head of sales and sales director. Two years later, Casey became one of the youngest CEOs in the luxury fashion sector, when she was asked to head up the global business of Lulu Guinness.

THE INTERIOR DESIGNER
Ilse Crawford is a creative director whose company, Studioilse, has created Soho House New York, the Electric Cinema, and the influential Babington House. Other notches in Ilse's belt include the launch of *Elle Decoration* in 1989, and a vice-presidency with Donna Karan Home (where she helped launch DKNY and Donna Karan Homeware). Ilse is also head of department at the renowned Design Academy Eindhoven. Her latest book, *Home Is Where the Heart Is*, explores ways in which we can integrate our basic emotional needs into design.

THE MARKETING GURU
As founder of luxury, fashion and lifestyle marketing agency Brand Couture, **Kirsten McNally** translates emerging consumer trends into brand experiences on a daily basis. In terms of hotels, Kirsten recognizes that simple pleasures and personal touches go a long way with the modern traveller. In a world of increasing global fashion homogeneity, she celebrates Mr & Mrs Smith's eclectic mix of hi- and lo-fi places for every mood.

THE MILLINER
If hats were a country, then **Philip Treacy** would be royalty. As a child in the west of Ireland, he was obsessed by his mother's sewing machine, and eventually studied for an MA in fashion design at the Royal College of Art. He went on to design hats for Lagerfeld at Chanel, Gianni Versace, Valentino and Alexander McQueen, winning five British Fashion Designer of the Year awards in the process. He was recently created design director for the interiors of hotel The G in Galway.

THE MODEL
Seven years of writing assignments and four years of fashion modelling have taken *GQ Style* associate editor **David Annand** on a pretty comprehensive tour of the world's hotels. In marble-floored palaces in the Arabian desert and in Milanese fleapits, David, who has modelled for Prada and Rolex, has whiled away many hours watching films dubbed into languages he does not speak, and getting drunk on his own. So it was a welcome respite to finally be allowed to take Mrs Smith along for the ride.

THE NOVELIST
Susie Boyt is the author of four critically acclaimed novels, including *The Last Hope of Girls* (shortlisted for the John Llewellyn Rhys prize) and *Only Human* (shortlisted for the Mind Book of the Year). She also writes a weekly shopping column, Consumer Culture, for the *Financial Times Weekend*. Susie lives in London with her family, and has never visited anywhere else she likes half as much.

THE RECORD-LABEL BOSS
After eight years in advertising, **Ben Sowton** co-founded events company Atomic, and the White House members' bar and restaurant in south London, then fulfilled a long-held ambition to set up a record label: Seamless Recordings, whose *Bargrooves* series has been described by *Wallpaper** as 'achingly sophisticated'. They also produce the Mr & Mrs Smith *Something for the Weekend* series.

THE TUNESMITH
Rob Wood is a DJ, journalist and music consultant. When not writing for magazines, he helps run digital music store TuneTribe.com, and can be spotted riding the wheels of steel at events like the Big Chill, Bestival and the Isle of Wight Festival. He's also responsible for putting together the *Something for the Weekend* compilation albums and writing Mr & Mrs Smith's TuneSmith music page.

THE TV DIRECTOR

A love of travel lured **Charles Martin** into television, with stints on *Holiday, Dream Ticket* and *The Travel Show*. His love for music and nightlife led him to directing: the opening titles for the first series of *Big Brother* are his populist claim to fame, his documentary on *Cream* nightclub his credible one. Having directed a few episodes of *The Smiths' Hotels for 2*, he went onto the award-winning *My Life as a Popat*, as his *Freaky* series hit Channel 4.

THE TV PRODUCER

Helen Veale is a TV producer who, together with her business partner, Laura Mansfield, runs Outline Productions. Outline produces the TV series based on the Mr & Mrs Smith guidebooks, along with hit parental-guidance show, *The House of Tiny Tearaways*. Previously, Helen was a freelance producer-director, and she has always enjoyed indulging in implausible amounts of Italian food and wine.

THE MR & MRS SMITH TEAM

James Lohan is one half of the couple behind the Mr & Mrs Smith brand. James's first company, Atomic, created London's infamous Come Dancing parties. He built on this success with Atomic Events and in March 2000, he co-founded the White House bar, restaurant and members' club in Clapham, which has become one of London's hippest establishments. James has visited more than 500 hotels and, since publication of the second book, has squeezed in a proposal at 101 Hotel in Iceland, and his marriage to Tamara at Ca's Xorc in Mallorca.

Tamara Heber-Percy, co-founder of Mr & Mrs Smith (and James's real-life Mrs Smith) graduated from Oxford with a degree in languages, then left the UK for a year in Brazil, where she launched a new energy drink. Since then, she has worked as a marketing consultant for international brands such as Ericsson, Honda, Unilever and Swissair, but she left the corporate world in 2002 to head up her own company, The County Register, an exclusive introductions agency, and to launch Mr & Mrs Smith.

Bloom, creators of the Mr & Mrs Smith brand and designers of the book, are one of the UK's freshest and most innovative design agencies. Originally founded in 2001 by three of the youngest heavyweights in the industry, Ben White, Gavin Blake and Harriet Marshall, Bloom is responsible for inspirational brand designs for some of Europe's and the USA's leading consumer-brand companies.

Associate editor **Sophie Dening** first got a taste for room service when she missed school to tour Europe with her opera-singer mother. Her travels have taken her from limin' in Tobago and wine-tasting in Provence to teaching 12-year-olds 'The Wheels on the Bus' in southwest China. She also works at *GQ Style*, and writes freelance for *High Life, Country Living* and *Harper's Bazaar*.

In 1990, publishing director **Andrew Grahame** launched the country's first corporate-fashion magazine. After moving into fashion shows, exhibitions and conferences, he transferred his talents to business finance, launching *Small Company Investor*. He started a promotions company in 1993, with clients such as Sony and Virgin, and after a spell as a restaurant/bar owner in Chelsea, he entered tourism, creating the award-winning London Pass and New York Pass. He is co-presenter on the Discovery Travel & Living programme *The Smiths' Hotels for 2.*

With a diverse portfolio of subjects from some of the world's most famous faces through to breathtaking and obscure locations, **Adrian Houston** has made a lot of noise in the photographic world. In fact, his meticulous eye for detail, combined with his intuitive, creative and relaxed approach, have established him as one of the UK's best-respected photographers. For more information and to view his portfolio, go to www.adrianhouston.co.uk.

Marketing and PR manager **Aline Keuroghlian** has worked in travel for more than ten years, with stints at Armani and Sir John Soane's Museum helping to cultivate her aesthetic eye. After university, she spent a couple of years guiding high-flying professionals across the Italian countryside for niche tour operator ATG Oxford, where she became head of marketing. Now she is putting both her sense and sensibility to good use by working with some of the most beautiful hotels in the world.

Editor **Juliet Kinsman** has led a nomadic lifestyle from the get-go; childhood stints in Africa, America and Canada, followed by a Home Counties schooling and a degree in social anthropology, left her yearning to explore the world properly. After spells working in New York, Greece and India, she decided London was sufficiently cosmopolitan for her to drop anchor in. When not racing round the world for *The Smiths' Hotels for 2* or the new online collections, she has shared her travel secrets in *The Observer, The Times, Marie Claire, Time Out* and *The Face.*

Scott Manson likes hotels, and writing about them, so who better to have as one of our chief wordsmiths (excuse the pun)? A former editor of *Ministry, Loaded* and BA's *High Life* magazine, he has travelled the world with DJs, rock stars and supermodels. Sometimes he didn't even have to carry their bags. He's also a regular travel writer for the *Evening Standard* and a contributor to the *Sunday Times Style* magazine.

Having grown up in the south of Spain, after three years at Manchester University, hotel collections manager **Katy McCann** moved to the Spanish capital, where she became editor of its biggest English publication, *In Madrid.* Drawn back to London by the English weather, she was tracked down by the Mr & Mrs Smith team to join on the hotel-relations side, which fits in perfectly with her love of travelling, her multilingual skills and her hope of opening up her own hotel some day.

Production manager **Laura Mizon** spent her younger years living in Spain and, after graduating from Manchester University, returned to the country of her childhood to spend four years at an independent record label in Madrid, promoting the emerging Spanish hip-hop movement. Soon after she joined Mr & Mrs Smith on a freelance basis in 2004, it became clear that Laura was to play a key role in the company; since then she has cultivated a roving existence researching hotels and destinations for its ever-growing collections.

Edward Orr has been working in investment banking and managing companies in their early stages for more than ten years. As a result he has had to stay in many hotels across five different continents – and, generally, he doesn't like them. This qualifies him not only to look after the finances of Mr & Mrs Smith, but also to have penned a few of the team reviews. He can happily confirm that Smith hotels really are special enough to be a treat, even for the most jaded corporate traveller.

Membership manager **Amber Spencer-Holmes** may be a Londoner, but she has form as a cosmopolitan type, having lived in Sydney and Paris before reading French and English at King's College London. Previous to joining Spy, Mrs TuneSmith (her husband is DJ Rob Wood) made waves in the music industry, running a number of well-respected record labels, before going on to launch the much-loved *Back to Mine* and *Bargrooves* compilation series, and the Mr & Mrs Smith *Something for the Weekend* CDs.

Deputy editor **Jim Whyte** spent ten years in marketing before fatefully asking *The Guardian* to send him somewhere cold. He was promptly dispatched to Siberia for the winter to file a series of travel articles. When he requested somewhere a bit warmer for his next assignment, they sent him to ride a camel across the Sahara. Now reacquainted with stylish and comfortable travel as a Mr & Mrs Smith editor, Jim is resolutely sticking to his first loves of yachts, sundowners and Italian ice cream.

(gift voucher)

Mr & Mrs Smith Get a Room! gift vouchers are available for an amount of your choosing, from a minimum of £50. Stylishly presented in a black Smith envelope, with a personalised letter, they can be used toward the purchase of accommodation at any participating Smith destinations; a list of the hotels and terms and conditions are available at **www.mrandmrssmith.com/hotel-gift-voucher.**

GET A ROOM!

Seven lucky reasons why Mr & Mrs Smith gift vouchers are a wonderful invention

1

Who wouldn't want to stay at a fabulous boutique hotel? This is one gift where one size definitely fits all... no dusting it off and having it on display when you next pay them a visit; they can relax in the knowledge that there's no bag for the charity shop in their boot to hide from you; and gone is that awkward asking if you still have the receipt.

2

If you just can't face logging onto another department-store website to look at another dreary wedding list, splash out on some Smith vouchers and the happy couple can start planning their second honeymoon just as the mundanity of real life starts to kick in. And better to be remembered for that than a fish poacher or Magimix.

3

If you're embarking on a new romance, send a Smith voucher as an anonymous token: if the object of your affections invites a parent, a mate or a pesky love rival, you know to cut your losses and run. It's tough, baby, but it's more effective than truth serum.

4

When it comes to a special occasion, from Valentine's to making up for an overlooked anniversary, you couldn't give better. Plus it's a guaranteed love-life spicer-upper if you feel things could do with a little extra fizz. Trust us: it's scientifically proven in 8 out of 10 tests.

5

If you're in need of a little self-gifting, but it's actually your beloved's birthday and not yours, treating them to a Mr & Mrs Smith voucher is fantastically yet discreetly non-altruistic: you get a weekend away, plus you get hailed as a generous soul – it's win-win. And if they invite someone else, see (3).

6

If a friend has just emerged, heartbroken, from a long-term relationship, get them one. They can have a relaxing weekend away with you, or they can use it to woo a new squeeze. Their love for you will last forever, even if their romances don't.

7

If you're fairly certain you're never going to be able to buy that villa in a far-flung land for your parents to retire to in rock-star style, then rest assured that a romantic weekend away on their next anniversary should still keep them sweet.

(music)

No more suffering his middle-of-the-road rock favourites or enduring her bubblegum-pop guilty pleasures, as we present these first-class tickets to soul-injected, rock-peppered, electrofunk-enhanced aural escapism...

VOLUME 1

Saint Etienne 'Nothing Can Stop Us'
Ralph Myerz & The Jack Herren Band 'Think Twice'
Rune Lindbaek 'Junta Jaeger'
Randy Crawford 'Cajun Moon'
Rae & Christian 'Spellbound'
McKay 'Tell Him'
Faze Action 'Broad Souls'
Chungking 'Les Fleurs'
Max Sedgley 'Happy'
Chris Rea 'Josephine'
Lambchop 'Up With People'
RSL 'Wesley Music'
Primal Scream 'Come Together'

VOLUME 2

Plantlife featuring Dena Deadly 'When She Smiles She Lights Up The Sky' (4 Hero mix)
Husky Rescue 'Summertime Cowboy'
The Superimposers 'Seeing Is Believing'
Grand Popo Football Club 'Men Are Not Nice Guys'
Black Grass 'Nice Up'
Chungking 'Voodoo' (Ellis Burnel remix)
The Beta Band 'It's Not Too Beautiful'
Alice Russell featuring TM Juke 'Hurry On Now'
Lazyboy & Roddy Frame 'Western Skies'
N*E*R*D 'Provider' (Zero 7 mix)
Sebastien Tellier 'La Ritournelle'
Feist 'One Evening'
Aretha Franklin 'Day Dreaming'
Damn! 'Got To Go'

SOMETHING FOR THE WEEKEND

A dance track from Ibiza; an anthem from Glastonbury; an encore at a gig on the Lower East Side – music signposts our lives. Like travel, it allows us to explore other cultures and exotic places; it provides the soundtrack to loves, losses and new discoveries. And, if we depend on holidays to escape our lives, to hide from work and bills, so, too, can we seek refuge within the chords and choruses of our favourite tracks. Just as the festival-goer has three days of hedonism away from his desk, the iPod owner shuts out the world to get personal with Nick Drake or Miles Davis.

The ultimate escape is, of course, to be found in those hotels where we can lose ourselves in exciting new surroundings – perhaps even by checking in as someone else entirely. That's why Mr & Mrs Smith promise you the perfect sounds to disappear to. Discover more new and vintage sounds with TuneSmith: www.mrandmrssmith.com/music.

VOLUME 3

Turner 'My Aeroplane Mania'
Bang Bang 'Don't Care'
Tullio De Piscopo 'Primavera (Stop Bajon)'
Ian Dury 'Wake Up & Make Love With Me'
Amadou & Mariam 'La Réalité'
Sugardaddy 'Chasing My Tail (album version)'
Bantu featuring Ayuba 'How Real (Can A Real, Real Be)'
The Supremes 'Come Together'
King Biscuit Time 'Kwangchow'
Louie Austen 'Feel Me!'
Javi P3Z Orquesta 'Ping Pong'
Keith 'Hold That Gun'
Grandadbob 'Hide Me' (original)

To find out more about seamless recordings and the *bargrooves* series, visit www.seamlessrecordings.com.

(applause)

thank you

Thanks once again to our team for their savvy, hard work, creativity and explorations: Adrian for his images, which are more breathtaking than ever, and to his assistant, Tom, and Hasselblad cameras; the editorial team for their way with words – Juliet, Sophie, Jim, Anna Wood, Scott Manson; Ed and Craig for keeping our finances on track; Katy and Laura for enduring so many nights away in search of the most special hotels; Bloom Design, for their brand genius and for making this book fit for the most discerning coffee table, with special thanks to Ben White, Lindsay Reynolds, Layla Kammeier and Arron Egan; Andrew for his bright ideas and for taking Smith to the small screen; Aline, our inspired marketing manager, and her assistant, Lucy; Kirsten and Jess at Brand Couture for yet more inspiration; Amber, our membership manager; and Peggy, Jasmine, Mary and Anton at Spy HQ. Also Chris Mair and Joseph at Airlock for our clever new web technology and online magazine; Lynton for his web wizardry; Ed Bussey, Peter Clements and Ian Taylor; Ben Sowton and Simon Dawson at Seamless Recordings, and Rob Wood for our third *Something for the Weekend* CD; Marin and the team at Travel Intelligence; Hugh, Carol and Lauren at Portfolio Distribution; Ed Ripley and all at Macmillan; all our stockists; Mark and the team at E-media; Graham and the team at Trichrom Ltd for printing the book; Turismo Andaluz for the Costa de la Luz images; David Hares for his Mallorca shots; Helen Veale at Outline, Stephanie Dennis at Bump, and Robert Curran at Discovery for making our TV show; Hallmark for getting this to you; all of our reviewers for sharing their tales. And last, but by no means least, huge thanks to anyone else who has helped make our long-awaited third book a reality: for additional research from our spies Jon Murphy, Sally Clarke, Cara Allen, Theresa De Lorenzi, Louiza Patikas; Ian Ridpath, author of the *Monthly Sky Guide,* for his astronomical nous; Stewart Wild, our eagle-eyed proofreader; and, of course, all those 'other halves' who accompanied reviewers, or helped with filling in the gaps.

Mr & Mrs Smith

index